OLD TESTAMENT MESSAGE

A Biblical-Theological Commentary

Carroll Stuhlmueller, C.P. and Martin McNamara, M.S.C.

EDITORS

Old Testament Message, Volume 2

GENESIS

Michael Maher, M.S.C.

Michael Glazier, Inc.
Wilmington, Delaware

Acknowledgement

We wish to thank *Biblical Archaeologist* for its kind permission to reproduce the art on pages 18, 90, and 220.

First published in 1982 by: MICHAEL GLAZIER, INC., 1723 Delaware Avenue, Wilmington, Delaware 19806

Distributed outside U.S., Canada & Philippines by: GILL & MACMILLAN, LTD., Goldenbridge, Inchicore, Dublin 8 Ireland

Library of Congress Catalog Card Number: 82-81221
International Standard Book Number
  Old Testament Message series: 0-89453-235-9
  GENESIS
  0-89453-237-5 (Michael Glazier, Inc.)
  7171-1166-0 (Gill & Macmillan, Ltd.)

Cover design by Lillian Brulc

Cartography by Lucille Dragovan

Printed in the United States of America

Contents

Editors' Preface

Old Testament Message brings into our life and religion today the ancient word of God to Israel. This word, according to the book of the prophet Isaiah, had soaked the earth like "rain and snow coming gently down from heaven" and had returned to God fruitfully in all forms of human life (Isa 55:10). The authors of this series remain true to this ancient Israelite heritage and draw us into the home, the temple and the marketplace of God's chosen people. Although they rely upon the tools of modern scholarship to uncover the distant places and culture of the biblical world, yet they also refocus these insights in a language clear and understandable for any interested reader today. They enable us, even if this be our first acquaintance with the Old Testament, to become sister and brother, or at least good neighbor, to our religious ancestors. In this way we begin to hear God's word ever more forcefully in our own times and across our world, within our prayer and worship, in our secular needs and perplexing problems.

Because life is complex and our world includes, at times in a single large city, vastly different styles of living, we have much to learn from the Israelite Scriptures. The Old Testament spans forty-six biblical books and almost nineteen hundred years of life. It extends through desert, agricultural and urban ways of human existence. The literary style embraces a world of literature and human emotions. Its history began with Moses and the birth-pangs of a new people, it came of age politically and economically under David and Solomon, it reeled under the fiery threats of prophets like Amos and Jeremiah. The people despaired and yet were re-created with new hope during the Babylonian exile. Later reconstruction in the homeland and then the trauma of apocalyptic movements prepared for the revelation of "the mystery hidden for ages in God who created all things" (Eph 3:9).

While the Old Testament telescopes twelve to nineteen hundred years of human existence within the small country of Israel, any single moment of time today witnesses to the reenactment of this entire history across the wide expanse of planet earth. Each verse of the Old Testament is being relived somewhere in our world today. We need, therefore, the *entire* Old Testament and all twenty-three volumes of this new set, in order to be totally a "Bible person" within today's widely diverse society.

The subtitle of this series—"A Biblical-Theological Commentary"—clarifies what these twenty-three volumes intend to do.

Their *purpose* is theological: to feel the pulse of God's word for its *religious* impact and direction.

Their *method* is biblical: to establish the scriptural word firmly within the life and culture of ancient Israel.

Their *style* is commentary: not to explain verse by verse but to follow a presentation of the message that is easily understandable to any serious reader, even if this person is untrained in ancient history and biblical languages.

Old Testament Message—like its predecessor, *New Testament Message*—is aimed at the entire English-speaking world and so is a collaborative effort of an international team. The twenty-one contributors are women and men drawn from North America, Ireland, Britain and Australia. They are scholars who have published in scientific journals, but they have been chosen equally as well for their proven ability to communicate on a popular level. This twenty-three book set comes from Roman Catholic writers, yet, like the Bible itself, it reaches beyond interpretations restricted to an individual church and so enables men and women rooted in biblical faith to unite and so to appreciate their own traditions more fully and more adequately.

Most of all, through the word of God, we seek the blessedness and joy of those
who walk in the law of the Lord!...
who seek God with their whole heart (Ps. 119:1-2).

Carroll Stuhlmueller, C.P.   Martin McNamara, M.S.C.

INTRODUCTION

Ancient Traditions for our Modern Day

The task of presenting the Book of Genesis in an intelligible, relevant and inspiring way to our sophisticated generation is indeed a challenge! The educated person of the twentieth century is endowed with intellectual curiosity, often combined with religious and ethical scepticism. He or she has acquired considerable knowledge of the physical universe and feels alienated by the very first chapters of Genesis which describe the creation of the world in terms that cannot be squared with the findings of the sciences. Stories about a God who worked like a potter, narratives that involve a tree of life and a talking serpent, and accounts of a world in which every form of suffering is absent give the impression that Genesis opens with a collection of mildly entertaining fairy-tales that may be calculated to amuse children, but which can be of little interest to enlightened adults.

One who continues to read beyond the first perplexing chapters of Genesis soon encounters lengthy genealogies that list strange names that mean nothing to us, and that can scarcely be expected to stimulate the reader's interest or to encourage one to persist in reading Genesis. Records of brutality which reflect a primitive savagery (*cf.,* 4:23-24; 34:25-29) shock the reader who knows a more civilized and

11

orderly society. Then there are passages like the story of
Tamar (chap. 38) which embarrass the morally sensitive,
and which are discreetly omitted from the list of liturgical
readings lest they scandalize rather than edify. The stories of
the patriarchs have been richly embroidered with folkloristic motifs, and although they may bear eloquent testimony
to the biblical writers' faith and literary ability, they presuppose ideas and values that are hardly palatable today. In
short, the Book of Genesis appears to the intelligent but
casual reader as a disorderly and heterogeneous body of
material, part of the cumbersome legacy which the Church
inherited from Judaism.

Nevertheless, Genesis, like the rest of the Old Testament,
bears witness to a people's search for God, and to the
reflections of spiritually sensitive persons on the world and
on human existence. Genesis is a prelude to the spiritual and
political history of Israel, and as such it is also part of our
history, since we remain in historical and spiritual continuity with Israel. We cannot, therefore, jettison the record
of the religious experiences of the people from whom we
sprang, and it is the duty of the expositor to make the
authentic message of Genesis available to the intelligent
Christian of our day. With this particular goal and this
particular reader in mind the present commentary can
afford to gloss over many of the more obstruse discussions
of the scholars, and will aim at summarizing the better
established conclusions of specialized research. Since our
goals are religious and practical rather than academic and
antiquarian, we need not delay over genealogical details and
tribal origins, or over archaeological minutiae and rem-
nants of political history. Instead we will focus attention on
the theological message of the text. In doing so we will not
betray the author's intent, since Genesis is primarily a theological work, a statement of faith, and an expression of
religious truths.

The authors of Genesis did not, for example, intend
chaps. 1-11 to be simply a factual account of how the world
came to be, or a history of the world's earliest inhabitants.

These chapters are the result of the author's grappling with life's most serious questions: What is man and what is woman? What is their relation to God and to the world? Why is life such a perplexing mixture of good and evil? Similarly the authors of chaps. 12-50 were not primarily interested in recounting the history of the family of Abraham, but in showing how God began to realize his plan for the redemption of all humankind by choosing one family, forming it into his own people, and guiding its destiny according to his own designs. Nevertheless, while it is true that Genesis is an expression of religious insights rather than a textbook of science or history or archaeology, we cannot read it intelligently unless we bring to it a number of scholarly presuppositions and convictions. We must, for example, have clear concepts about the origins of the Book of Genesis as it now exists if we are to appreciate the different literary styles and theological outlooks which can be detected in the narratives.

The Composition of Genesis

It is generally agreed among contemporary scholars that the first five books of the Bible, known as the Pentateuch, resulted from a long process of growth; many hands were involved in the composition.

For over a hundred years now scholars have noticed differences of vocabulary, style and theological interest in different passages of the Pentateuch, and have concluded that these point to a diversity of authors. A number of "doublets" or even "triple traditions" — parallel passages where the same story is told two or three times — seem to indicate that different versions of the same story have been recorded in different sources, and perhaps in different localities. For example, we have two accounts of creation (Gen 1:1—2:4a and 2:4b-25) which must represent two independent sources. Gen 12:10-20; 20:1-18; 26:6-11 offer three versions of a story about a frightened husband who hands over his wife to another man in order to save his own life. Repetitions and contradictions within the same story suggest that originally independent sources have been woven together in the narrative as it now exists. We find, for example, in the Flood story that Gen 6:5 and 6:12 make the same point, and 7:7 and 7:13 assert the same fact, while 7:4, 12, 17 contradict the statements in 7:24 and 8:3b. The simplest explanation of these surprising facts indicates that the Flood story as it has come down to us resulted from different traditions combined by a redactor who was not as interested in forming an even and harmonious text as a modern editor might be.

The sources which scholarly research has discovered in the Pentateuch are referred to by the initials J, E, D and P, and we shall devote a few moments to the characteristics, stylistic and theological, which distinguish them. Since, however, the Genesis material does not seem to have been modified or enriched by the D authors we can omit discussion of this source.

The Yahwist (J)

The Yahwist (J) source was given its name by the German scholars who noticed its preference for *Yahweh* (in German Jahweh, hence the initial J) as a name for God. This strand of tradition was composed in the tenth century B.C.

It begins with an account of creation (Gen 2:4b-31), and extends through the patriarchal and Exodus stories to the wandering in the desert.

In producing this wide survey of history the Yahwist was able to utilize many pre-existing traditions, oral and written, which were preserved and transmitted in the songs and ballads and cultic narrations which were part of the tribal, national and religious festivals of the people. His undeniable genius lay in his ability to select, synthesize, and arrange these traditions into a continuous and coherent literary composition remarkable for its artistic merit as well as for its monumental proportions, for its profound theological perception as well as for its keen insight into human nature.

The Yahwist is no mere retailer of the products of other people's brains. Critics rank him among the giants of world literature, and recognize in him a storyteller of great genius and a poet who has given us some passages of rare freshness and beauty. Yet, however admirable the Yahwist's literary achievement may be, it is not so important for us as his theological and religious insights. In the patriarchal narratives (Gen 12-50), for example, the author shows how God guided the destiny of Israel's ancestors. In his primeval history (2:4a—11:9) he reached back to times for which no historical reminiscences were available, in order to portray the beginnings of the great family of humankind in which Israel was to play a special role. In those early chapters the Yahwist confronts humanity's basic and perennial problems, and explains the origins of the world and of man and woman, the origin of sin and division and pain in the world, and the progressive alienation from God in a world where people had been destined to live in harmony with one another and their maker. In order to convey the idea of God's familiar communion with the human family, the Yahwist sprinkles the early chapters with abundant *anthropomorphisms*, that is, with descriptions of God in purely human terms. (See, for example, Gen 2:7, 8, 21; 3:8, 21; 7:16c; 11:7.) In the patriarchal narrative God is portrayed as having a close relationship with his chosen ones. He spoke directly to Abraham (12:1-3) and made a covenant with him (Chap. 15). He accepted Abraham's hospitality at the patriarch's tent in Mamre (18:1-15), and entered into dialogue with him about the fate of Sodom (18:22-33).

The stories attributed to the Yahwist articulate remarkably coherent insights into God's relationship with the world and with the human family, and they do so with such characteristic literary and theological style that we can perceive the stamp of a single author who was at once a profound theologian and a master of the literary art.

The Elohist (E)

The Elohist (E) tradition gets its name from the fact that it uses the name *Elohim* for God until the revelation of the name Yahweh in Exod 3:14. The E compilation seems to have been the work of scribes who in the ninth century B.C. collected the traditions of the Northern Kingdom of Israel.

The Elohist contributed nothing to the primeval history (Gen 1-11), and probably appears for the first time in a fragmentary fashion in Gen 15. The first complete E narrative occurs in 20:1-18. The striking account of the sacrifice of Isaac (Gen 22), which finds no counterpart in J, shows that the Elohist could, on occasion, show himself to be a story-teller of the calibre of the Yahwist. In the Joseph story (Gen 37-50) the J and E strands are so closely intertwined that attempts to separate them often leave one in the realm of probability rather than certainty.

It is generally agreed that the Elohist does not exhibit the same literary talent as J, although some E passages, like Gen 22, are remarkable for their vivid and dramatic structure. On a theological level E avoids J's anthropomorphisms, that is, the tendency to present God in human traits. Whereas J pictures God walking in the garden to meet Adam (3:8) or deciding to go down to see what people are doing on earth (11:7), the God of E communicates in dreams and visions (20:3, 6; 21:12; 28:12, etc.) or through the voice of an angel (21:17; 22:11, 15), or in theophanies or divine apparitions where God reveals himself in splendour and majesty (Exod 19:16-19).

The Elohist shows a particular sensitivity to moral issues and he occasionally modifies stories in order to eliminate less edifying incidents that might be considered objectionable in his day. A parade example of this procedure occurs in Gen 20 where the author adapts some elements of the corresponding J story to his own more refined moral standards.

The Priestly Source (P)

The Priestly (P) strand of tradition was the latest to be composed; it derives its name from the fact that it originated with priestly scribes during and after the Babylonian exile (c. 539-450 B.C.). Although the majestic account of creation with which the Priestly strand of the tradition begins (Gen 1:1-2:4a) shows that its authors could write prose of a high literary quality, their style is generally formal, measured, unimaginative and repetitive.

Among the primary marks of the Priestly author's theology are his absolute monotheism and his almost total avoidance of anthropomorphisms. Both characteristics are evident in the creation narrative in Gen 1. God is depicted as alone and without rival, and as distant from the world of mortals. Another remarkable feature of the Priestly Source is the succession of genealogical tables which punctuate the narrative (*cf.,* 5:1-28, 30-32, 10:1-32; 11:10-30, etc.) and which actually structure his Genesis story. It is by means of genealogies that P gradually eliminates the nations in whom he is not interested, and focuses the reader's attention on those who have a part in God's design.

Classical source criticism which has accepted the existence of J, E, D and P traditions in the Pentateuch has been seriously challenged in recent years. A number of critics, for example, would claim that there never was an independent E source. Nevertheless, the majority of Old Testament scholars still accept the documentary hypothesis, and in the present commentary we will work on the conviction that several independent sources have been fused to form our present Genesis text.

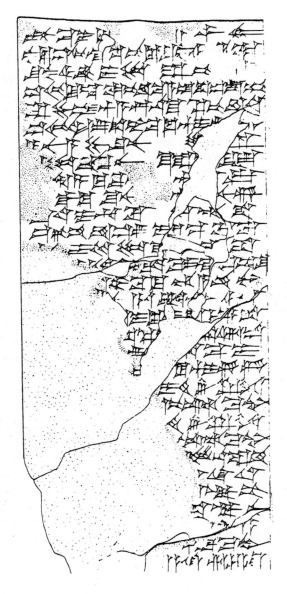

Tablet I, column i of the Babylonian Epic of Atrahasis. Written before 1700 B.C., this epic is a Primeval History which presents a flood story in a context similar to that of Gen 1-9.

I. SONG OF CREATION
1:1—2:4a (P)

IN THE BEGINNING
1:1-5

> **1** In the beginning God created the heavens and the earth. ²The earth was without form and void, and darkness was upon the face of the deep; and the Spirit of God was moving over the face of the waters.
>
> ³And God said, "Let there be light"; and there was light. ⁴And God saw that the light was good; and God separated the light from the darkness. ⁵God called the light Day, and the darkness he called Night. And there was evening and there was morning, one day.

Although the opening chapter of Genesis was long regarded as a factual account of the origin of the world and of the human family, it is now almost universally recognized as primarily a profession of faith, a poetic affirmation of Israel's religious convictions. Any attempt to reconcile the data of this chapter with the findings of modern science is misguided and futile. The Priestly authors to whom we owe this passage most probably believed that it incorporated the most advanced scientific thinking of their day, but their primary intention in writing was to declare God's sovereignty over an orderly world which he had freely created, and which corresponds perfectly to his plan and purpose.

This Priestly creation narrative is generally regarded as a gem of religious poetry. It is true that the same phrases recur again and again, and that the structure of the passage is sober, or even austere, in its regularity. One notices, for example, how the account of the work of each day of creation follows a strict pattern: 1) Introduction: "And God said"; 2) Divine command: "Let there be..."; "Let the waters...the earth", etc.; 3) The fulfillment of the command: "and there was..."; "and it was so"; 4) Divine evaluation: "God saw that it was good"; 5) Rounding off phrase: "And there was evening..." Yet, in spite of this rather rigid structure this chapter has a grandeur of its own, and its measured but majestic language gives expression to sublime theological reflection.

The above (RSV) translation of v. 1 follows the traditional rendering of the verse, and sees in it an independent sentence which is in effect a summary of the whole chapter. This summary is then unfolded and elucidated in the rest of the chapter which describes the orderly manner in which God went about the task of creating "the heavens and the earth." The latter phrase embraces all created things that are the object of human perception and that make up the ordered universe. The Hebrew word *bara'* which is translated as 'created,' although used invariably with God as its subject (*cf.,* Isa 40:26; 41:20; 45:7,8), does not necessarily mean making something from nothing. It follows then that v. 1 does not solve the problem of whether the world was created from nothing (*creatio ex nihilo*) or not. The question did not arise for the author who was content to say that God made all things that now exist, and that he did so in a way that cannot be compared with any human activity.

From a syntactic point of view, however, v. 1 can be translated and understood in quite a different manner. It may be seen as an introductory clause which is completed by v. 2, and it can be translated as follows: "When God began to create the heavens and the earth, the earth was without form etc..." This reading allows us to see in the formless mass that preceded God's creative word the raw material from which he created an ordered world. This understanding of the creative process corresponds to the view of creation that was common in the ancient Babylonian myths from which the Priestly authors quarried. But while this reading of vv. 1-2 is admissible I prefer the traditional view that sees v. 1 as an independent phrase which makes a general statement about God's creative activity, thus forming a solemn theological opening to the whole Bible.

The alliterative Hebrew words *tohu - wa bohu* which are rendered "without form and void" (v. 2) suggest desolation and barrenness, formlessness and chaos. With these onomatopoeic words the author describes how things were before God's creative act produced the ordered world we know. *Darkness* is mentioned as a feature of the primordial chaos, and *the deep* which was enveloped in darkness was that unbridled mass of water that covered the whole chaotic world. Commentators regularly note that *tehom*, the Hebrew word for *the deep*, is etymologically related to *Tiamat*, the personified monster who is represented in the Babylonian creation myths as resisting the creating gods. In the Priestly story, however, the concept of opposition to God's creative will is totally absent, and the deep is simply that mass of water that would be separated into the waters above and the waters under the firmament (*cf.,* vv. 6-9). The statement that *the Spirit of God was moving over the face of the waters* has traditionally been taken to mean that the life-giving power and energy of God was hovering over the gloomy chaos, eager, as it were, to bestow the warmth and life that would transform the amorphous watery mass into a productive and habitable world. This time-honoured understanding of the verse is solidly based on the fact that the "Spirit of God" is indeed a life-giving agency (*cf.,* Job 33:4; Ps 33:6), while the Hebrew verb translated "moving" is used in Deut 32:11 to express care and concern. Although this traditional interpretation cannot be ruled out of court many modern commentators claim that it does not faithfully convey the Priestly author's meaning. The phrase *ruah elohim* which is rendered "Spirit of God," should, say the critics, be translated as "a divine wind," or better "a mighty wind." This "mighty wind" sweeping over the face of the waters is merely another element of the pre-creational chaos, a factor to be controlled by the act of creation rather than a divine influence preceding the creative *fiat*.

The phrase *and God said* introduces each work of creation and forms a kind of refrain running right through the chapter. The idea of creation by divine word alone appears in Egyptian texts in the early third millennium B.C., and it suggests the effortless ease with which the deity brought all things into being. The Priestly authors use this concept to show that the transcendent God remains totally distinct from creation, and that his sovereign unchangeable will and omnipotent word called the world into existence (*cf.,* Ps 33:6-9). It must be noted, however, that the Priestly author also speaks of God as creating by direct act (*cf.,* vv. 7, 16, 21, etc.). *Light* (v. 3) is the indispensable condition for life, and was the first element to be created. The ancient orientals did not think of light as necessarily connected with the heavenly bodies, and they regarded it as having an existence of its own. We find, for example, that Job (38:19-20) envisaged light and darkness having each its separate dwelling place where it was stored away, as it were, when not required. The Priestly author was interested, not in the question of the immediate source of light, but in asserting the fact that light is a created element, and that it is one of God's gifts to the world. The formula *And God saw that it was good* occurs seven times in the Priestly creation story (1:4, 10, 12, 18, 21, 25, 31). It expresses God's verdict of approval on each day's work, it declares that the world corresponds to God's design, and it is calculated to arouse in the reader an optimistic view of the world in which each element serves a divine purpose. The mention of God's separating activity in vv. 6, 7, 14 and 18 assures us that the Creator brought order and design into the emerging world and gradually overcame the primeval chaos. For the ancients the act of giving its name to something (*cf.,* vv. 5, 8, 10) was an expression of control over that particular thing. By giving their names to day and night (v. 5) God was assigning them their roles in creation and setting in motion the regular coming and going of day and night. Even darkness was given its place in God's universe (*cf.,* Ps 104:20), and it is not to be regarded as the abode of evil or as the threatening unknown that it was for the ancients.

HEAVEN AND EARTH
1:6-13

⁶And God said, "Let there be a firmament in the midst of the waters, and let it separate the waters from the waters." ⁷And God made the firmament and separated the waters which were under the firmament from the waters which were above the firmament. And it was so. ⁸And God called the firmament Heaven. And there was evening and there was morning, a second day.

⁹And God said, "Let the waters under the heavens be gathered together into one place, and let the dry land appear." And it was so. ¹⁰God called the dry land Earth, and the waters that were gathered together he called Seas. And God saw that it was good. ¹¹And God said, "Let the earth put forth vegetation, plants yielding seed, and fruit trees bearing fruit in which is their seed, each according to its kind upon the earth." And it was so. ¹²The earth brought forth vegetation, plants yielding seed according to their own kinds, and trees bearing fruit in which is their seed, each according to its kind. And God saw that it was good. ¹³And there was evening and there was morning, a third day.

The *firmament* is the sky which the ancients visualized as a gigantic metallic vault (*cf.,* Job 37:18) or as an inverted bowl, which was suspended over the earth. It was seen as a firmly hammered expanse capable of supporting vast reservoirs of water (*cf.,* Ps 148:4) which could, at God's command, be allowed to pour out upon the earth through "windows" (*cf.,* Gen 7:11; 8:2). The firmament served as a boundary between *the waters which were under the firma-ment and the waters which were above the firmament* (v. 7). These former waters included, in the minds of the ancients, the seas, and the waters under the earth (*cf.,* 7:11; Exod 20:4, etc.), which burst through apertures in the earth's surface as springs and rivers. The separation and ordering of the chaotic primordial waters (*cf.,* v.1) was an important step in the process of bringing order into the developing world.

Two works of creation are assigned to the third day, probably because the author was interested in showing that the whole process of producing an ordered universe was completed in six days, so that on the seventh day the Lord would rest. Further progress is made in the task of giving form to the world when *the waters under the heavens* recede behind boundaries established for them by God (*cf.,* Ps 104:7-9; Jer 5:22), so that the dry land can emerge. The author, like all his contemporaries, visualized the earth as a flat disc resting on the subterranean waters (*cf.,* Ps 24:2) and sustained in position by mighty pillars (*cf.,* Job 9:6). One may notice that the words *let the earth put forth vegetation* (v. 11) differ from the formula "let there be..." which introduced the other works of creation recorded so far (*cf.,* vv. 3, 6, 9). It is as if the author wished to indicate that the fertile earth has a part in the creative act, and that the growth of vegetation is a continuation of the work of creation. However, it is clear from the narrative that the earth is productive only because God wills it, and to the extent that he wills it. The earth's fertility is not something that can be personified and deified as it had so often been by Israel's neighbours. By listing various categories of vegetation (v. 11) the author seems to be making the point that all kinds of plants and trees are produced by God, and that *each according to its kind,* that is, each within its own species, has its place within God's ordered plan.

THE HEAVENLY BODIES
1:14-19

> [14]And God said, "Let there be lights in the firmament of the heavens to separate the day from the night; and let them be for signs and for seasons and for days and years, [15]and let them be lights in the firmament of the heavens to give light upon the earth." And it was so. [16]And God made the two great lights, the greater light to rule the day, and the lesser light to rule the night; he made the stars also. [17]And God set them in the firmament of the heavens to give light upon the earth, [18]to rule over the day and over the night, and to separate the light from the darkness. And God saw that it was good. [19]And there was evening and there was morning, a fourth day.

The process of peopling the heavens and the earth now begins, and the "setting" (v. 17) of "lights" (v. 14) in the skies renders permanent the distinction that had already been established between night and day (v. 5). By referring to the sun and moon as "lights," and by declaring that they were created to render a service to man and woman, the author is engaging in an implicit polemic against the mythologies of the Middle East which attributed divine status to the heavenly bodies. The custom of worshipping "the host of heaven" seems to have had a remarkable hold on the Israelite mind, so that preachers and prophets had to warn against it continually (*cf.,* Deut 4:19; 17:3; Job 31:26-28; Isa 47:13). By stating that the heavenly bodies are mere light-bearers, component parts of the universe that fulfill a divinely ordained function in the world, the author dissociates himself from the mythological mentality, and strips the sun and moon of all divine qualities, thus preserving the clear line of distinction between God and creation. When it is said that the "lights" serve as "signs" (v. 14) the reference seems to be to unusual phenomena such as eclipses which were regarded by the ancients as presaging future events. The sun and moon determined "seasons" in that they enabled the ancients to establish sacred and profane dates so that cult and work could be regulated.

LIVING CREATURES
1:20-23

> [20]And God said, "Let the waters bring forth swarms of living creatures, and let birds fly above the earth across the firmament of the heavens." [21]So God created the great sea monsters and every living creature that moves, with which the waters swarm, according to their kinds, and every winged bird according to its kind. And God saw that it was good. [22]And God blessed them, saying, "Be fruitful and multiply and fill the waters in the seas, and let birds multiply on the earth." [23]And there was evening and there was morning, a fifth day.

Now that the chaotic waters are restrained, the heavens supported by the solid firmament, the dry land firmly established, and fertile with all kinds of vegetation and food, and light available to nurture life, all the conditions are ripe for the appearance of living things on earth. So the waters are peopled with a rich variety of aquatic life, and all kinds of birds are made to fly in the heavens. The verb *bara'*, which as we remarked earlier (see comment to v. 1 above, p. 20), indicates divine activity that is absolutely without analogy, is here for the first time applied to the creation of specific creatures. This fact suggests that something unprecedented is taking place and that the production of living creatures involves direct divine intervention. The author wished to assert that all living things in the seas and in the skies owe their existence to God. But no doubt his readers would have taken a special interest in *the great sea monsters* (v. 21), since these strange beings figured prominently in the mythologies of both Canaan and Mesopotamia. In these literatures the chaotic sea, personified as a monster, confronted the creator God and was subdued only after a struggle. Echoes of this myth are found in several Old

Testament passages (*cf.,* Isa 27:1; 51:9; Job 26:13; Ps 74:13-15). For the author of Gen 1, however, the sea monster is no longer an adversary of God, but a creature of his hand, with its own place among the living creatures of the sea.

The sea-life and the birds of the sky not only receive the customary words of divine approval, but enjoy a special blessing from God, and are given a mandate to *be fruitful and multiply* (v. 22). This formula is characteristic of the Priestly author (*cf.,* v. 28; 8:17; 9:1, 7) and it suggests that the procreative power within living things is a divinely ordained gift, and that the function of transmitting life is carried on under divine blessing.

ANIMALS AND HUMAN LIFE
1:24-31

24And God said, "Let the earth bring forth living creatures according to their kinds: cattle and creeping things and beasts of the earth according to their kinds." And it was so. 25And God made the beasts of the earth according to their kinds, and everything that creeps upon the ground according to its kind. And God saw that it was good.

26Then God said, "Let us make man in our image, after our likeness; and let them have dominion over the fish of the sea, and over the birds of the air, and over the cattle, and over all the earth, and over every creeping thing that creeps upon the earth." 27So God created man in his own image, in the image of God he created him; male and female he created them. 28And God blessed them, and God said to them, "Be fruitful and multiply, and fill the earth and subdue it; and have dominion over the fish of the sea and over the birds of the air and over every living thing that moves upon the earth." 29And God said, "Behold, I have given you every plant yielding seed which is upon the face of all the earth, and every tree with seed in its fruit; you shall have them for food. 30And to every beast of the earth, and to every bird of the air, and to everything that creeps on the earth, everything that has the breath of life, I have given every green plant for food." And it was so. [31]And God saw everything that he had made, and behold, it was very good. And there was evening and there was morning, a sixth day.

Just as two works were assigned to the third day (vv. 9-13) so now two creative acts, the creation of animals and of humanity, are said to have been performed on the sixth day. If the phrase *let the earth bring forth living creatures* seems to suggest that animals are in some way the offspring of mother earth the following statement that *God made the beasts of the earth* shows that they are the objects of a direct creative act. The divine assertion of the goodness of the animals (v. 25) clearly marks the end of this work of creation, and gives us time to draw our breath before going on to the account of the creation of humanity.

God's Masterpiece

The new formula, *Let us make man and woman in our image* (v. 26), which introduces the final step in the process of creation imparts special solemnity to the account of the creation of man and woman. The precise meaning of the plural verb in this phrase has eluded the commentators although it has never ceased to exercise their ingenuity. The opinion, held by many early Church writers, that the plural pointed to the plurality of Persons in the Trinity, is of historical interest, but it tells us nothing about the original meaning of the text. It is often said that the plural is simply a "plural of majesty" which is found in royal proclamations, and which is meant to convey the authority and dignity of the royal speaker. However, many scholars hold that the "plural of majesty" or the "royal we" is not a usual Hebrew form, and they hesitate to accept it as a satisfactory explanation in this case. The more commonly held explanation today understands the text against the background of a heavenly court where God was surrounded by advisers. This concept of God's majesty is retained in several Old Testament passages (*e.g.,* 1 Kgs 22:19-22; Ps 82, 1; 89:6-8; Job 1:6), and in later theology the heavenly advisers became known as angels. It can be objected that this image of the heavenly court may have been originally polytheistic, and that the Priestly author, who is so deliberately monotheistic in his teaching, would have avoided it. But it is possible that he saw in the old image of God deliberating with his heavenly advisers a means of indicating the special attention which God gave to his creation of man and woman. However we explain the plural form in the words *Let us make man and woman in our image*, the phrase as a whole is meant to convey the idea that humanity, the high point of creation, was brought into being as a result of a special divine choice and decision.

Since the word *image* (*selem* in Hebrew) can be used of something physical like a statue, and since it ordinarily suggests an exact copy of something material, it is difficult to see how man and woman can be said to be made in the image of the transcendant God. Similarly, it is not easy to explain how man and woman, part of whose make-up is so obviously material, can be said to be *in the likeness* of the immaterial God. Certainly the Priestly author did not think of God as being in human form. Neither did he think that anything in nature could be an image of God (*cf.,* Exod 20:4-6). He would not have thought that the divine likeness is to be found in man and woman's spiritual nature alone, since the ancient Israelites conceived of human beings as a unity and not as beings composed of separable physical and spiritual parts. A clue as to what the idea meant to the biblical writers may be gathered from the fact that this phrase is followed by a divine commission which gave man and woman dominion over all living creatures (v. 26b). It seems that man and woman can be said to be in the image of God because they enjoy a share in God's sovereignty over the world, and because this participation in the divine dominance distinguishes them from all other creatures and raises them above the animal world. Created in God's image, man and woman's unique dignity and destiny entitled them to act as God's viceregents in the world, to maintain order in God's good creation, to be partners with God in the ongoing development of the universe, and, in that sense, to subdue the earth (v. 28). Insignificant though man and woman might appear in the midst of God's majestic creation they have been made "little less than God" and given "dominion over the works of God's hands" (*cf.*, Ps 8; Sir 17:2-4). However, their dominion over the world must be modelled on God's, and can never be a dominion of caprice or exploitation, but one of justice and benevolence.

Male and Female

Humanity, which was created in the image of God, was created *male and female*. Sexual distinction is of divine origin, woman and man are of equal dignity in God's presence, and both share in the privilege and task of participating in God's dominion over the world. This understanding of woman's status in the world is most remarkable against the background of a culture where woman was subservient to man and valued merely as childbearer and worker.

If sexual distinction is part of the divine design for creation, sexual activity is also part of God's good world. It is the duty of the sexually differentiated partners to be fruitful and to multiply, and in fulfilling this duty they enjoy a special blessing (v. 28). By using the divinely given power of procreation they do not enter into mystic communion with the gods, as the promoters of the fertility cults of the Middle East suggested. Unlike Israel's neighbours who divinized the power of procreation, the biblical writers regarded fertility as a gift of God, and they saw sexual activity as something to be carried out in obedience to a divine decree.

Food For Man And Beast

Although God in his solicitude provided food for all living things, the diet of both man and animals was restricted to vegetation. Seed-bearing plants and fruits were reserved for man and woman, while grasses provided the animals with sustenance (vv. 29-30). Only in a fallen world and after the Flood will the Priestly author permit the eating of meat (see comment on 9:3-4; below p. 74). Like all his contemporaries this author believed that vegetation and fruits did not fall within the domain of life, so that no violence was involved in the process of procuring them as food. In the world as we know it, life is supported at the price of life, but the author of our present passage visualized a time when human beings did not shed animal blood, and when animal did not prey on animal in order to survive. Just as the prophet pictured the messianic era as one of peace and harmony where "the wolf shall dwell with the lamb" (*cf.,* Isa 11:6-9), so did the Priestly author imagine the primeval age as a peaceable kingdom without violence of any kind.

On the sixth day the work of creation was completed. Chaos has now been totally subdued, order and harmony have been established, and every element of the creative universe has been given its place and function. Each individual stage in the creative process has been declared good, and the entire cosmos has received the divine verdict of "very good." God has made everything beautiful in its time (*cf.,* Qoh 3:11). The Priestly author ends his story of creation with a note of unrestrained approval, and leaves it to the Yahwist account of chapters 2-3 to explain the undeniable fact that evil and suffering now mar God's beautiful world.

THE SEVENTH DAY
2:1-4a

> **2** Thus the heavens and earth were finished, and all the host of them. ²And on the seventh day God finished his work which he had done, and he rested on the seventh day from all his work which he had done. ³So God blessed the seventh day and hallowed it, because on it God rested from all his work which he had done in creation.
>
> ⁴These are the generations of the heavens and the earth when they were created.

The repeated assertion that God had completed the task of creation in six days (vv. 1-2) prepares for the statement that God rested on the seventh day. The writer does not call the seventh day "Sabbath," although the link between the Sabbath and God's rest is suggested by the fact that the Hebrew verb for *rested* is *shabath*. Even though we are told that "God blessed the seventh day and hallowed it" (v. 3) the writer does not actually say that God instituted the Sabbath. However, since God *hallowed* the day, that is, sanctified it, and set it in a particular relationship to himself, it must have a special significance. When the Priestly author wrote, the Sabbath had in fact become one of the distinguishing characteristics of the Jews (*cf.,* Ezek 20:12, 20) and had become a sign of their covenant bond with Yahweh (*cf.,* Exod 31:12-17, P). It is obvious then why he should wish to trace the origins of the Sabbath back to creation, and why he should wish to portray God's rest on the seventh day as the model which the Israelites follow when they observe the Sabbath.

The formula *These are the generations of the heavens and the earth* seems to mean something like "this is the story of the origins of the heavens and the earth." The phrase *These are the generations* (Hebrew *toledoth*) occurs ten times in the Book of Genesis (2:4a; 5:1; 6:9; 10:1; 11:10; 11:27; 25:12, 19; 36:1; 37:2), and each time it marks a new stage in the development of the Priestly story.

God's First Redemptive Act

The Priestly creation story in its sublime and dignified style develops a theology of goodness. The one God, with whom no other creating power exists, and against whom no rival power stands, out of goodness and love created an ordered universe in which each component part contributed to the harmony and beauty of the whole. In this newly created world peace and order reigned, plants provided food, and all creatures lived in an atmosphere where violence was unknown. At the peak of creation were man and woman, whose grandeur consists in the fact that, as God's representatives, they exercise a purposeful control over the natural world. The whole story invites the reader to join the author of the Book of Revelation in proclaiming:

> "Worthy art thou, our Lord and God,
> to receive glory and honour and power,
> for thou didst create all things,
> and by thy will they existed and were created"(Rev. 4:11).

This prayer which is addressed to God as the author of creation is a particularly appropriate response to Gen 1, where God, and not the world nor humanity, is at the centre of the story. It is God who created, spoke, separated, blessed, gave light and life, and proclaimed everything good. Clearly this chapter is theology — a word about God. It is a word or story about God's first intervention in the world, and about the beginning of a history in which God shaped human destiny. It is, in short, God's first redemptive act, and it was seen as such in biblical passages like Ps 136:4-25; Isa 42:5-9; 44:24-26, which place God's creative actions side by side with his saving interventions on behalf of Israel. Texts like these suggest that there is a continuity between creation and God's actions in the history of salvation, and they assure us that the God who revealed his power and goodness by creating our world continues to manifest the same characteristics in saving it.

II. ADAM AND EVE
IN THE GARDEN
2:4b-3:24 (J)

Readers who leave the Priestly account of creation (Gen 1:1-2:4a) and go on to read the Yahwistic narrative that has been traditionally called the story of the Creation and Fall (2:4b-3:24), suddenly find themselves in a totally different literary atmosphere. The stereotyped formulae of chap. 1 give way to a picturesque narrative where a variety of vivid scenes are blended together to produce a story of charm and simplicity. Anthropomorphisms which were almost totally absent in the Priestly account are frequent in chaps. 2-3, where God is portrayed as moulding clay, planting trees, breathing, walking, etc. While it is true that the author of chap. 1 incorporated some mythological motifs into his account, the Yahwist shows a much closer dependence on extra-biblical texts, and has blended several popular elements from mythological sources into his story. Such themes as the formation of people from clay, a blissful garden of God, magical trees, talking serpents, and cherubs guarding the gates, are the stuff that myths are made of, and they belonged to the folklore from which the biblical author drew.

MORTAL HUMANITY
2:4b-7

> In the day that the Lord God made the earth and the heavens, [5]when no plant of the field was yet in the earth and no herb of the field had yet sprung up—for the Lord God had not caused it to rain upon the earth, and there was no man to till the ground; [6]but a mist went up from the earth and watered the whole face of the ground— [7]then the Lord God formed man of dust from the ground, and breathed into his nostrils the breath of life; and man became a living being.

Whereas in the preceding chapter the story of creation began with a watery chaos, the present narrative begins with an arid land that was incapable of producing any kind of growth. The *mist* (or flood) *that went up from the earth* was useless, since there was no one to channel it into fertilizing courses. So the world was desolate and barren when God *formed humankind*, the first object of his creative activity, from *dust of the ground*. The verb *formed*, representing the first of the author's numerous anthropomorphisms, suggests the image of a potter moulding clay, while the statement that humankind (*adam* in Hebrew) was made from the ground, (*adamah* in Hebrew) includes a pleasant play on words that points to an intimate bond between humans and the earth. We find the motif of people being created from clay in both Egyptian and Mesopotamian mythologies, and the Yahwist takes up this traditional imagery to express the fragile condition of human beings and their dependence on God. Creaturehood is apparent in human origins, and the clay bespeaks mortality. Having come from the dust people will inevitably return to it (*cf.,* 3:19; Job 4:19; 10:9; Qoh 12:7). Nevertheless, when the author says that God breathed into adam's nostrils the breath of life, he is not only saying that adam enjoys life as a gift from God, but is also suggesting that human beings enjoy a share in God's own life. If this is so, then the Yahwist's teaching is not so far removed from that of the Priestly writer who declared that man and woman are made in God's image and likeness. In any case, the present author will go on to show that humble and fragile man and woman were called into companionship with their creator and enjoyed a privileged life in God's presence.

A GARDEN IN EDEN
2:8-9

> 8And the Lord God planted a garden in Eden, in the east; and there he put the man whom he had formed. 9And out of the ground the Lord God made to grow every tree that is pleasant to the sight and good for food, the tree of life also in the midst of the garden, and the tree of the knowledge of good and evil.

The Hebrew word rendered *garden* in our English texts became *paradeisos* in the Greek version. This word, from which, of course, we get our word Paradise, has connotations of abundance and pleasure. The garden was in fact a symbol of God's generosity in providing for the first human beings whom he had made. The name *Eden* means "pleasure" in Hebrew, and would have conjured up for the original readers images of bliss and contentment. To say that the garden was *in the east* could only mean to the Palestinian that it was located in Mesopotamia.

Among the abundant trees of the garden was the *tree of life*. Several Middle Eastern mythologies knew of a tree of life whose fruits could grant immortality, and no doubt the biblical author borrowed the idea from them. However, the tree of life has no role in the drama that was to be played out in the garden, and it is only mentioned again at the very end of the story.

THE FOUR RIVERS
2:10-14

> [10]A river flowed out of Eden to water the garden, and there it divided and became four rivers. [11]The name of the first is Pishon; it is the one which flows around the whole land of Havilah, where there is gold; [12]and the gold of that land is good, bdellium and onyx stone are there. [13]The name of the second river is Gihon; it is the one which flows around the whole land of Cush. [14]And the name of third river is Tigris, which flows east of Assyria. And the fourth river is the Euphrates.

It is the generally accepted view of scholars that these verses, which interrupt the flow of the Yahwist's narrative, are a later addition to the text. The four rivers do not feature in the unfolding of the narrative, and they are introduced here to suggest that the garden enjoyed an abundance of water. The editor who inserted the verses doubtless wished to localize Eden. His mention of the Tigris and Euphrates shows that he believed it to be in the East (*cf.*, v. 8). Pishon and Gihon cannot be identified, but must be lesser rivers in Mesopotamia.

TILL IT AND KEEP IT
2:15-17

> [15]The Lord God took the man and put him in the garden of Eden to till it and keep it. [16]And the Lord God commanded the man, saying, "You may freely eat of every tree of the garden; [17]but of the tree of the knowledge of good and evil you shall not eat, for in the day that you eat of it you shall die."

The commission given to Adam to till and keep the delightful garden shows that from the very beginning work was an essential part of the human condition. While enjoying the fertile garden as God's gift Adam could develop his own capacities and unfold the rich potentialities of God's beautiful world. Since in recent times we have become conscious of the scandalous way in which we waste the natural resources of the earth, and of the thoughtless way in which we pollute the air we breathe and the water we must drink, commentators on our present passage often remark that the command to till the earth and keep it points to our responsibility as the custodians of the world which is God's gift. We must indeed develop the world, and we must use all the discoveries of science and technology in doing so. We cannot, however, use the world just for our own profit and convenience. We must "keep" the earth, and prudently conserve its riches, we must avoid exploitation and waste which are simply a desecration of what God has placed at our disposal.

It is remarkable that *the tree of the knowledge of good and evil* is not mentioned in the Old Testament outside the garden of Eden story. The phrase *good and evil* has no moral overtones, and it seems to refer to the totality of knowledge (*cf.*, 31:24, 29; 2 Sam 13:22; etc.). What is meant then in the exclusion of the tree of knowledge from human control seems to be that man and woman cannot acquire universal knowledge. Such knowledge would give a mastery over their own existence, and would place them in a position of self-sufficiency and autonomy with regard to God. In seeking such knowledge and autonomy man and woman would overstep the limits decreed for them by God, and the punishment for such arrogance is expressed in terms of death.

A HELPER FIT FOR MAN
2:18-25

> [18]Then the Lord God said, "It is not good that the man should be alone; I will make him a helper fit for him." [19]So out of the ground the Lord God formed every beast

of the field and every bird of the air, and brought them to the man to see what he would call them; and whatever the man called every living creature, that was its name. 20The man gave names to all cattle, and to the birds of the air, and to every beast of the field; but for the man there was not found a helper fit for him. 21So the Lord God caused a deep sleep to fall upon the man, and while he slept took one of his ribs and closed up its place with flesh; 22and the rib which the Lord God had taken from the man he made into a woman and brought her to the man. 23Then the man said,

> "This at last is bone of my bones
>   and flesh of my flesh;
> she shall be called Woman,
>   because she was taken out of Man."

24Therefore a man leaves his father and his mother and cleaves to his wife, and they become one flesh. 25And the man and his wife were both naked, and were not ashamed.

The story of the creation of the animals is told not so much for its own sake as to emphasize, by contrast, the dignity and the role of woman. God in his kindness saw that *it is not good that man should be alone* in the world, and that he needed a suitable partner with whom he would find fellowship. Man is by nature a social being who needs interpersonal relationships if he is to develop his human potential. So God, who was interested in his well-being, provided him with *a helper fit for him*. This phrase appears in the NEB as *I will provide a partner for him*, a rendering which seems to catch the flavour of the original Hebrew. As man's partner, woman enjoys equality with him. Of the same nature as man, yet different from him, she complements his being, and enters into a relationship of mutual love and respect with him. Thus the present narrative portrays woman as a being who is appreciated for her own worth, and not just as one who is capable of satisfying man's needs and instincts.

The curious story of God's creating woman from the rib of the unconscious Adam (v. 21) is highly anthropomorphic, and may be inspired by an ancient Sumerian tale. Perhaps the extraordinary sleep that overcame Adam when God was about to provide him with a partner may suggest the mysterious nature of God's creative activity (*cf.,* Ps 139:13-15; 2 Macc 7:22). The statement that woman was created from a rib conveys the idea that man provides the raw material from which woman is made, and that she is therefore of the same nature as he. Man's reaction at the sight of his new companion was one of enthusiasm and joy, and he voiced his feelings in what are the first lines of poetry in the Bible (v. 23). Although there is no real etymological basis for the association of the Hebrew word *ishshah* (woman) and *ish* (man), the author, in typically Yahwistic fashion, uses the similarity in the sound of the words to explain that woman gets her name from the fact that she was taken from man. We may add, incidentally, that the Yahwist's play on words is reproduced in English in the words wo*man* and *man.*

Since man and woman are complementary beings there is a mysterious attraction between them that impels them to break the bonds that tie them to their parents' home in order to *become one flesh.* The concept of becoming one flesh must not, of course, be understood in the narrow sense of sexual union, but must be taken to refer to that full union of persons that enables two individuals to find fulfilment in each other. We may note, however, that it is unlikely that the author of this verse, who wrote in the polygamous environment of Israel in the tenth century B.C., intended to teach the doctrine of monogamous marriage or to exclude divorce. Later Israel continued to accept both polygamy and divorce, and it was not until Jesus interpreted Gen 2:24 that the ideal of the indissoluble union of husband and wife was seen as strictly binding (*cf.,* Mark 10:2-12).

The assertion that *the man and his wife were both naked* (v. 25) points to the childlike innocence and to the state of bliss in which the first couple lived in the idyllic garden in which God had placed them. The statement does not refer primarily to the absence of sexual awareness or of sexual disorder, but to the relationship of mutual trust and respect that united the first couple. Only after their sin when this harmonious relationship would be broken would man and woman become aware of their nakedness (*cf.,* 3:7).

TEMPTATION AND DISOBEDIENCE
3:1-7

> **3** Now the serpent was more subtle than any other wild creature that the Lord God had made. He said to the woman, "Did God say, 'You shall not eat of any tree of the garden'?" ²And the woman said to the serpent, "We may eat of the fruit of the trees of the garden; ³but God said, 'You shall not eat of the fruit of the tree which is in the midst of the garden, neither shall you touch it, lest you die.'" ⁴But the serpent said to the woman, "You will not die. ⁵For God knows that when you eat of it your eyes will be opened, and you will be like God, knowing good and evil." ⁶So when the woman saw that the tree was good for food, and that it was a delight to the eyes, and that the tree was to be desired to make one wise, she took of its fruit and ate; and she also gave some to her husband, and he ate. ⁷Then the eyes of both were opened, and they knew that they were naked; and they sewed fig leaves together and made themselves aprons.

This little passage with its fast-moving dialogue is recognized as one of the masterpieces of Old Testament literature. With the portrayal in chapter two of man and woman in the idyllic garden where they had access to all its trees except the tree of the knowledge of good and evil the stage is set for a new and dramatic episode. Onto that stage, as if from nowhere, crawls the subtle serpent (v. 1). In the Yahwist's mind the serpent is not the embodiment of the demonic or of evil that it was to become in later Jewish and Christian tradition (*cf.,* Wis 2:24; John 8:44; 2 Cor 11:3; Rev 12:9), for he categorizes it as one of *the wild creatures that God had made*, and he distinguishes it from the other animals only by its uncanny cleverness. Some commentators think that the serpent was chosen for its nefarious role in the temptation story because of its association with idolatrous fertility rites in which sexual promiscuity was an important feature. According to this theory the author of the temptation story was engaging in a subtle polemic against these rites. It is probable, however, that we need not look for such a recondite meaning in the text. The loathsome serpent that endangers human life (*cf.,* 49:17; Isa 14:29; Job 20:16) and whose treacherous sublety was proverbial (*cf.,* Prov 30:19; Matt 10:16), was quite a natural choice for the sinister role that was given to it in the garden scene.

The astute serpent approached the woman in a gingerly fashion, and asked her an apparently innocuous question (v. 1). Yet that question represented a deliberate distortion of the divine command, because God had not denied access to *all* the trees of the garden to Adam (*cf.,* 2:16-17). The woman firmly corrected the serpent's misrepresentation of God's command, but did not completely silence the serpent. The tempter went on to deny that death would be the inevitable consequence of rejection of the limitation which God imposed on man and woman (vv. 4-5). The serpent thus called the word of God into question, insinuated that God jealously wished to retain the gift of immortality for himself, and implied that the Creator had imposed an unwarranted restriction on humankind. All this struck at the roots of the first couple's trusting relationship with God, and prepared the way for the serpent's positive affirmation that transgression of God's decree would not bring death but would have the effect of making man and woman *like God, knowing good and evil.* "Becoming like God" and "knowing good and evil" have much the same meaning, for they both imply an usurpation of divine prerogatives, and a striving after an autonomy that belongs to God alone. The prospect of gaining that knowledge of complete mastery over one's own destiny could not be other than enticing to the woman, and in defiance of God's express command she ate the forbidden fruit. The man soon joined her in her disobedience, and became a willing accomplice in her rejection of God's authority. It is not said that the woman actually enticed her husband to eat, so that the statement in Sir 25:24 that "woman is the origin of sin" does not fully correspond to the Yahwist's presentation of the case. The Genesis narrative does not excuse the man of culpability, and the blunt statement "and he ate" points to a deliberate transgression that gives man a share in his wife's guilt.

The primeval couple's dream of unlimited knowledge and of the accompanying independence was soon shattered. They had been told that their eyes would be opened, and that they would see God. But when their eyes were opened after their transgression they became conscious only of a shameful nakedness. The naked condition which before their sin caused no embarrassment (*cf.*, 2:25) now caused an acute sense of shame which was the expression of guilt. Ill at ease in each other's presence the couple realized that their sin which had shattered their relationship with God had also put an end to their own mutual relationship of trust and harmony.

JUDICIAL INQUIRY
3:8-19

> [8]And they heard the sound of the Lord God walking in the garden in the cool of the day, and the man and his wife hid themselves from the presence of the Lord God among the trees of the garden. [9]But the Lord God called to the man, and said to him, "Where are you?" [10]And he said, "I heard the sound of thee in the garden, and I was afraid, because I was naked; and I hid myself." [11]He said, "Who told you that you were naked? Have you eaten of the tree of which I commanded you not to eat?" [12]The man said, "The woman whom thou gavest to be with me, she gave me fruit of the tree, and I ate." [13]Then the Lord God said to the woman, "What is this that you have done?" The

woman said, "The serpent beguiled me, and I ate." [14]The
Lord God said to the serpent,
"Because you have done this,
  cursed are you above all cattle,
  and above all wild animals;
upon your belly you shall go,
  and dust you shall eat
  all the days of your life.
[15]I will put enmity between you and the woman,
  and between your seed and her seed;
he shall bruise your head,
  and you shall bruise his heel."
[16]To the woman he said,
"I will greatly multiply your pain in childbearing;
  in pain you shall bring forth children,
yet your desire shall be for your husband,
  and he shall rule over you."
[17]And to Adam he said,
"Because you have listened to the voice of your wife,
  and have eaten of the tree
of which I commanded you,
  'You shall not eat of it,'
cursed is the ground because of you;
  in toil you shall eat of it all the days of your life.
[18]thorns and thistles it shall bring forth to you;
  and you shall eat the plants of the field.
[19]In the sweat of your face
  you shall eat bread
till you return to the ground,
  for out of it you were taken;
you are dust,
  and to dust you shall return."

The Lord did not abandon his world because of the
disobedience of the man and woman. He continued to "walk
in the garden," and even sought out the couple who had
ignored his decree. But the guilty pair who knew they had
incurred the Creator's wrath tried to avoid an encounter

with him (v. 8). The Hound of Heaven, however, went in quest of his creatures, and the omniscient God called out, "Where are you?" Entering into dialogue with the confused couple he suggested by means of a rhetorical question that the couple's nakedness, their sense of shame, and their guilt, could only be the result of their disobedience (v. 11.) But the man was not prepared to make an open avowal of guilt, and instead mingled self-justification and evasion of responsibility with a reluctant confession of disobedience (v. 12). The woman in her turn followed the typical procedure of the guilty one, found a scapegoat, and pointed the finger of blame at the serpent (v. 13). God did not enter into dialogue with the serpent but went on to pass the verdict of punishment on the serpent, on the woman, and on man, in that order, that is, in the order in which the three were involved in the process of sinning.

The account of the sentences meted out to the guilty ones has a definite etiological intent, that is to say, it is meant to explain existing realities and some of the enigmas of life. The fact that serpents crawl on the ground and seem to eat dust (*cf.,* Isa 65:25; Mic 7:17), and that there exists an undying enmity between the serpent and humankind, are explained as the result of a divine curse (v. 14). The pains of childbirth and woman's subordinate status in ancient Middle Eastern society are interpreted as a punishment for the first woman's part in the initial rebellion against God's will (v. 16). The wearisome nature of work, which was originally a pleasant duty (*cf.,* 2:15), and the drudgery involved in the peasant's life, are said to be the consequence of the sin of the father of the human race (vv. 17-19).

He Shall Bruise Your Head (v. 15)

Ever since St. Irenaeus (about 200 A.D.) saw in v. 15 a prophecy of Christ's victory over Satan this verse has enjoyed a privileged place in the Christian interpretation of the Old Testament. When taken literally the verse seems to say no more than that the serpent species ("your seed, oh serpent") will struggle violently and unremittingly with every generation of humans (the woman's seed). The New English Bible translation — "they (the seed or descendants of the woman) shall strike at your (the serpent's) head, and you shall strike at their heel" — seems to convey the original meaning. There is no suggestion that one party in the struggle will emerge victorious. To say that victory for humankind is implied in the fact that a human being will crush the head of the serpent while the latter will only wound the heel of the other, seems to be going beyond the meaning of the text. In accord with the imagery called for by the situation, the biblical words simply oppose humankind's crushing of the serpent's head to the latter's deadly sting.

How then did Christian commentators come to see in this verse a *Protoevangelium*, or the first promise of salvation for the human race? The translation "he shall bruise your head" which we find in the RSV, and which goes all the way back to the ancient Greek version of the Scriptures known as the Septuagint, personalizes the "seed" or the descendants of Eve. This translation, which is allowed, but not demanded by the Hebrew, opened the way for the Christian interpreters who took the "he" of the phrase just quoted to refer to Christ, the representative of the human race, the victor over the serpent who was identified with Satan (*cf.,* Wis 2:24; Rom 5:12; John 8:44; etc.).

The Latin translation known as the Vulgate further complicated the issue by rendering this famous line as "*she* shall bruise your head." Basing themselves on this false reading many Christian commentators saw in the Genesis verse a prophecy of the role of Mary in human redemption. Since the Christian tradition which found Christological and Mariological implications in Gen 3:15 is based on faulty translations of the Hebrew originals, modern commentators have no qualms about denying that there is any prediction of messianic salvation in that verse. The author did not go beyond the mutual hostility that exists between human beings and the serpent, and he explained that hostility according to his lights. However, we Christians can extend the original author's meaning, and, regarding the serpent as a symbol of sin and evil, we can see Christ as the "seed of Eve" who vanquished that enemy of humankind.

The words "you are dust, and to dust you shall return" (v. 19) with which God's verdict on man and woman ends clearly implies that death is not a natural event but rather the consequence of sin. This idea is not fully reconcilable with the statement that humankind is made of clay (2:7) and therefore by nature destined to corruption. The Old Testament in general regarded death as the natural destiny of all humans (*cf.,* 2 Sam 14:14), and Sir 25:24 is the earliest text to state explicitly that death is the result of sin. This idea is developed at some length by St. Paul in Rom 5:12-20; cf. 1 Cor 15:22.

UNCEREMONIOUS EXPULSION
3:20-24

> [20]The man called his wife's name Eve, because she was the mother of all living. [21]And the Lord God made for Adam and for his wife garments of skins, and clothed them.
>
> [22]Then the Lord God said, "Behold, the man has become like one of us, knowing good and evil; and now, lest he put forth his hand and take also of the tree of life, and eat, and live for ever" — [23]therefore the Lord God sent him forth from the garden of Eden, to till the ground from which he was taken. [24]He drove out the man; and at the east of the garden of Eden he placed the cherubim, and a flaming sword which turned every way, to guard the way to the tree of life.

Having announced the inevitability of death for man and woman, the author passes on abruptly, and not without some element of paradox, to announce that the man called his wife Eve. In its Hebrew form this name has an affinity with the word for life, and was therefore an appropriate name for her who was to be "*the mother of all the living.*"

The *garments of skins* which God made for the couple he had condemned shows that in spite of their rebellion the Lord still showed concern for them. Even in their fallen state man and woman are the object of God's grace and solicitude, and even though sin alienates the creature from the Creator it does not bring about an absolute separation.

In placing the words *behold the man has become like one of us, knowing good and evil* (v. 22) on God's lips, the author is saying with a certain note of irony that the first couple had, in a sense, become like God, in that they had refused to accept their status as creatures, and rejected obedience in order to live autonomously. But their action had dire consequences, and expulsion from the garden and exclusion from the tree of life showed that the arrogant couple had lost the happy relationship with God which they had enjoyed. The *cherubim* who guarded the entrance to the garden (v. 24) are legendary beings, winged animals with a human face, that are known from Babylonian and Canaanite monuments as guardians of royal palaces and temples. The cherubim and a flaming sword — probably personified lightning — bring the story of Eden to an end, and leave us with the gloomy message that Paradise is irretrievably lost to humankind, and that the human race can never, except by divine grace, regain the familiar companionship with the Creator which it once enjoyed.

A Symbolic Story

Gen 2-3 has no direct parallel in the mythology of the Ancient Near East. But the chapters incorporate many mythological motifs by which the author conveys a profound message about man and woman, their relationship to God and their moral responsibility in the world. "The man" and "the woman" of the story represent "Everyman" and "Everywoman" and in their experience of temptation, sin, regret, punishment, and new hope, we see a reflection of our own lives and experiences. But these two chapters must be read as part of the universal history (Gen 1-11) that forms the first great section of the Book of Genesis, and only when one has read that whole section can one fully appreciate the meaning of the story of the Fall.

III. THE SPREAD OF SIN
4:1—6:4

THE FIRST MURDER
4:1-16 (J)

4 Now Adam knew Eve his wife, and she conceived and bore Cain, saying "I have gotten a man with the help of the Lord." ²And again, she bore his brother Abel. Now Abel was a keeper of sheep, and Cain a tiller of the ground. ³In the course of time Cain brought to the Lord an offering of the fruit of the ground, ⁴and Abel brought the firstlings of his flock and of their fat portions. And the Lord had regard for Abel and his offering, ⁵but for Cain and his offering he had no regard. So Cain was very angry, and his countenance fell. ⁶The Lord said to Cain, "Why are you so angry, and why has your countenance fallen? ⁷If you do well, will you not be accepted? And if you do not do well, sin is couching at the door; its desire is for you, but you must master it."

⁸Cain said to Abel his brother, "Let us go out to the field." And when they were in the field, Cain rose up against his brother Abel, and killed him. ⁹Then the Lord said to Cain, "Where is Abel your brother?" He said, "I do not know; am I my brother's keeper?" ¹⁰And the Lord said, "What have you done? The voice of your brother's

blood is crying to me from the ground. [11]And now you are cursed from the ground, which has opened its mouth to receive your brother's blood from your hand. [12]When you till the ground, it shall no longer yield to you its strength; you shall be a fugitive and a wanderer on the earth." [13]Cain said to the Lord, "My punishment is greater than I can bear. [14]Behold, thou hast driven me this day away from the ground; and from thy face I shall be hidden; and I shall be a fugitive and a wanderer on the earth, and whoever finds me will slay me." [15]Then the Lord said to him, "Not so! If any one slays Cain, vengeance shall be taken on him sevenfold." And the Lord put a mark on Cain, lest any who came upon him should kill him. [16]Then Cain went away from the presence of the Lord, and dwelt in the land of Nod, east of Eden.

Eve's joyful exclamation *I have gotten a man* gives a popular etymology to the name Cain, which is similar in sound to the verb *qanah*, to get or acquire. The words *with the help of the Lord* suggest the idea that all life is a gift from God (*cf.,* v. 25; 16:2; 29:31; Ps 127:3; etc.) and that it is the mother's privilege to share in a special way in the creative act. The name *Abel* means "breath" or "puff," an appropriate name for one whose life was so suddenly cut short.

We are not told why the brothers made their offerings to God (v. 4), but we must presume that they did so in order to secure well-being for themselves and for their flocks or crops. The shepherd offered a victim from his flock while the tiller offered some of the produce of the land, reminding us that each culture gives rise to its own form of worship, and that the externals of religion must always respond to the experiences and needs of the believers. Our terse story fails to explain why the Lord had regard for Abel's offering or why he rejected that of Cain. There is no suggestion that Cain's earlier deeds had been evil (*cf.,* 1 John 3:12), or that his offering was made without faith (*cf.,* Heb 11:4). The author simply wishes to tell us that the younger son was preferred to the older, and this theme of the choice of the younger son taking precedence over the firstborn will occur several times in his story (*cf.,* 21:1-13; 25:19-34; 38:27-30). The imaginative phrase *his countenance fell* paints a telling picture of the envy and resentment that overcame Cain when his sacrifice was not accepted. But the God who rejected Cain's sacrifice did not reject Cain himself. There is in the words *Why are you angry?* which the Lord addressed to the agitated Cain a touch of paternal tenderness, and there is an encouraging ring to the question that follows: *if you do well, will you not be accepted?* Sin may be couching like some predatory beast trying to get control of Cain's life, but he can resist its attraction, for even in his fallen state the individual has the power to say no to sin.

Cain's fratricidal act took place *in the field* where no one could witness the foul deed (v. 8). (Since vv. 1-2 tell us that Cain and Abel were the only children born to Adam and Eve there could be no one to witness it in any case. But this does not bother the author who is more interested in getting on with the story than in producing a perfectly coherent narrative.) God's question *Where is Abel your brother?* reminded the murderer that his responsibility before God involved responsibility for his brother. Cain's truculent and insolent reply, *Am I my brother's keeper?* includes a direct lie, and witnesses to a hardening attitude to sin. If Adam and Eve shrank in shame before God and tried to excuse themselves of guilt (*cf.,* 3:10-13) Cain shows no sign of repentance. Cain's petulant disavowal of responsibility for his brother avails him nothing, since no one can escape the eyes of God who sees all. The words of the divine accusation, *The voice of your brother's blood is crying to me from the ground* (v. 10), must be understood against the background of the Old Testament view that life is in the blood (Lev 17:11-14), and that blood and life belong to God alone (*cf.,* comment on 9:4, below p. 74). If expulsion from the land he had desecrated with his brother's blood seemed a punishment beyond endurance to Cain (vv. 13-14), it was not only because of the natural inhospitality of the wilderness, but also because the desert was a place of violence where every stranger was an enemy until they could prove otherwise, and where the lone wanderer had little chance of survival. Cain's anguished cry *whoever finds me will slay me* was no exaggeration and could be taken literally. But even the life of the murderer remains in the care of God, and the Lord did not abandon Cain. The merciful Judge mitigated the sentence he had passed on the sinner, and guaranteed to take revenge on anyone who might murder him. It is not clear what kind of mark God put on Cain. But it was a sign that the chastened fratricide enjoyed the special protection of his God. Marked with this sign he set out to the land called *Wandering* (in Hebrew, *Nod*), to live in isolation and without peace.

It has been remarked that the Cain and Abel passage mentions seven times that the protagonists were brothers. The story makes the point that each person *is* his brother's or sister's keeper, and it shows that every offence committed against one's neighbour brings about an alienation from God. Cain can be seen as a model of the average human being who can be led by envy, anger, or greed to a practical denial of family bonds, and his punishment is a reminder that even what we do in secret against our neighbour has a bearing on our relationship with God.

THE GENEALOGY OF CAIN
4:17-24 (J)

17Cain knew his wife, and she conceived and bore Enoch; and he built a city, and called the name of the city after the name of his son, Enoch. 18To Enoch was born Irad; and Irad was the father of Mehujael, and Mehujael the father of Methushael, and Methushael the father of Lamech. 19And Lamech took two wives; the name of the one was Adah, and the name of the other Zillah. 20Adah bore Jabal; he was the father of those who dwell in tents and have cattle. 21His brother's name was Jubal; he was the father of all those who play the lyre and pipe. 22Zillah bore Tubalcain; he was the forger of all instruments of bronze and iron. The sister of Tubalcain was Naamah.

23Lamech said to his wives:
"Adah and Zillah, hear my voice;
  you wives of Lamech, hearken to what I say;
I have slain a man for wounding me,
  a young man for striking me.
24If Cain is avenged sevenfold,
  truly Lamech seventy-sevenfold."

In this the first of a series of genealogies that appear in the Genesis text (*cf.,* 5:1-32; 11:10-32; etc.) the Yahwist traces the family tree of Cain. The image of Cain given in this passage is quite different from the one we found in the murder story which immediately preceded it (vv. 2-16). The Cain who had become a fugitive and a wanderer (vv. 12, 16) is now portrayed as the father of those who built cities and who made the kind of cultural and technical progress that can only take place in organized community life. We notice too that Jubal, one of Cain's descendants, is in the present narrative said to have been "the father of those who dwell in tents and have cattle" (v. 20). The earlier story, however, had told us that Abel was a shepherd (v. 2), who, we must presume, dwelt in tents and moved about with his flocks. The genealogy of Cain, then, seems to have been an ancient independent tradition which the Yahwist introduced into his story, not so much for its genealogical and chronological value, as for its importance as an account of the beginnings of various institutions and as a summary of the earliest cultural achievements.

To Cain himself is attributed the establishment of urban life (v. 17), and among his descendants were the first pastoral nomad (v. 20), the inventor of stringed and wind musical instruments (v. 21), and the first smith (v. 22). It is sometimes said that Lamech's polygamy (v. 19) was intended by the author to be seen as a further sign of the progress of sin in the fallen world. But since polygamy was an accepted custom in the Yahwist's day this is most unlikely.

The evaluation of the line of Cain in vv. 17-24 is very positive, and the descendants of him who was earlier portrayed as an unrepentant murderer are singled out as the inventors who contributed greatly to humankind's technical progress. The passage tells a story of successful secular enterprise, and it may be a reminder to us that God's gifts are also distributed to the ungodly, and that we in our own day benefit by the inventions of scientists and discoverers who find no God on their horizon.

The memorable if violent song of Lamech (vv. 23-24) records the boastful cry of a vengeful tribesman who takes pride before his womenfolk in the savage revenge he has taken on his vanquished enemies. The purpose of the song in the Yahwist's story is to tell of the progress of violence and bloodshed in the world, and to show how human pride and self-assertiveness lead to an ever-increasing rupture in the peace and harmony that characterized the world when God created it. The song breathes arrogance and caprice, and it reflects a barbarous society where a spirit of savagery reigned, and where might was right. And yet the human situation described in the song is not so different from our own competitive society that is so often ruled by a spirit of dog-eat-dog, and where the ruthless and the arrogant so often sing the song of victory. However, Lamech's readiness to exact seventy-seven fold vengeance, and indeed every expression of revenge and violence, are condemned by Jesus who taught that one must be ready to forgive seventy-seven times (*cf.,* Matt 18:22).

CALLING THE NAME OF THE LORD
4:25-26 (J)

> [25]And Adam knew his wife again, and she bore a son and called his name Seth for she said, "God has appointed for me another child instead of Abel, for Cain slew him." [26]To Seth also a son was born, and he called his name Enosh. At that time men began to call upon the name of the Lord.

The words "God has appointed for me another child" (v. 25) which Adam's wife spoke at the birth of her third son remind one of the exclamation "I have gotten a man with the help of the Lord" (v. 1) with which she greeted the birth of Cain. In both cases the child is seen as a gift from God. The name which the mother gave her new son suggests this idea too, for the name Seth resembles the Hebrew verb *shath*, which means to grant. The present passage traces the line of Seth for only one generation, but the family tree of this son who was to continue the line of Adam will be pursued in the Priestly genealogy of chapter 5.

The fact that the Yahwist traces the worship of Yahweh back to primeval times (v. 26) is surprising in view of the fact that Exod 3:14 (E) and 6:3 (P) inform us that the name Yahweh was first revealed to Moses. But in saying that people *began to call upon the name of the Lord* (*Yahweh* in the Hebrew text) the Yahwist wishes to assert that the true God, the God whom Israel knew as Yahweh, was worshipped at the earliest stages of human history. The notice that God was worshipped at this point in the Genesis story is also a reminder that although humankind had sinned and rebelled against God it had not abandoned him completely and was not totally estranged from him.

THE PRE-FLOOD PATRIARCHS
5:1-32 (P)

5 This is the book of the generations of Adam. When God created man, he made him in the likeness of God. [2]Male and female he created them, and he blessed them and named them Man when they were created. [3]When Adam had lived a hundred and thirty years, he became the father of a son in his own likeness, after his image, and named him Seth. [4]The days of Adam after he became the father of Seth were eight hundred years; and he had other sons and daughters. [5]Thus all the days that Adam lived were nine hundred and thirty years; and he died.

6When Seth had lived a hundred and five years, he became the father of Enosh. 7Seth lived after the birth of Enosh eight hundred and seven years, and had other sons and daughters. 8Thus all the days of Seth were nine hundred and twelve years; and he died.

9When Enosh had lived ninety years, he became the father of Kenan. 10Enosh lived after the birth of Kenan eight hundred and fifteen years, and had other sons and daughters. 11Thus all the days of Enosh were nine hundred and five years; and he died.

12When Kenan had lived seventy years, he became the father of Mahalalel. 13Kenan lived after the birth of Mahalalel eight hundred and forty years, and had other sons and daughters. 14Thus all the days of Kenan were nine hundred and ten years; and he died.

15When Mahalalel had lived sixty-five years, he became the father of Jared. 16Mahalalel lived after the birth of Jared eight hundred and thirty years, and had other sons and daughters. 17Thus all the days of Mahalalel were eight hundred and ninety-five years; and he died.

18When Jared had lived a hundred and sixty-two years he became the father of Enoch. 19Jared lived after the birth of Enoch eight hundred years, and had other sons and daughters. 20Thus all the days of Jared were nine hundred and sixty-two years; and he died.

21When Enoch had lived sixty-five years, he became the father of Methuselah. 22Enoch walked with God after the birth of Methuselah three hundred years, and had other sons and daughters. 23Thus all the days of Enoch were three hundred and sixty-five years. 24Enoch walked with God; and he was not, for God took him.

25When Methuselah had lived a hundred and eighty-seven years, he became the father of Lamech. 26Methuselah lived after the birth of Lamech seven hundred and eighty-two years, and had other sons and daughters. 27Thus all the days of Methuselah were nine hundred and sixty-nine years; and he died.

[28]When Lamech had lived a hundred and eighty-two years, he became the father of a son, [29]and called his name Noah, saying, "Out of the ground which the Lord has cursed this one shall bring us relief from our work and from the toil of our hands." [30]Lamech lived after the birth of Noah five hundred and ninety-five years, and had other sons and daughters. [31]Thus all the days of Lamech were seven hundred and seventy-seven years; and he died.

[32]After Noah was five hundred years old, Noah became the father of Shem, Ham, and Japheth.

Having parted company with the Priestly writers at 2:4a where they rounded off their creation story, we now rejoin them as they recall the creation of man and woman (vv. 1-2) and then go on to list the generations that link the beginnings of humankind with the Flood (vv. 3-32). The phrase "This is the book of the generations of..." occurs frequently as an introduction to Priestly genealogical lists (see above, p. 17), and the rest of the terminology in vv. 1-2 clearly echoes the Priestly account of the creation of the first couple (*cf.,* 1:26-27). The genealogy follows a rigid pattern, stating:

a) the age of each patriarch at the time of his first son's birth;

b) the number of years he lived after that event, and the fact that he had other sons and daughters;

c) his age when he died.

This genealogy says nothing about the descendants of Cain. However, the author includes among the descendants of Seth individuals whom the Yahwist had listed in Cain's family tree (*cf.,* 4:17-24). Thus, for example, the names Enoch and Lamech appear in both rosters (*cf.,* 4:17-19; 5:21-24, 28-31), while Mehujael and Methushael (4:18) are simply variants of Mahalalel (5:12) and Methuselah (5:21). It seems then that both authors had available to them the same traditional source material which had been modified in the course of transmission. The tradition known to the

Yahwist began the genealogical line with Cain, whereas that known to the Priestly writers began with Seth.

There is marked similarity between the genealogies in Gen 4-5 and the so-called Babylonian "King-lists." These lists enumerate a series of eight kings who reigned from the beginning of kingship in Mesopotamia until the coming of a great flood. The regnal years of the kings vary from 43,200 to 18,600. In comparison with this the 969 years of Methuselah (Gen 5:27), who outdid all the other descendants of Adam in longevity, seem quite modest. The seventh king in the Babylonian list was allowed into the company of the gods, just as Enoch, the seventh member of the Priestly list, was taken by God (Gen 5:24). The last king on the Babylonian roll became the central figure in the flood story, just as did Noah, the last individual in the Priestly list (Gen 5:32). It is very probable that the Priestly genealogy is in some way based on the Mesopotamian list, but what the connection between the two traditions is is by no means clear.

This rather dreary Priestly catalogue, seemingly irrelevant to us moderns, is not devoid of theological interest. It shows, for example, that the blessing given to the first couple (*cf.,* 1:28; 5:2) was not without effect, and that the human race multiplied quickly upon the earth. The repeated comment that each member of the list had "other sons and daughters" brings out this point. The remark that Adam "became the father of a son in his own likeness, after his image" (v. 3) reminds us that like Adam (*cf.,* 1:26-27) all human beings are in the image of the Creator. Successive generations of humans enjoy the dignity of entering into communion with God, and share in his dominion over the created world.

In his reference to Enoch (5:21-24) the author modifies his regular formula. He informs us that this worthy person *walked with God* (v. 24), that is, that he lived in fellowship with God and that his life was one of total loyalty to his Lord. Later on the same writer will apply the same term to the righteous Noah (*cf.,* 6:9). By attributing a life-span of 365 years — the number of days in a year — to Enoch the

Priestly writer may have intended to suggest his moral perfection. The fact that Enoch "was not, for God took him" (v. 24) shows that because of his righteous life he escaped death which is the lot of every descendant of Adam. Like Elijah who was taken up in a whirlwind (*cf.,* 2 Kgs 2:1, 9-11) Enoch was taken directly into the divine presence. It is not surprising that one about whom such extraordinary things were said should find a place in later Jewish literature (*cf.,* Sir 44:16; 49:14), in the New Testament (*cf.,* Jude 14-15), and in the apocryphal literature where we find writings entitled the "Books of Enoch."

The etymology of the name Noah is probably to be sought in the Hebrew verb *nuah* which means to rest. The genealogy (v. 29), however, chooses to link the name with the vaguely similar *naham*, which means to comfort or bring relief. Perhaps the author intended his favourable interpretation of Noah's name as a reference to the latter's sacrifice (*cf.,* 8:20-22) which would relieve the earth from the curse that had been pronounced over it (*cf.,* 3:17). Or perhaps the name is to be linked with the more mundane fact that Noah was to be the discoverer of wine (*cf.,* 9:20-24) which gladdens human hearts (*cf.,* Ps 104:15) and brings relief from the daily toil.

PRIDE AND CORRUPTION
6:1-4 (J)

> **6** When men began to multiply on the face of the ground, and daughters were born to them, [2]the sons of God saw that the daughters of men were fair; and they took to wife such of them as they chose. [3]Then the Lord said, "My spirit shall not abide in man for ever, for he is flesh, but his days shall be a hundred and twenty years." [4]The Nephilim were on the earth in those days, and also afterward, when the sons of God came in to the daughters of men, and they bore children to them. These were the mighty men that were of old, the men of renown.

Leaving the Priestly author's genealogy (5:1-32) we come upon this curious piece of ancient mythology (6:1-4). The *sons of God* who cohabitated with human women are those divine beings who formed God's heavenly retinue (*cf.*, comment on 1:26 p. 29). Without doubt the concept of other divine beings besides God is polytheistic in origin, and it sits uncomfortably in Israel's scheme of things. Nevertheless the biblical authors freely adapted the concept of an "assembly of the gods," and the Yahwist uses it here in a matter-of-fact fashion. We are surprised to find that the condemnation spoken by God (v. 3) is addressed not only to the guilty *sons of God* and their human partners, but to all men and women. However, we must not press the writer for logic. His purpose in telling the story is to convey the idea that although man and woman may attempt to cross the boundaries that separate them from the divine world, they always remain creatures, mortal and perishable, who depend for life on the continued gift of God's spirit (*cf.*, 2:7; Ps 104:29). The mention of the *Nephilim* echoes the common folkloristic theme that describes the people of yore as mighty warriors, gigantic in size and of extraordinary strength (*cf.*, Num 13:33).

Whatever may have been the original meaning of these intriguing verses it is clear that the Yahwist wished us to see in the promiscuous union of the heavenly beings with mortal woman yet another example of humankind's attempts to overstrip the limits imposed on it by God. This strange union marks a new stage in the increasing lawlessness of the world, and represents a widening of the breach in the relationship between God and humankind.

IV. THE FLOOD
6:5—8:12

Although stories of world-destroying floods were widely diffused in the mythologies of many cultures, it is only when we turn to the literature of Israel's Mesopotamian neighbours that we find a flood story that shows any close resemblance to the Noah narrative. The most extensive and the best preserved of the Babylonian stories is the *Epic of Gilgamesh*, which dates back almost to 2,000 B.C. Modern scholars agree that the biblical authors have borrowed extensively from this famous epic, and that they have done little to hide their borrowing. Yet the biblical writers did more than borrow. They completely reworked the ancient myth, adapted it to the spirit of Israel's faith, and gave a religious meaning to an amoral tale.

Gen 6-8 offers us a long passage where even the amateur literature critic has a field-day. For here the repetitions and inconsistencies which prove the presence of combined sources are so obvious that one needs no specialist training to discover them. One notices *repetitions* by comparing 6:5 (J) with 6:11-12 (P); 6:13, 17 (P) with 7:4 (J); 7:7 (J) with 7:13 (P); 7:21 (P) with 7:22 (J); etc., etc. One discovers *inconsistencies* by comparing 6:19-20; 7:15-16 (P) with 7:2-3 (J); 7:4, 12 (J) with 7:24 (P); 8:6-12, 13b (J) with 8:14-16 (P), etc. It is obvious then that the Yahwistic and Priestly sources have been combined to form one story. Yet the resulting narrative runs quite smoothly, and the reader is not bothered by the inconsistencies it contains.

Historicity

Are we to believe that "all the high mountains under the heavens were covered" by the flood (7:19)? Was every living creature except Noah and his family blotted out from the earth (7:21-23)? In other words, was the Flood a cosmic catastrophe? From what we said earlier about the Mesopotamian origins of the biblical story, it is clear that these questions must be transferred to the sources which the Yahwist and Priestly writers borrowed, since the incorporation of the source material into the biblical narrative added nothing to its historical value. Now, floods were frequent in the flat Tigris-Euphrates valley, and it is very probable that Mesopotamian flood stories are based on unusually disastrous local inundations that made a lasting impression on the popular memory, and that, in the course of time, were magnified out of all proportion into catastrophes of universal dimensions. The story of a universal flood, then, in its Babylonian version and its biblical form, is almost totally devoid of historical value.

ABSOLUTE DEGENERATION
6:5-8 (J)

⁵The Lord saw that the wickedness of man was great in the earth, and that every imagination of the thoughts of his heart was only evil continually. ⁶And the Lord was sorry that he had made man on the earth, and it grieved him to his heart. ⁷So the Lord said, "I will blot out man whom I have created from the face of the ground, mand and beast and creeping things and birds of the air, for I am sorry that I have made them." ⁸But Noah found favor in the eyes of the Lord.

This theological comment links the Flood story with the preceding verses, and forcefully expresses a divine judgment on erring humankind. But it was not only the abominable mating described in vv. 1-4, but also the disobedience in the Garden, Cain's fratricide, and the violence of Lamech, that justify the harsh verdict that is attributed to God himself: "every imagination of the thoughts of the human heart was only evil continually" (v. 5). The anthropomorphic statement *the Lord was sorry that he had made man and woman* (v. 6; *cf.,* v. 7) suggests divine grief and dismay at the extent to which sin had dominated the human race. There could scarcely be a more telling denunciation.

MAKE YOURSELF AN ARK
6:9-22 (P)

⁹These are the generations of Noah. Noah was a righteous man, blameless in his generation; Noah walked with God. ¹⁰And Noah had three sons, Shem, Ham, and Japheth.

¹¹Now the earth was corrupt in God's sight, and the earth was filled with violence. ¹²And God saw the earth, and behold, it was corrupt; for all flesh had corrupted their way upon the earth. ¹³And God said to Noah, "I have determined to make an end to all flesh; for the earth is filled with violence through them; behold, I will destroy them with the earth. ¹⁴Make yourself an ark of gopher wood; make rooms in the ark, and cover it inside and out with pitch. ¹⁵This is how you are to make it: the length of the ark three hundred cubits, its breadth fifty cubits, and its height thirty cubits. ¹⁶Make a roof for the ark, and finish it to a cubit above; and set the door of the ark in its side; make it with lower, second, and third decks. ¹⁷For behold, I will bring a flood of waters upon the earth, to destroy all flesh in which is the breath of life from under heaven; everything that is on the earth shall die. ¹⁸But I will establish my covenant with you; and you shall come into the ark, you, your sons, your wife, and your sons'

wives with you. [19]And of every living thing of all flesh, you shall bring two of every sort into the ark, to keep tham alive with you; they shall be male and female. [20]Of the birds according to their kinds, and of the animals according to their kinds, of every creeping thing of the ground according to its kind, two of every sort shall come in to you, to keep them alive. [21]Also take with you every sort of food that is eaten, and store it up; and it shall serve as food for you and for them." [22]Noah did this; he did all that God commanded him.

The typically Priestly phrase *these are the generations of* (*see above* p. 58) indicates that we now continue our story with the Priestly author as our guide. This author has not prepared us for this succinct characterization of the world as totally corrupt. He left us with a world that was very good (1:31) and where all created beings lived in harmony (1:29-30). Now that same world has become totally corrupt and full of violence. The author does not try to explain how the change took place. The entry of evil into the world remains for him a mystery.

One of the characteristics of the Priestly author is his interest in precise chronology and in exact measurements, and both interests are reflected in the flood story. Since a cubit was about 18 inches, or a little less than half a metre, the information that the ark was 300x50x30 cubits (v. 15) gives us an idea of its colossal size. The Hebrew word *mabbul*, which is translated as *flood of waters* (v. 17) occurs only in the Flood story and in Ps 29:10, and it refers to a kind of heavenly ocean that is situated above the firmament (*cf.,* Gen 1:7). The divine threat of disaster by means of the catastrophic flood-waters (v. 17) is somewhat moderated by the promise of a covenant which God would establish with Noah (v. 18). He and his family were, by God's goodness, to be saved from the cosmic disaster so that through them humanity would continue into a new era.

CLEAN AND UNCLEAN
7:1-5 (J)

> 7 Then the Lord said to Noah, "Go into the ark, you
> and all your household, for I have seen that you are
> righteous before me in this generation. ²Take with you
> seven pairs of all clean animals, the male and his mate;
> and a pair of the animals that are not clean, the male and
> his mate; ³and seven pairs of the birds of the air also, male
> and female, to keep their kind alive upon the face of all
> the earth. ⁴For in seven days I will send rain upon the
> earth forty days and forty nights; and every living thing
> that I have made I will blot out from the face of the
> ground." ⁵And Noah did all that the Lord had com-
> manded him.

While the Priestly author stated that Noah was to take
two of every kind of living creature into the ark (6:19-20) the
Yahwist distinguishes between *clean* and *unclean* animals
and birds, and specifies that seven pairs of the former and
only one pair of the latter were to be taken aboard the
house-boat. The Priestly author made no distinction
between clean and unclean, since according to his scheme of
things such a distinction was unknown until it was revealed
at Sinai (*cf.,* Lev 11; Deut 14). The Yahwist, however,
presumed that this distinction belonged to the nature of
things from the beginning, and he was also convinced that
sacrifices were offered to Yahweh from the earliest times
(*cf.,* 4:3-4; 8:20-22; 12:7, etc.). According to his thought
pattern, then, a greater number of clean animals and birds
were to be taken aboard the ark since they would be
required for food and sacrifice, whereas the sole purpose for
taking unclean species was to preserve them from
extinction.

UNIVERSAL DESTRUCTION
7:6-24

⁶Noah was six hundred years old when the flood of waters came upon the earth. ⁷And Noah and his sons and his wife and his sons' wives with him went into the ark, to escape the waters of the flood. ⁸Of clean animals, and of animals that are not clean, and of birds, and of everything that creeps on the ground, ⁹two and two, male and female, went into the ark with Noah, as God has commanded Noah. ¹⁰And after seven days the waters of the flood came upon the earth.

¹¹In the six hundredth year of Noah's life, in the second month, on the seventeenth day of the month, on that day all the fountains of the great deep burst forth, and the windows of the heavens were opened. ¹²And rain fell upon the earth forty days and forty nights. ¹³On the very same day Noah and his sons, Shem and Ham and Japheth, and Noah's wife and the three wives of his sons with them entered the ark, ¹⁴they and every beast according to its kind, and all the cattle according to their kinds, and every creeping thing that creeps on the earth according to its kind, and every bird according to its kind, every bird of every sort. ¹⁵They went into the ark with Noah, two and two of all flesh in which there was the breath of life. ¹⁶And they that entered, male and female of all flesh, went in as God had commanded him; and the Lord shut him in.

¹⁷The flood continued forty days upon the earth; and the waters increased, and bore up the ark, and it rose high above the earth. ¹⁸The waters prevailed and increased greatly upon the earth; and the ark floated on the face of the waters. ¹⁹And the waters prevailed so mightily upon the earth that all the high mountains under the whole heaven were covered; ²⁰the waters prevailed above the mountains, covering them fifteen cubits deep. ²¹And all flesh died that moved upon the earth, birds, cattle, beasts, all swarming creatures that swarm upon the earth, and

every man; [22]everything on the dry land in whose nostrils
was the breath of life died. [23]He blotted out every living
thing that was upon the face of the ground, man and
animals and creeping things and birds of the air; they
were blotted out from the earth. Only Noah was left, and
those that were with him in the ark. [24]And the waters
prevailed upon the earth a hundred and fifty days.

In the remainder of the Flood story the J and P strands
are so closely intertwined that it is not practical to present
them separately. The Priestly concern with the chronology
appears in vv. 6 and 11. According to J the cause of the
catastrophic deluge was rain that lasted *forty days and forty
nights* (v. 12), while according to P the flood was caused by
the fact that *all the fountains of the great deep burst forth,
and the windows of the heavens were opened* (v. 11). The P
statement evokes the creation narrative which tells of the
separation of the waters above from the waters below (*cf.,
1:6-7 P*), and implicitly suggests that the flood was a reversal
of the creative process. For when the waters beneath the
earth were released from the boundaries that held them in
check, and when the heavenly ocean poured through the
windows of the firmament, the waters above once again
merged with the waters below, the whole cosmic order was
shattered, and creation sank into chaos.

The touching remark that the Lord shut Noah into the
ark (v. 16b) is a typical Yahwistic anthropomorphism. It
suggests that God not only directed the whole operation,
but also that he took special care of his chosen Noah. The
result of the calamitous deluge is described of vv. 21-23, and
the remark that *only Noah was left, and those that were with
him in the ark* (v. 23b) is a stark summary of the cosmic
disaster that sin had brought about.

THE WATERS ABATED
8:1-12

8 But God remembered Noah and all the beasts and all the cattle that were with him in the ark. And God made a wind blow over the earth, and the waters subsided; [2]the fountains of the deep and the windows of the heavens were closed, the rain from the heavens was restrained, [3]and the waters receded from the earth continually. At the end of a hundred and fifty days the waters had abated; [4]and in the seventh month, on the seventeenth day of the month, the ark came to rest upon the mountains of Ararat. [5]And the waters continued to abate until the tenth month; in the tenth month, on the first day of the month, the tops of the mountains were seen.

[6]At the end of forty days Noah opened the window of the ark which he had made, [7]and sent forth a raven; and it went to and fro until the waters were dried up from the earth. [8]Then he sent forth a dove from him, to see if the waters had subsided from the face of the ground; [9]but the dove found no place to set her foot, and she returned to him to the ark, for the waters were still on the face of the whole earth. So he put forth his hand and took her and brought her into the ark with him. [10]He waited another seven days, and again he sent forth the dove out of the ark; [11]and the dove came back to him in the evening, and lo, in her mouth a freshly plucked olive leaf; so Noah knew that the waters had subsided from the earth. [12]Then he waited another seven days, and sent forth the dove; and she did not return to him any more.

According to the P version of events the flood came to an end when the Lord sent a wind over the earth that caused the water to subside, and at the same time, restrained the waters beneath the earth and those above the heavens (vv. 1b-2a). The Yahwist on the other hand says simply that the rains ceased, allowing the flood to subside gradually (vv. 2b-3a). The mountains of Ararat upon which the ark came to rest when the flood had abated must be localized in the area that is now Armenia.

The Babylonian counterpart of the Flood tells how the survivor of the deluge sent out consecutively a dove, a swallow and a raven, to determine whether the flood had ended, and how he knew that the dry land had appeared when the raven, did not return. This motif is taken up by the Priestly writer (v. 7), and much more effectively by J (vv. 8-12), who skillfully builds the story up to a climax. On its first flight the dove which Noah sent out found no resting place on the submerged world. It returned from its second outing with a fresh olive branch which indicated that the flood was abating, and that new growth was appearing on earth. The failure of the dove to return after the third sending led Noah to the joyful conclusion that *the waters had subsided from the earth* (v. 11).

V. A NEW BEGINNING
8:13—11:32

NOAH WENT FORTH
8:13-22

[13]In the six hundred and first year, in the first month, the first day of the month, the waters were dried from off the earth; and Noah removed the covering of the ark, and looked, and behold, the face of the ground was dry. [14]In the second month, on the twenty-seventh day of the month, the earth was dry. [15]Then God said to Noah, [16]"Go forth from the ark, you and your wife, and your sons and your sons' wives with you. [17]Bring forth with you every living thing that is with you of all flesh—birds and animals and every creeping thing that creeps on the earth—that they may breed abundantly on the earth, and be fruitful and multiply upon the earth." [18]So Noah went forth, and his sons and his wife and his sons' wives with him. [19]And every beast, every creeping thing, and every bird, everything that moves upon the earth, went forth by families out of the ark.

[20]Then Noah built an altar to the Lord, and took of every clean animal and of every clean bird, and offered burnt offerings on the altar. [21]And when the Lord smelled the pleasing odor, the Lord said in his heart, "I will never

again curse the ground because of man, for the imagination of man's heart is evil from his youth; neither will I
ever again destroy every living creature as I have done.
[22]While the earth remains, seedtime and harvest, cold and
heat, summer and winter, day and night, shall not cease."

Verses 13b and 20-22 form the Yahwist's contribution to
this passage. The assertion in v. 13a that the waters had
finally subsided on the first day of a new year is of great
theological interest to the Priestly author who wishes to
suggest that after the flood a new era began in world history,
and that Noah was like a new Adam introducing a new
phase in the human story. God's command to Noah to leave
the ark with all his human and animal companions is formulated in terms that remind one immediately of the terminology of the Priestly creation story (*cf.*, 8:17 and 1:22, 24-25,
28). The writer thus subtly reinforces the idea that Noah's
exit from the ark marked a new beginning for the world.

The Babylonian flood stories ended with an account of a
sacrifice to the gods, and the Epic of Gilgamesh tells that the
ravenous gods "smelled the savor" of the sacrifice and
"crowded about the sacrificer." Having disembarked from
the ark Noah too offered sacrifice, slaughtering, no doubt,
some of the clean animals which he had taken aboard the
ark (*cf.*, 7:2). The remark that *the Lord smelled the pleasing
odor of the sacrifice* (v. 21) had, as we noticed, its origin in
pagan mythology, and it undoubtedly reflects the primitive
notion that the sacrifices offered to the gods provided them
with the food they required. This crude idea seems to be
echoed in some Old Testament passages (*cf.*, Lev 21:6,8;
22:25; Num 28:2), but it was later clearly rejected (*cf.*, Ps
50:12-13). The Yahwist used the ancient terminology to
show that God accepted Noah's sacrifice (*cf.*, Exod 29:18;
Lev 1:9), and was once again reconciled with the human
race. The J Flood story which began with God grieving in
his heart because of humankind's rebelliousness (*cf.*, 6:6)
ends with the Lord pondering in his heart and deciding
never again to destroy sinful humans. Human beings may be

weak and incorrigible, but God will always look on them with mercy (v. 21b). The constant rhythm of the seasons (v. 22) is a sign of the Lord's faithfulness, and a guarantee that he will never abandon the world or its inhabitants. On that note of unrestrained hope the Yahwist ends his Flood story.

A COVENANT WITH NOAH
9:1-17 (P)

9 And God blessed Noah and his sons, and said to them, "Be fruitful and multiply, and fill the earth. ²The fear of you and the dread of you shall be upon every beast of the earth, and upon every bird of the air, upon everything that creeps on the ground and all the fish of the sea; into your hand they are delivered. ³Every moving thing that lives shall be food for you; and as I gave you the green plants, I give you everything. ⁴Only you shall not eat flesh with its life, that is, its blood. ⁵For your lifeblood I will surely require a reckoning; of every beast I will require it and of man; of every man's brother I will require the life of man. ⁶Whoever sheds the blood of man, by man shall his blood be shed; for God made man in his own image. ⁷And you, be fruitful and multiply, bring forth abundantly on the earth and multiply in it."

⁸Then God said to Noah and to his sons with him, ⁹"Behold, I establish my covenant with you and your descendants after you, ¹⁰and with every living creature that is with you, the birds, the cattle, and every beast of the earth with you, as many as came out of the ark. ¹¹I establish my covenant with you, that never again shall all flesh be cut off by the waters of a flood, and never again shall there be a flood to destroy the earth." ¹²And God said, "This is the sign of the covenant which I make between me and you and every living creature that is with you, for all future generations: ¹³I set my bow in the cloud, and it shall be a sign of the covenant between me and the earth. ¹⁴When I bring clouds over the earth and the bow is seen in the clouds, ¹⁵I will remember my

covenant which is between me and you and every living creature of all flesh; and the waters shall never again become a flood to destroy all flesh. [16]When the bow is in the clouds, I will look upon it and remember the everlasting covenant between God and every living creature of all flesh that is upon the earth." [17]God said to Noah, "This is the sign of the covenant which I have established between me and all flesh that is upon the earth."

The first words that God spoke to the survivors of the flood renew the blessing given at creation (9:1-7; *cf.,* 1:28). In the world that had been purified by the Flood, procreation begins anew under a divine benediction, and humankind is reconfirmed in its position as sovereign of the created universe. However, the human rule over animals will be one of fear (v. 2), and part of every human's food will be provided at the expense of animal life (v. 3). Thus the slaughter of living things is permitted so that the paradisiacal peace is ended (*cf.,* 1:29-30), and violence is accepted as a normal ingredient of life in the new world. The prohibition against eating *flesh with its life, that is, its blood* (v. 4), is based on the idea that blood is the seat of life (*cf.,* Lev 17:11, 14), and since all life belongs to God (*cf.,* 1 Sam 2:6; Ps 36:9, Job 4:9, etc.), blood, the bearer of life, may not be consumed by humans (*cf.,* Lev 17:10-14; Deut 12:16, 24, etc.). But if all life belongs to God, human life is especially sacred to him, so that whoever kills another human being forfeits his own life (vv. 5-6).

In the society to which the ancient Hebrews belonged, relations between individuals and between groups were regulated by covenants, which were essentially agreements or pacts. After the Flood, God made a covenant, not only with Noah and his descendants, but with all living creatures (vv. 8-17). This covenant was unconditional in that it assured the human race of God's unfailing protection without imposing any obligations or conditions on man and woman. The rainbow which is a natural symbol of light and hope, was seen as a suitable sign of the divine favor involved in the covenant. It was to be a reminder to God of his promise to preserve the world and all living things in existence, and for humankind it was a pledge of the divine faithfulness that gives to the world a sense of security and stability.

CURSED BE CANAAN
9:18-27 (J)

18The sons of Noah who went forth from the ark were Shem, Ham, and Japheth. Ham was the father of Canaan. 19These three were the sons of Noah; and from these the whole earth was peopled.

20Noah was the first tiller of the soil. He planted a vineyard; 21and he drank of the wine, and became drunk, and lay uncovered in his tent. 22And Ham, the father of Canaan, saw the nakedness of his father, and told his two brothers outside. 23Then Shem and Japheth took a garment, laid it upon both their shoulders, and walked backward and covered the nakedness of their father; their faces were turned away, and they did not see their father's nakedness. 24When Noah awoke from his wine and knew what his youngest son had done to him, 25he said,
"Cursed be Canaan;
   a slave of slaves shall he be to his brothers."
26He also said,
   "Blessed by the Lord my God be Shem;
      and let Canaan be his slave.
27God enlarge Japheth,
      and let him dwell in the tents of Shem;
      and let Canaan be his slave."

In vv. 20-27 we seem to have an independent narrative that originally had no connection with the Flood story, and that may have been an etiological tale that explained the origin of viniculture and the discovery of the intoxicating effects of wine. The Bible in general took a positive view of wine which it regarded as one of God's gifts to man and woman (*cf.,* Ps 104:15; Deut 7:13; Prov 3:10), and in the present narrative there is no note of censure in the remark that Noah became drunk (v. 21). The centre of attention is rather the father's nakedness which became the occasion of Ham's shameful and unfilial behavior (v. 22). The extreme modesty of the other two brothers in the presence of their father's nakedness (v. 23) is in marked contrast to the vulgar levity of Ham.

In this curious account Ham, *the father of Canaan* (vv. 18-22), must be seen as the representative of the Canaanites who preceded the Israelites as the occupants of Palestine. Ham's immodesty symbolizes the sexual depravity that was involved in the Canaanite fertility rites which are so frequently condemned in the Bible (*cf.,* Hos 4:14; Deut 23:17-18; Jer 2:20-25, etc.). So when Canaan is cursed because of the shameless conduct of his father Ham (vv. 25-26), all his descendants are condemned, and their immoral practices are stigmatized. The actual curse which envisages Canaan as a slave to his brothers was probably formulated at a time when the Canaanites were actually subject to their "brothers," the Israelites, who were descended from Shem. Japheth (v. 27) seems to represent other non-Israelites who settled in Palestine (*cf.,* Gen 23; 1 Sam 26:6), that is, dwelt in the tents of Shem, as v. 27 so poetically puts it. These peaceful inhabitants are pictured as sharing in the blessings of Shem and his descendants the Israelites, and in their lordship over the socially and politically inferior Canaanites.

THE TABLE OF NATIONS
10:1-32 (PJ)

10   These are the generations of the sons of Noah, Shem, Ham, and Japheth; sons were born to them after the flood.

²The sons of Japheth: Gomer, Magog, Madai, Javan, Tubal, Meshech, and Tiras. ³The sons of Gomer: Ashkenaz, Riphath, and Togarmah. ⁴The sons of Javan: Elishah, Tarshish, Kittim, and Dodanim. ⁵From these

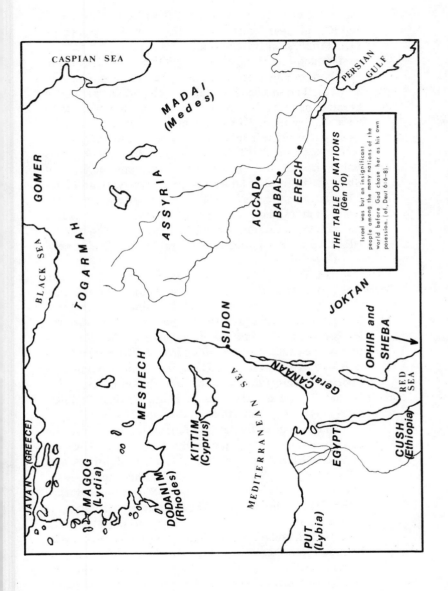

THE TABLE OF NATIONS (Gen 10)

Israel was but an insignificant people among the many nations of the world before God chose her as his own possession. (cf. Deut 6:6-8).

the coastland peoples spread. These are the sons of
Japheth in their lands, each with his own language, by
their families, in their nations.

⁶The sons of Ham: Cush, Egypt, Put, and Canaan.
⁷The sons of Cush: Seba, Havilah, Sabtah, Raamah, and
Sabteca. The sons of Raamah: Sheba and Dedan. ⁸Cush
became the father of Nimrod; he was the first on earth to
be a mighty man. ⁹He was a mighty hunter before the
Lord; therefore it is said, "Like Nimrod a mighty hunter
before the Lord." ¹⁰The beginning of his kingdom was
Babel, Erech, and Accad, all of them in the land of
Shinar. ¹¹From that land he went into Assyria, and built
Nineveh, Rehoboth-Ir, Calah, and ¹²Resen between
Nineveh and Calah; that is the great city. ¹³Egypt became
the father of Ludim, Anamim, Lehabim, Naphtuhim,
¹⁴Pathrusim, Casluhim (whence came the Philistines),
and Caphtorim.

¹⁵Canaan became the father of Sidon his first-born,
and Heth, ¹⁶and the Jebusites, the Amorites, the Girga-
shites, ¹⁷the Hivites, the Arkites, the Sinites, ¹⁸the Arvadites, the Zemarites, and the Hamathites. Afterward the
families of the Canaanites spread abroad. ¹⁹And the territory of the Canaanites extended from Sidon, in the direction of Gerar, as far as Gaza, and in the direction of
Sodom, Gomorrah, Admah, and Zeboiim, as far as
Lasha. ²⁰These are the sons of Ham, by their families,
their languages, their lands, and their nations.

²¹To Shem also, the father of all children of Eber, the
elder brother of Japheth, children were born. ²²The sons
of Shem: Elam, Asshur, Arpachshad, Lud, and Aram.
²³The sons of Aram: Uz, Hul, Gether, and Mash.
²⁴Arpachshad became the father of Shelah; and Shelah
became the father of Eber. ²⁵To Eber were born two sons:
the name of the one was Peleg, for in his days the earth
was divided, and his brother's name was Joktan. ²⁶Joktan
became the father of Almodad, Sheleph, Hazarmaveth,
Jerah, ²⁷Hadoram, Uzal, Diklah, ²⁸Obal, Abimael,
Sheba, ²⁹Ophir, Havilah, and Jobab; all these were the

sons of Joktan. ³⁰The territory in which they lived extended from Mesha in the direction of Sephar to the hill country of the east. ³¹These are the sons of Shem, by their families, their languages, their lands, and their nations.

³²These are the families of the sons of Noah, according to their genealogies, in their nations; and from these the nations spread abroad on the earth after the flood.

This rather daunting list of persons, national groups and cities turns our attention to the nations who were known to the ancient Israelites. The list is based not on racial and linguistic divisions, but on the geographic location and political connections of the various peoples mentioned. The Priestly author's formula "These are the generations of the sons of Noah" (*cf.*, above p. 15) brings back into focus the sons of Noah (v. 1) whom we have already encountered at 6:10 (P) and 9:18 (J). Having introduced the sons in the order Shem, Ham and Japheth the text goes on to alter that order as it develops their genealogies. By first recording the lineage of Japheth (vv. 2-5) and Ham (vv. 6-20), the author cleared the field, as it were, for the family tree of Shem (vv. 21-30), among whose descendants we find Eber (v. 25), the ancestor of the Hebrews.

The "sons of Japheth" (vv. 2-5) include peoples who were located in the area stretching from the Caspian Sea in the East, through Asia Minor, and as far west as the Aegean Sea. Among the peoples who can be identified with some degree of confidence are *Madai*, the Medes, whose kingdom was situated in the general area that is now Iran, *Javan*, the Greeks, *Kittim* and *Dodanim* who represent the peoples of Cyprus and Rhodes respectively.

To the "sons of Ham" (vv. 6-20) belong some African races, Arabian tribes from the area around the Red Sea and the inhabitants of Canaan. Among the African nations mentioned are *Cush*, which is to be identified with Ethiopia, *Egypt*, and *Put*, which is Lybia. The mention of the Semitic *Canaanites* among the sons of Ham is surprising, and may be due to the fact that Egypt controlled the land of Canaan for centuries before Israel first settled there.

The genealogical table is broken by the Yahwist's verses (8-12) which record the exploits of a certain Nimrod who cannot be positively identified with any hero known to us from the ancient world. He was remembered as the founder of several mighty cities, including *Babel* (Babylon) and *Nineveh*, the capital of Assyria. It may be that the Yahwist identified Nimrod with Tukulti-Ninurta I, the thirteenth century B.C. Assyrian king who conquered Babylonia.

Apart from the Arkites, the Sinites, and the Arvadites, the peoples mentioned in vv. 15-18 are well known from the Bible as the peoples who were displaced when the Israelites took over Canaan (*cf.,* 15:21; Deut 7:1, etc.). Verse 19 interrupts the genealogical flow of the story in order to outline the borders of Canaan.

The peoples who belonged to the line of Shem (vv. 21-31) were situated in the territory that stretches from the area east of Babylonia, across the Tigris-Euphrates valley and into the Arabian peninsula. Among these peoples we find (v. 22) the names of some well-known races: *Elam* or the Elamites were settled in the mountains east of the Tigris-Euphrates; *Asshur* is, of course, Assyria; and *Aram* refers to the Arameans who had their homeland in northern Mesopotamia. *Eber* (v. 25) is the eponymous ancestor of the Hebrews, this is to say, he is the representative of the Hebrew people who are said to spring from him and who bear his name. In his usual way the Yahwist plays on the name *Peleg*, relating it to the Hebrew verb *peleg*, to divide (v. 25). The statement that in Peleg's days "the earth was divided" is enigmatic and scholars can only guess at its meaning. The reference may be to the division and scattering that took place after the episode of the tower of Babel (*cf.,* 11:1-9), or to the great irrigation canals which in ancient times criss-crossed the land in the Tigris-Euphrates valley.

We may now ask if this rather turgid catalogue of names is of any theological or religious significance. An important point which the authors may have wished to make is that the divine blessing given to Noah after the Flood (*cf.*, 9:1) was amply fulfilled in the many peoples who descended from him. Another obvious message to be gleaned from the genealogy is that all those who populated the world after the Flood were descended from the one father, Noah, so that all the nations that are spread abroad over the earth (*cf.*, 10:32b) are united by a common parentage. The catalogue also shows that if Israel, the people descended from Eber, was to be chosen from among all the nations, it owed this not to its own special qualities, but to God's free choice (*cf.*, Deut 7:6-8) and to his continued guidance.

THE TOWER OF BABEL
11:1-9 (J)

11 Now the whole earth had one language and few words. [2]And as men migrated from the east, they found a plain in the land of Shinar and settled there. [3]And they said to one another, "Come, let us make bricks, and burn them thoroughly." And they had brick for stone, and bitumen for mortar. [4]Then they said, "Come, let us build ourselves a city, and a tower with its top in the heavens, and let us make a name for ourselves, lest we be scattered abroad upon the face of the whole earth." [5]And the Lord came down to see the city and the tower, which the sons of men had built. [6]And the Lord said, "Behold, they are one people, and they have all one language; and this is only the beginning of what they will do; and nothing that they propose to do will now be impossible for them. [7]Come, let us go down, and there confuse their language, that they may not understand one another's speech." [8]So the Lord scattered them abroad from there over the face of all the earth, and they left off building the city. [9]Therefore its name was called Babel, because there the Lord confused the language of all the earth; and from there the Lord scattered them abroad over the face of all the earth.

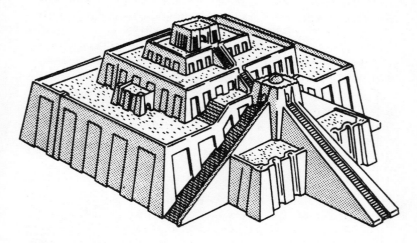

Reconstruction of the ziggurat at Ur, a three-storeyed temple-tower that was dedicated to the moon-god Sin.

In this intriguing passage we seem to have an independent folkloristic tale which the Yahwist inserted into the story. Babylonia, or *Shinar* (v. 2) as it was called in ancient times, provides the background to the story, and Babylon is the city (v. 4) which features in the narrative (*cf.,* v. 9). The *tower* (v. 4) was a *ziggurat* or stepped pyramidal temple-tower of colossal proportions. Such temples formed a prominent feature of many ancient Babylonian cities, and the original story which the Yahwist adopted may have been intended to explain the origin of some ruined or unfinished monument.

In itself the building of a city or a tower would not seem to be a reprehensible enterprise. But in our present story the project is seen as an expression of a human effort to organize the world and found a great empire independently of God. It was humankind's attempt to *make a name* or to win glory for itself while flouting the supreme authority of God. The Lord's reaction to this self-assertion is recorded in typically Yahwistic anthropomorphic terms, and not without a wry sense of humor and a note of satire (vv. 5-7). The words *let us go down* (v. 7) reflect a polytheistic background (*cf.,* comments on 1:26 and 6:1-4; above p. 29, 61). The splendid structure which was to win a name for those who planned it seemed so tiny to the God who sits in the heavens and laughs at the schemes of his creatures (*cf.,* Ps 2:4), that he had to come down to examine it. Because the ambitious building of the city was only the beginning of what humankind would do if it succeeded in this first grandiose project, God decided to frustrate the plan, and thus prevent further manifestations of rebellion. God's decision to intervene is, therefore, not only punitive, but also an expression of parental concern for sinful humanity. He prefers to punish now lest he be forced to destroy later. By confusing the language of the builders so that they could not understand each other, the Lord forced them to abandon their scheme and to separate from each other to form individual nations. The etymology given in v. 9 for Babel or Babylon — *bab-illu,* gate of God in Accadian — is, from a linguistic point of view, incorrect. But by linking the name Babel with the Hebrew verb *balal* which means to confuse or mix, the author indulges in a pleasant play on words, and suggests the effect which God's punitive action had on the builders.

The story of the Tower of Babel explains the origin of the multiplicity of languages that divides the human race into distinct groups and nations. But the author's main purpose in telling the story was to show that humankind's attempt to organize the world without reference to God's supreme will ended in confusion and frustration. Furthermore, man's challenge to God's supreme dominion not only brought about alienation from God, but also resulted in a disintegration of the unity of the human race. The multiplicity of nations and the divisions among them are signs of God's judgment on rebellious humankind. However, God's punishment is not everlasting, so that the prophets could foresee a time when the scattering of Babel would be reversed, and when all nations would come together in unity and peace (*cf.*, Isa 2:2-4).

THE DESCENDANTS OF SHEM
11:10-32 (PJ)

[10]These are the descendants of Shem. When Shem was a hundred years old, he became the father of Arpachshad two years after the flood; [11]and Shem lived after the birth of Arpachshad five hundred years, and had other sons and daughters.

[12]When Arpachshad had lived thirty-five years, he became the father of Shelah; [13]and Arpachshad lived after the birth of Shelah four hundred and three years, and had other sons and daughters.

[14]When Shelah had lived thirty years, he became the father of Eber; [15]and Shelah lived after the birth of Eber four hundred and three years, and had other sons and daughters.

[16]When Eber had lived thirty-four years, he became the father of Peleg; [17]and Eber lived after the birth of Peleg

four hundred and thirty years, and had other sons and daughters.

[18]When Peleg had lived thirty years, he became the father of Reu; [19]and Peleg lived after the birth of Reu two hundred and nine years, and had other sons and daughters.

[20]When Reu had lived thirty-two years, he became the father of Serug; [21]and Reu lived after the birth of Serug two hundred and seven years, and had other sons and daughters.

[22]When Serug had lived thirty years, he became the father of Nahor; [23]and Serug lived after the birth of Nahor two hundred years, and had other sons and daughters.

[24]When Nahor had lived twenty-nine years, he became the father of Terah; [25]and Nahor lived after the birth of Terah a hundred and nineteen years, and had other sons and daughters.

[26]When Terah had lived seventy years, he became the father of Abram, Nahor, and Haran.

[27]Now these are the descendants of Terah. Terah was the father of Abram, Nahor, and Haran; and Haran was the father of Lot. [28]Haran died before his father Terah in the land of his birth, in Ur of the Chaldeans. [29]And Abram and Nahor took wives; the name of Abram's wife was Sarai, and the name of Nahor's wife, Milcah, the daughter of Haran the father of Milcah and Iscah. [30]Now Sarai was barren; she had no child.

[31]Terah took Abram his son and Lot the son of Haran, his grandson, and Sarai his daughter-in-law, his son Abram's wife, and they went forth together from Ur of the Chaldeans to go into the land of Canaan; but when they came to Haran, they settled there. [32]The days of Terah were two hundred and five years; and Terah died in Haran.

If the genealogy in 10:21-31 had portrayed Shem as the
father of many nations the present text narrows the vision
and follows a direct line from Shem, son of Noah, to Abraham who was to become the father of the chosen race.
Verses 10-26 are the work of the Priestly author, and are
similar in many ways to the list in chapter 5 (P). As that
chapter counted ten generations before the Flood the present list enumerates ten generations from Noah to Abraham,
and the structure of the two chapters is very much alike. It
must be noted, however, that the life-span attributed to the
individuals mentioned in chapter 11 is much shorter than
that of the pre-Flood patriarchs of chapter 5.

The Yahwist has already mentioned Arpachshad, Shelah,
Eber and Peleg (*cf.,* 10:22, 24) among the descendants of
Shem, and these now occur as the first four names in the
present list (11:10-18). The Priestly author then takes up
another tradition and continues the line of Shem to Terah,
father of Abraham (vv. 19-26). The names of some of the
individuals mentioned in this list (*e.g.,* Serug, vv. 20-23;
Nahor, vv. 22-25; Terah, vv. 24-28; Haran, v. 26) occur as
the names of readily identifiable cities in north-west Mesopotamia, the place where the Hebrew patriarchs are said to
have originated. This, however, raises no problems since the
identity of place and personal names was not uncommon in
the Middle East of that time.

Verse 27 (P) introduces us to the immediate family of
Abraham. Both the Yahwist (v. 28; *cf.,* 15:7) and the Priestly
writer (v. 31) assure us that *Ur of the Chaldeans* was the
birthplace of Terah. Scholars note that the Chaldeans, a
branch of the Aramean race, did not arrive in Mesopotamia
until late in the second millennium B.C., so that the mention
of that tribe at the time of Abraham is anachronistic. Some
scholars maintain that the very mention of Ur in connection
with Abraham is out of place. The main reason for this
contention is that the later Genesis stories mention only the
north-western Mesopotamian connections of the patriarchs
(*cf.,* 24:10; 27:43; 28:2; 29:4, etc.) and show little knowledge
of the southern Tigris-Euphrates valley where Ur is located.

Plausible though this argument may be it does not render untenable the biblical statement that Abraham originated in Ur. We know, for example, that Ur and Haran were sister-cities, that the inhabitants of both cities worshipped the same deity, the moon-god Sin, and that there were regular goings and comings between the two cities. There is therefore nothing inherently improbable in the idea that Abraham and his family moved from one city to the other. Furthermore, we know that the so-called Third Dynasty of Ur was destroyed towards the end of the twentieth century B.C. by the Elamites, who moved in from the east, and by the Amorites, a nomadic people who infiltrated from the steppes to the west. It is quite probable that Terah's family belonged to one of the Amorite groups who settled in Ur at that time (*cf.,* Ezek 16:3, 45), and that Abraham later departed from that disturbed and declining city for the more peaceful Haran to the north. This would explain why Ur was the starting point of Abraham's pilgrimage, and it would indicate that his story began somewhere in the middle of the nineteenth century B.C.

The name Abram by which the patriarch is known in all the traditions before Gen 17:5 has appeared in Mesopotamian texts from about 2000 B.C., and it means "the father (*i.e.,* the father-god) is exalted." The remark that *Sarai was barren* (v. 30) prepares us for the story of the birth of Isaac (18:9-14; 21:1-7) and underlines the paradox involved in the promise of many children that will be made to Abraham (*cf.,* 12:2-7; 15:5).

A Gracious God

The first eleven chapters of Genesis paint a tragic picture of humankind, and show that left to itself the human race was prone to sin and destined to get enmeshed in greater and greater evils. Although humankind was created good by God and privileged to live in familiar friendship with him, the human proclivity to sin manifested itself in the disobedience of the first couple, and then spread like a contagion to every area of human life. Once sin had gained a foothold in the world its increasing power over humankind was revealed in the fratricide of Cain, in the hardened vengeance of Lamech, in the union of the sons of God with human maidens and in the pretentious attempt to build the Tower of Babel. So steep was the human decline into moral disintegration that the Yahwist could sum up the situation by saying that every imagination of the human heart was evil continually (6:5). So universal was this deterioration that the Priestly author could say that "the earth was filled with violence" (6:11).

However, the editors who placed Gen 1-11 at the beginning of the Bible did not intend them to be read alone. The fact that the outline of universal history that is sketched in these chapters ends with the spotlight on Abram and Sarai shows that these chapters form a prologue to the history of salvation that begins with Abram and Sarai. In fact, the God of Gen 1-11 who had to punish rebellious humankind also showed his concern for the sinful Adam and Eve (3:21), placed a protecting mark on the first murderer (4:15), blessed a purified world (8:21; 9:1), and pledged that he would never again destroy the world (9:8-17). This same God will continue to reveal his power and graciousness in the history of Abraham and Sarah and their descendants, and through them God will bring salvation to the whole world.

VI. ABRAHAM, THE CHOSEN
12:1—20:18

THE CALL OF ABRAHAM
12:1-9 (JP)

12 Now the Lord said to Abram, "Go from your country and your kindred and your father's house to the land that I will show you. ²And I will make of you a great nation, and I will bless you, and make your name great, so that you will be a blessing. ³I will bless those who bless you, and him who curses you I will curse; and by you all the families of the earth shall bless themselves."

⁴So Abram went, as the Lord had told him; and Lot went with him. Abram was seventy-five years old when he departed from Haran. ⁵And Abram took Sarai his wife, and Lot his brother's son, and all their possessions which they had gathered, and the persons that they had gotten in Haran; and they set forth to go to the land of Canaan. When they had come to the land of Canaan, ⁶Abram passed through the land to the place at Shechem, to the oak of Moreh. At that time the Canaanites were in the land. ⁷Then the Lord appeared to Abram, and said, "To your descendants I will give this land." So he built there an altar to the Lord, who had appeared to him. ⁸Thence he removed to the mountain on the east of Bethel, and

Obverse and reverse of a tablet from Ebla containing a hymn to "the Lord of heaven and earth." The tablets unearthed at Ebla (Tell-Mardikh) in Syria in 1976 date from about 2500 B.C. Scholars cannot yet evaluate the bearing of these important but controversial texts on the Patriarchal stories.

pitched his tent, with Bethel on the west and Ai on the east, and there he built an altar to the Lord and called on the name of the Lord. ⁹And Abram journeyed on, still going toward the Negeb.

With the call of Abraham a new era of salvation dawns, and the first stage of human redemption begins. Abraham, about whose religious background we know nothing more than that his ancestors were idolators (*cf.,* Josh 24:2), and about whose personal qualities before his call we know nothing at all, was, without prior warning, called to abandon homeland and kindred, to entrust his destiny to God's guidance, and to set out for an undisclosed destination (12:1). With nothing more than a divine promise to rely on, the seventy-five year old patriarch (*cf.,* v. 4b, P) was called on to exchange the known for the unknown. But the Lord who called and commanded also promised, and assured his chosen one of a great future. The key-word in the divine promise is *bless,* a word which occurs five times as verb or noun in God's commitment (vv. 2-3). The promise to make Abraham a *great nation* is the first of many promises to the patriarchs which assures them of innumerable descendants (*cf.,* 13:16; 15:5; 17:5-6; 18:18, etc.). The promise of a *great name* refers to the fame which would come to Abraham through the many descendants who would arise from him and Sarah. Abraham will *be a blessing* (v. 2b), that is, the model of divine blessing, and so obviously favored by God that others would say "May God bless us as he has blessed Abraham" (*cf.,* 48:20). This is also the meaning of v. 3b as rendered in the text of RSV: *and by you all the families of the earth will bless themselves.* But this half-verse can also be translated as follows: *in you all the families of the earth will be blessed.* This makes Abraham the source of blessing for all nations (*cf.,* Sir 44:21), and gives to the promise made to him a universal note. So, having had our view directed to all peoples in chap. 10, and having narrowed our focus to one family and one couple in 11:10-32, we now encounter the individual Abraham, only to have our gaze turned again to all the families of the earth who will share in the blessing promised to him and Sarah. The assurance *I will bless those who bless you, and him who curses you I will curse* (v. 3a) effectively establishes Abraham as the mediator of God's blessing to those, and only to those, who approve of what he stood for. Thus, in practice, the descendants of Abraham and Sarah, the Israelites, were destined to be a "light to the nations" (*cf.,* Isa 42:6; Luke 2:32), and their faith would be a challenge to all.

With the simple laconic statement *So Abraham went as the Lord had told him* (v. 4) the author portrays Abraham as wholly at God's disposal and totally obedient to his will. We should like to know what form the divine call took, how Abraham felt as he wrenched himself from his familiar surroundings, and what were the actual motives that inspired his departure. But the author is silent on all these matters. He makes no suggestion that Abraham was disgusted with the polytheism of his surroundings or that he went in search of a purer religion. He is satisfied with showing that Abraham had unreserved trust in the divine word. This Yahwistic idea is aptly echoed by the Christian author who wrote: "By faith Abraham obeyed when he was called to go out to a place which he was to receive as an inheritance; and he went out, not knowing where he was to go" (Heb 11:8).

Shechem (v. 6), about one mile east of the modern Nablus, was an ancient Canaanite city dating back to the third millenium. It became a centre of Israelite cult in the early period of the settlement (*cf.,* Josh 24:1; 1 Kgs 12:1). Although the site is more closely connected with Jacob in the patriarchal traditions (33:18-20; 35:4), the present passage tells us that Abraham received a divine revelation there and that he built an altar there, thus laying claim to the site for his God. The *oak* (or terebinth) *of Moreh* must have been one of those sacred trees which were supposed by the ancients to have been a place where divine instruction was received, and it was here that the Lord spoke to Abraham and communicated his promises to him. The remark that *the Canaanites were in the land* is not only a declaration of fact, but also underscores the strangeness of the promise made to Abraham in v. 7: *To your descendants I will give this land.* For how could the wandering nomad Abraham, with his small band of tribal followers, hope to disinherit a well established people who dwelt in walled cities? The most that the incoming nomads could hope for would be a settlement in the more sparsely populated and mountainous areas of Canaan. But the divine promise extended to all the land, and was to be repeated several times in the patriarchal story (13:15; 15:7, 18; 17:8). Obviously such a promise could be realized only by God himself.

Leaving Shechem, Abraham moved on to the mountain east of Bethel and settled there. Bethel, whose name signifies "House of God," and which was situated about fourteen miles north of Jerusalem, was a sacred place before Abraham's arrival, and was to be a prominent cult centre in Israelite times (Judg 20:18, 26; 21:2; 1 Kgs 12:28-33; Amos 3:14; 4:4, etc.). The assertion that Abraham built an altar there *to Yahweh* is anachronistic, a retrojection from a later age (*cf.,* comment on 4:26; above p. 56). Abraham's acts of worship at Bethel and Shechem were for later Israelites a justification of their own cultic activity at those shrines, which, although tainted in their Canaanite origins, were hallowed by the patriarch's act of worship.

In typical semi-nomadic fashion Abraham did not settle in the central hill country of Palestine around Shechem or Bethel, but moved south to the Negeb, that expansive area that extends from Beer-sheba in southern Judah to the Gulf of Aqaba. The region was settled and cultivated during certain periods of history, and was always attractive to semi-nomads who could pasture their flocks in the vicinity of the wells and springs that are found there.

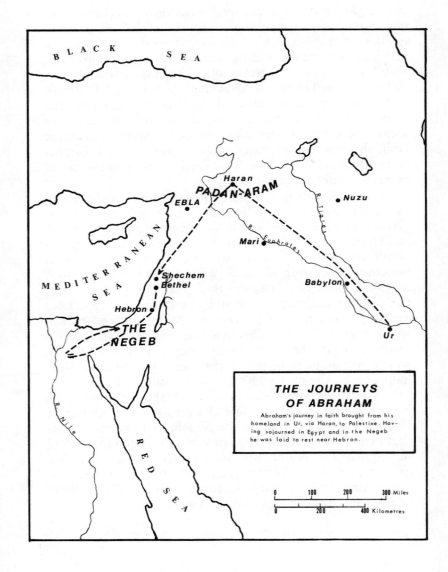

THE JOURNEYS
OF ABRAHAM

Abraham's journey in faith brought from his homeland in Ur, via Haran, to Palestine. Having sojourned in Egypt and in the Negeb he was laid to rest near Hebron.

THE ANCESTRESS IN DANGER
12:10-20 (J)

¹⁰Now there was a famine in the land. So Abram went down to Egypt to sojourn there, for the famine was severe in the land. ¹¹When he was about to enter Egypt, he said to Sarai his wife, "I know that you are a woman beatiful to behold; ¹²and when the Egyptians see you, they will say, 'This is his wife'; then they will kill me, but they will let you live. ¹³Say you are my sister, that it may go well with me because of you, and that my life may be spared on your account." ¹⁴When Abram entered Egypt the Egyptians saw that the woman was very beautiful. ¹⁵And when the princes of Pharaoh saw her, they praised her to Pharaoh. And the woman was taken into Pharaoh's house. ¹⁶And for her sake he dealt well with Abram; and he had sheep, oxen, he-asses, menservants, maidservants, she-asses, and camels.

¹⁷But the Lord afflicted Pharaoh and his house with great plagues because of Sarai, Abram's wife. ¹⁸So Pharaoh called Abram, and said, "What is this you have done to me? Why did you not tell me that she was your wife? ¹⁹Why did you say, 'She is my sister,' so that I took her for my wife? Now then, here is your wife, take her, and be gone." ²⁰And Pharaoh gave men orders concerning him; and they set him on the way, with his wife and all that he had.

Having heard the Lord's promise to give the land of Canaan to Abraham's descendants (v. 7), one is surprised to read that the patriarch soon abandoned that land and set out to Egypt (v. 10). The recipient of the divine promise was forced to set out for Egypt in order to save himself from starvation. Such a migration by a clan leader and his followers was by no means an uncommon occurrence in the early second millennium B.C., as we learn from Egyptian sources that tell of Semitic nomads entering into the Nile Valley in search of food. The patriarchal narratives recall several groups who journeyed to Egypt in order to ward off famine (41:54-57; 43; 47:4). Such migrants became temporary residents with limited rights, but without the normal privileges of citizens, while, like Abraham, they sojourned (12:10) in the fertile Nile Valley.

Different forms of the dramatic story of the endangered ancestress occur in 12:10-20 (J), 20:1-18 (E) and 26:6-11 (J). The identification of the husband and wife or of the king involved may vary, or the locale of the episode may change, and the various authors' retouching of the stories because of their particular moral sensibilities may be observed; but the basic motifs of wife-sister theme and the preservation of the ancestress remain in all three.

The image of Sarah as a beautiful woman who would arouse the kind of attention suggested in 12:11-12 does not presuppose the information given by P in 12:4b and 17:17, according to which Sarah would have been sixty-five years old when she went with her husband to Egypt. In the civilization to which Abraham belonged, the husband of a beautiful woman would be in considerable danger from local princes or prosperous individuals who would be on the look out for attractive additions to their harems. Such gentlemen would not violate the sanctity of marriage by taking a married woman into their courts, but they would not be above eliminating a husband who would frustrate their designs on his wife. So although Abraham's utilitarian decision to persuade Sarah to pass as his sister and thus run the risk of becoming a member of Pharaoh's harem, if not noble, it is at least understandable.

In recent times scholars have drawn attention to the fact that the wife-sister theme reflects a legal custom that was in vogue around the time of Abraham in Hurrian societies in northern Mesopotamia, the area which Abraham and his entourage regarded as their homeland (*cf.*, 11:31; 12:4). According to this custom, a husband who legally adopted his wife as his sister not only gained greater control over her but also gave greater status to his marriage in the eyes of his acquaintances. At the same time he gave the wife-sister privileges and protection over and above those of an ordinary wife. When the Yahwist wrote, the legal implications of this custom were forgotten, but tradition retained the wife-sister motif. The Yahwise took up the tradition and used it i such a way as to attribute a shrewd deception to Abraham.

That Abraham's premonitions about the possible reaction of the Egyptian courtiers towards his wife were correct is proved by vv. 14-15, which show that the hapless Sarah was taken into the harem of the Pharaoh. The mention of camels among the generous gifts which Abraham received in return for his wife (v. 16) is an anachronism, since the first camel nomads did not appear for another 600 years, about the year 1200 B.C.

Verses 17-19 raise a number of problems for modern readers who look for logic and coherence in a story. Why, we might ask, did God afflict Pharaoh who did nothing that would be regarded as reprehensible in the society in which he lived? How did Pharaoh come to associate the plague with Sarah? How did he know that she was Abraham's wife? But the Yahwist was not interested in these questions of detail. His main interest was in showing that when the honour of the ancestress and the purity of the race that was to spring from her were in jeopardy, God intervened to save his elect, and to ensure that his plan would not be frustrated. The Yahwist does not feel obliged to justify Abraham's deceit, or to gloss over the sharp rebuke the patriarch received from the outraged Pharaoh. He may even have found a certain delight in showing how deftly the quick-witted Abraham extricated himself from a sticky situation, even if he had to run the risk of betraying his wife in order to do so.

MELCHIZEDEK, KING AND PRIEST OF SALEM
CHAP. 14

Since chap. 13 is not difficult to understand, and since it contributes little of theological value to the Genesis story, we need not discuss it in this commentary where our space is limited. Chap. 14 on the other hand is one of the most perplexing passages in the book of Genesis, and scholars differ widely in their views about its historical value and about its meaning. We can therefore leave discussion of most of the chapter to those who have a special interest in the history and archaeology of the ancient Middle East. We will focus our attention on the final section of the chapter which is of greater relevance to readers for whom this series of commentaries is intended.

14:17-24

[17]After his return from the defeat of Ched-or-laomer and the kings who were with him, the king of Sodom went out to meet him at the Valley of Shaveh (that is, the King's Valley). [18]And Melchizedek king of Salem brought out bread and wine; he was priest of God Most High. [19]And he blessed him and said,
"Blessed be Abram by God Most High,
    maker of heaven and earth;
[20]and blessed be God Most High,
    who has delivered your enemies into your hand!"
And Abram gave him a tenth of everything. [21]And the king of Sodom said to Abram, "Give me the persons, but take the goods for yourself." [22]But Abram said to the king of Sodom, "I have sworn to the Lord God Most High, maker of heaven and earth, [23]that I would not take a thread or a sandal-thong or anything that is yours, lest you should say, 'I have made Abram rich.' [24]I will take nothing but what the young men have eaten, and the share of the men who went with me; let Aner, Eshcol, and Mamre take their share."

Having rescued Lot from the kings who had taken him captive (vv. 11-16), Abraham, on his return, was greeted by the king of Sodom (vv. 17, 21-24). The story of the encounter between the patriarch and the king is, however, interrupted by the account of a meeting between Abraham and

Melchizedek, king of Salem, who is introduced unexpectedly into the narrative (vv. 18-20).

The name *Melchizedek* is an old Canaanite one, meaning "(the god) Zedek is my king," or possibly "my king is upright" (*cf.*, Heb 7:2), and the name *Salem*, the city over which he ruled, is to be identified with Jerusalem. That Melchizedek enjoyed the prerogatives of both king and priest should not surprise us, since the combination of kingship and priesthood in the same individual was not unusual in the ancient Near East, including Israel (*cf.*, 2 Sam 6:12-14, 17-19; 24:25; 1 Kgs 8:5, 62-64). The title *God Most High*, by which Melchizedek's god was known, designated the supreme deity of the Canaanite pantheon, the monarchic head of the many local gods worshipped in Canaan in Abraham's day. The epithet *maker of heaven and earth* is attested in Canaanite and Phoenician texts, and it suggests the god's dominion over all other gods and over all the world. The fact that Abraham could swear *to the Lord God Most High, maker of heaven and earth* (v. 22) shows how naturally the early Israelites accepted the Canaanite divine title as descriptive of their own God. The *bread and wine* which Melchizedek brought to Abraham (v. 18) may simply have been regarded as refreshment for the returning victor and his troops, or they may have been intended for a ritual meal between the two allied princes, Abraham and Melchizedek, who wished to renew and confirm their mutual trust. Such a meal might involve a sacrificial offering (*cf.*, 31:43-54) but there is no mention of this in the text, so that the story offers no real basis for the Christian interpretation which found in Melchizedek's bread and wine a foreshadowing of the Eucharist.

The author who inserted this episode into the Abraham story was primarily interested in linking the patriarch with Jerusalem and with its priest-king. By showing that the ancestor of the nation had acknowledged the priest-king of Jerusalem and paid tithes to him (v. 20) the writer is suggesting that Abraham's descendants have every reason to acknowledge the Davidic kings in Jerusalem and to pay tithes to the Jerusalem priesthood. In later times the author of Ps 110 portrayed Melchizedek as the prototype of the ideal Davidic king who would establish the universal kingship of Yahweh. At a still later date the author of the Epistle to the Hebrews was to use the Melchizedek story to prove that the priesthood of Jesus was superior to that of the Levitical priests (*cf.*, Heb 7).

The story of Abraham's encounter with the king of Sodom which was interrupted at the end of v. 17 is taken up at v. 21. The king and the patriarch outdo each other in foregoing their rights. The king disclaims any interest in the property that Abraham and his followers might have recovered from the retreating raiders. His only concern was that the people who had been taken captive should be returned safely. Abraham, for his part, cedes the booty he had captured lest he give the impression of having grown rich at another man's expense. The high-minded patriarch's only wish was that his companions in the battle against the foreign kings should receive a reward for their efforts.

ABRAHAM BELIEVED
15:1-6 (J)

> **15** After these things the word of the Lord came to Abram in a vision, "Fear not, Abram, I am your shield; your reward shall be very great." ²But Abram said, "O Lord God, what wilt thou give me, for I continue childless, and the heir of my house is Eliezer of Damascus?" ³And Abram said, "Behold, thou hast given me no offspring; and a slave born in my house will be my heir." ⁴And behold, the word of the Lord came to him, "This man shall not be your heir; your own son shall be your heir." ⁵And he brought him outside and said, "Look toward heaven, and number the stars, if you are able to number them." Then he said to him, "So shall your descendants be." ⁶And he believed the Lord; and he reckoned it to him as righteousness.

Many commentators claim that the first Elohist contribution to the Pentateuch is to be found in this chapter. But if this is so the Elohist material is so closely interwoven with the Yahwistic tradition that separation of the two strands is no longer possible.

The formula *the word of the Lord came to Abram in a vision* (v. 1; *cf.,* v. 4) was to become almost a technical phrase to indicate the revelation received by a prophet (*cf.,* Isa 1:1; Ezek 1:1; Amos 1:1, etc.). The reassuring phrase *fear not* frequently accompanies God's self-disclosure to individuals (*cf.,* Judg 6:23; Isa 41:10; Luke 1:30), and is calculated to allay the sense of terror which God's self-manifestation causes in human beings. The divine declaration *I am your shield* conveys the idea that God is the faithful protector and deliverer of his chosen servant (*cf.,* Pss 3:3; 18:2; 30, etc.), and that one who entrusts oneself to God and to his will enjoys security and peace. However, Abraham, who remained childless in spite of an earlier promise that he would become a great nation (*cf.,* 12:2; 13:16), found no peace in the divine reassurance. Despondent and sceptical, he declared the divine word devoid of meaning. The Hebrew phrase which the RSV renders as *the heir of my house is Eliezer of Damascus* is corrupt and beyond confident translation. But the reliability of this reading is supported by a similar phrase in v. 3: *a slave born in my house will be my heir*. Both texts reflect a custom that is known to us from Hurrian documents dating from the fifteenth century B.C. which were discovered at Nuzi in north-east Mesopotamia, the general area from which the patriarchs came. According to this custom a childless husband might adopt a stranger, even a slave, as his "son" and heir. It seems that in vv. 2-3 Abraham is referring to this legal custom when he declares that God's promise of children remains unfulfilled, and that he himself feels forced to adopt a son who will inherit his property. The Lord's reaction to Abraham's expression of perplexity and doubt was to reassure him that the slave would not be his heir and to reaffirm the promises of innumerable descendants which he had already made (vv. 4-6). The statement that Abraham *believed the Lord* (v. 6) means that he abandoned his own dismal diagnosis of the situation, put his trust in God's word, and allowed the Lord to fulfill his promise in his own time and in his own way. The patriarch's act of trust was reckoned to him as righteousness. Since Abraham is already known to us as a righteous man, that is, as one who lived in a right relationship with God and whose life was governed by the divine will, we may take this phrase to mean that Abraham's acceptance of the renewed promise was seen as a further manifestation of his fellowship with God. Because of his trusting attitude to God's promise Abraham became the prototype of a person of faith (*cf.*, Rom 4:3; Gal 3:6), and the model of all those who live confidently in the sometimes obscure light of God's word.

A COVENANT WITH ABRAHAM
15:7-21 (J)

⁷And he said to him, "I am the Lord who brought you from Ur of the Chaldeans, to give you this land to possess." ⁸But he said, "O Lord God, how am I to know that I shall possess it?" ⁹He said to him, "Bring me a heifer three years old, a she-goat three years old, a ram three years old, a turtledove, and a young pigeon." ¹⁰And he brought all these, cut them in two, and laid each half over against the other; but he did not cut the birds in two. ¹¹And when birds of prey came down upon the carcasses, Abram drove them away.

¹²As the sun was going down, a deep sleep fell on Abram; and lo, a dread and great darkness fell upon him. ¹³Then the Lord said to Abram, "Know of a surety that your descendants will be sojourners in a land that is not theirs, and will be slaves there, and they will be oppressed for four hundred years; ¹⁴but I will bring judgment on the nation which they serve, and afterward they shall come out with great possessions. ¹⁵As for yourself, you shall go to your fathers in peace; you shall be buried in a good old

age. [16]And they shall come back here in the fourth generation; for the iniquity of the Amorites is not yet complete."

[17]When the sun had gone down and it was dark,
behold, a smoking fire pot and a flaming torch passed
between these pieces. [18]On that day the Lord made a
covenant with Abram, saying, "To your descendants I
give this land, from the river of Egypt to the great river,
the river Euphrates, [19]the land of the Kenites, the Keniz-
zites, the Kadmonites, [20]the Hittites, the Perizzites, the
Raphaim, [21]the Amorites, the Canaanites, the Girga-
shites and the Jebusites."

Abraham, whose faith had been so unreservedly praised
in v. 6, now expresses doubts about the possibility of pos-
sessing the land which God promised him (vv. 7-8). But God
silenced the patriarch's doubts by sealing a covenant with
him. The rather curious directions given to Abraham (v. 9)
describe the preparations for an elaborate covenant ritual of
the type that was known among peoples of the ancient Near
East as late as the time of Jeremiah (*cf.,* Jer 34:18). The
cutting of the animals as described in v. 10 was an essential
part of that age-old ritual, and it prepared for a dramatic act
of high symbolic significance. For the parties in the covenant passed between the dissected animal parts and invoked
on themselves a fate like that of the animals should they
violate the terms of the agreement. In the covenant between
God and Abraham described here, only God, symbolized as
"a smoking fire pot and a flaming torch" (*cf.,* Exod 13:21-
22), passed between the sundered parts (v. 17). Since God
simply committed himself to fulfill a promise without
imposing any reciprocal obligations on Abraham, he alone
performed the rite of self-imprecation involved in going
between the pieces of animal flesh. The substance of the
divine promise is expressed in vv. 18-19, where the promise
of land which had already been made (*cf.,* 12:7; 13:15) is
renewed. Yahweh promised to dispossess the powerful
inhabitants of Canaan in order to give their land to his
chosen people.

The *birds of prey* mentioned in v. 11 must be regarded as ill omens, and the biblical author probably saw them as portents of the future captivity in Egypt. Verses 13-16 explain that such a captivity would be only temporary, and that the Israelites' long delay in acquiring possession of the promised land was due to the fact that "the iniquity of the Amorites was not yet complete" (v. 16). This cryptic statement is based on the idea that God only punishes a people when they have reached a certain measure of sinfulness and have thus become ripe for judgment (*cf.,* 2 Macc 6:14; 1 Thess 2:16). God bides his time, as it were, in judging the nations, but his designs for his chosen people are not frustrated, even though their execution may be delayed for four hundred years.

THE BIRTH OF ISHMAEL
16:1-16 (JP)

16 Now Sarai, Abram's wife, bore him no children. She had an Egyptian maid whose name was Hagar; ²and Sarai said to Abram, "Behold now, the Lord has prevented me from bearing children; go in to my maid; it may be that I shall obtain children by her." And Abram hearkened to the voice of Sarai. ³So, after Abram had dwelt ten years in the land of Canaan, Sarai, Abram's wife, took Hagar the Egyptian, her maid, and gave her to Abram her husband as a wife. ⁴And he went in to Hagar, and she conceived; and when she saw that she had conceived, she looked with contempt on her mistress. ⁵And Sarai said to Abram, "May the wrong done to me be on you! I gave my maid to your embrace, and when she saw that she had conceived, she looked on me with contempt. May the Lord judge between you and me!" ⁶But Abram said to Sarai, "Behold, your maid is in your power; do to her as you please." Then Sarai dealt harshly with her, and she fled from her.

⁷The angel of the Lord found her by a spring of water in the wilderness, the spring on the way to Shur. ⁸And he said, "Hagar, maid of Sarai, where have you come from

and where are you going?" She said, "I am fleeing from my mistress Sarai." [9]The angel of the Lord said to her, "Return to your mistress, and submit to her." [10]The angel of the Lord also said to her, "I will so greatly multiply your descendants that they cannot be numbered for multitude." [11]And the angel of the Lord said to her, "Behold, you are with child, and shall bear a son; you shall call his name Ishmael; because the Lord has given heed to your affliction. [12]He shall be a wild ass of a man, his hand against every man and every man's hand against him; and he shall dwell over against all his kinsmen." [13]So she called the name of the Lord who spoke to her, "Thou art a God of seeing"; for she said, "Have I really seen God and remained alive after seeing him?" [14]Therefore the well was called Beerlahairoi; it lies between Kadesh and Bered.

[15]And Hagar bore Abram a son; and Abram called the name of his son, whom Hagar bore, Ishmael. [16]Abram was eighty-six years old when Hagar bore Ishmael to Abram.

When Sarah despaired of seeing the fulfillment of God's promise to grant her children, she gave her maid to Abraham as a substitute wife through whom he would beget an heir. In doing so she seems to have been following a Mesopotamian custom that she and Abraham would have known in the land of their origins. For we learn from Mesopotamian laws that were operative in patriarchal times, that a barren wife could present her husband with a maid through whom he could bear children. Such children would, however, through legal fiction, be regarded as the offspring of the wife. So when Sarah proposed to adapt this procedure in order to acquire the children whom God, in spite of his promises, seemed to deny her, Abraham went along with the scheme. The childless couple, no longer content to leave things to God, took human measures to hurry things along. Their course of action, surprising though it may seem to us, enjoyed the sanction of custom, and from a moral point of view was totally acceptable within the context of their culture.

When the promoted slave-girl became pregnant with her master's child she looked with contempt on the barren Sarah (v. 4). However, Mesopotamian law stipulated that a slave who bore a child to her master and then claimed equality with her mistress, should be returned to her slave status. The aggrieved Sarah appealed to this statute, and compelled Abraham to restore the unfortunate Hagar to her place among the slaves (vv. 5-6). In this shabby domestic wrangle none of the participants is presented in a favourable light. Hagar appears as an insensitive young woman who was unworthy of the dignity that had been bestowed on her by her mistress. Sarah allowed her conduct to be dictated by jealousy and revenge. As for Abraham, although he acted under domestic pressure and according to the accepted customs of the times, his treatment of Hagar cannot be said to conform to a high standard of justice and decency. Perhaps the Yahwist, to whom we owe almost all this story, wished to paint the polygamous scene in its most negative colours in order to express his disapproval of the whole system of polygamy.

The *angel of the Lord* appeared to the desperate Hagar as she fled into the wilderness to escape from the misery of life under a jealous Sarah (vv. 6b-7); it is identified with God later on in the story (v. 13). The term "angel of the Lord," or "the Lord's messenger" (NAB), softens the usually bold anthropomorphisms of the Yahwist, while allowing us to understand that Yahweh himself is the subject of the story. In many Genesis passages where this title appears the angel is not clearly distinguished from Yahweh himself, and the term seems to be used simply in order to preserve the transcendence of God (*cf.,* 21:17; 22:11-12; 24:7, 40, etc.). The angel spoke to the distressed Hagar in terms that remind one of the divine promises to Abraham, and assured her that she would be the mother of many descendants (v. 10; *cf.,* 13:16; 15:5). The name Ishmael which Hagar was to give her son (v. 11), when understood according to its popular etymology — "God hears" — would always be a reminder that God heard the cry of the despairing Hagar and came to her aid. We shall find two somewhat different explanations of the name Ishmael in later Genesis stories (*cf.,* 17:20; 21:17).

Verse 12 must be understood as characterizing the semi-nomadic tribes who inherited the desert areas on Israel's borders, and who were regarded as the descendants of Ishmael (*cf.,* 25:12-18). Ishmael, as the ancestor of these tribes, is here described as *a wild ass of a man.* He and his descendants, like the wild ass (*cf.,* Job 39:5-8), are portrayed as leading a free and independent life, roaming where they please in search of food, and despising the "soft" life-style of the settled population. The rest of the verse portrays Ishmael as one who will live in continual strife with all peoples, and who will be feared and opposed as a marauder and plunderer. Thus the Ishmaelites, the cousins of the Israelites, are portrayed as a restless, warlike, proud and uncontrollable people. They will appear in the Joseph story as merchants who can get involved even in the slave trade (*cf.,* 37:25-28).

Verses 13-14 are rather obscure and partly corrupt. The idea seems to be, however, that Hagar identified Yahweh with the *God of seeing* (*El Roi* in Hebrew), who may have been worshipped at an ancient sanctuary known as *Beer-la-hai-roi,* i.e. *the well of one who sees and lives.* The RSV rendering of 13b is conjectural. It reflects Hagar's awe, and may be compared with Jacob's reactions as recorded in 28:16 and 32:30.

COVENANT AND CIRCUMCISION
17:1-14 (P)

> **17** When Abram was ninety-nine years old the Lord appeared to Abram, and said to him, "I am God Almighty; walk before me, and be blameless. ²And I will make my covenant between me and you, and will multiply you exceedingly." ³Then Abram fell on his face; and God said to him, ⁴"Behold, my covenant is with you, and you shall be the father of a multitude of nations. ⁵No

longer shall your name be Abram, but your name shall be Abraham; for I have made you the father of a multitude of nations. [6]I will make you exceedingly fruitful; and I will make nations of you, and kings shall come forth from you. [7]And I will establish my covenant between me and you and your descendants after you throughout their generations for an everlasting covenant, to be God to you and to your descendants after you. [8]And I will give to you, and to your descendants after you, the land of your sojournings, all the land of Canaan, for an everlasting possession; and I will be their God."

[9]And God said to Abraham, "As for you, you shall keep my covenant, you and your descendants after you throughout their generations. [10]This is my covenant, which you shall keep, between me and you and your descendants after you: Every male among you shall be circumcised. "You shall be circumcised in the flesh of your foreskins, and it shall be a sign of the covenant between me and you. [12]He that is eight days old among you shall be circumcised; every male throughout your generations, whether born in your house, or bought with your money from any foreigner who is not of your off-spring, [13]both he that is born in your house and he that is bought with your money, shall be circumcised. So shall my covenant be in your flesh an everlasting covenant. [14]Any uncircumcised male who is not circumcised in the flesh of his foreskin shall be cut off from his people; he has broken my covenant."

This chapter gives us the Priestly version of the covenant with Abraham which the Yahwist has already described in chap. 15. The divine title *God Almighty* (v. 1), which renders the Hebrew *El Shaddai*, comes to us through the Greek version where *Shaddai* was translated as "all powerful." The original meaning of the word *Shaddai* eludes the scholars, and we find no reference to a deity of that name among Israel's neighbours. In the pre-Mosaic stories the Priestly author frequently refers to the God of Israel under this title (*cf.,* 28:3; 35:11; 43:14; 48:3; 49:25; Exod 6:3).

The covenant as described in this chapter involves obligations for both God and Abraham. On his part God renewed his promises of numerous descendants and of the land of Canaan (vv. 4-8; *cf.,* 12:2, 7; 13:14-17; 15:5, 18). The patriarch, and his descendants after him, were obliged to practise circumcision as a sign of God's covenant with them (vv. 9-14). When the author links the name Abraham with the idea that the patriarch is to be *the father of a multitude of nations* (v. 5), he is merely giving a fanciful interpretation of the name. For the name "Abraham" is simply a dialectic variant of the name Abram by which the patriarch was known until now, and it means "my father (the god) is exalted." By explaining the name to mean "father of a multitude of nations," the author is indulging in theological word-play that links the patriarch's name with the promise given in 12:20. The phrase *to be God to you and to your descendants after you* (v. 7) reminds one of the covenant formula "you shall be my people and I will be your God" (Jer 7:23; 11:4; 24:7; Ezek 11:20, etc.), which expresses the special relationship that exists between God and his covenant partners.

As we noted when considering the covenant with Noah (see the comments on 9:8-17, above p. 74), covenants were always validated by some external signs. According to our present narrative circumcision was the sign of God's covenant with Abraham (vv. 10-14), and it was to serve as a reminder of Abraham's acceptance of God's word. Although circumcision was practised in Egypt and among the Semitic peoples who inhabited Canaan before the arrival of the Israelites, the peoples of Mesopotamia did not observe that rite. Originally the practice of circumcision may have been associated with puberty rites. Among the Israelites, however, it took place at infancy (*cf.,* v. 12; Lev 12:3), and it took on a religious significance. By the time of the Babylonian exile, that is, about the time of the Priestly author's literary activity, circumcision, like the Sabbath, had become one of the signs that distinguished the Israelites from their captors. It was a sign of allegiance to Yahweh and a witness of one's adherence to the covenant. The present passage shows how serious the obligation to practise circumcision was, when it declares that anyone who refused to undergo the rite was to be *cut off from his people* (v. 14), that is, excluded from the sacred community and regarded as having rejected the covenant.

A SON FOR SARAH
17:15-27 (P)

[15]And God said to Abraham, "As for Sarai your wife, you shall not call her name Sarai, but Sarah shall be her name. [16]I will bless her, and moreover I will give you a son by her; I will bless her, and she shall be a mother of nations; kings of peoples shall come from her." [17]Then Abraham fell on his face and laughed, and said to himself, "Shall a child be born to a man who is a hundred years old? Shall Sarah, who is ninety years old, bear a child?" [18]And Abraham said to God, "O that Ishmael might live in thy sight!" [19]God said, "No, but Sarah your wife shall bear you a son, and you shall call his name Isaac. I will establish my covenant with him as an everlasting covenant for his descendants after him. [20]As for Ishmael, I have heard you; behold, I will bless him and make him fruitful and multiply him exceedingly; he shall be the father of twelve princes, and I will make him a great nation. [21]But I will establish my covenant with Isaac, whom Sarah shall bear to you at this season next year."

[22]When he had finished talking with him, God went up from Abraham. [23]Then Abraham took Ishmael his son and all the slaves born in his house or bought with his money, every male among the men of Abraham's house, and he circumcised the flesh of their foreskins that very day, as God had said to him. [24]Abraham was ninety-nine years old when he was circumcised in the flesh of his foreskin. [25]And Ishmael his son was thirteen years old when he was circumcised in the flesh of his foreskin.

26That very day Abraham and his son Ishmael were circumcised; 27and all the men of his house, those born in the
house and those bought with money from a foreigner,
were circumcised with him.

Just as Abraham's name had been changed (v. 5) so is
Sarai's name now altered to Sarah, although no explanation
of the new name is given as had been done in the case of
Abraham. Actually Sarai and Sarah are simply different
forms of the same name. However, a change of name usually
signifies a turning point in a person's life (*cf.,* John 1:42;
Matt 16:17-18), and here the author wishes us to see the
change in Sarai's name as marking the point where her
future role as mother of the child of promise was made
explicit. Abraham's reaction to God's extraordinary promise that his aging wife would become a mother (v. 16) was a
mixture of belief and doubt. He *fell on his face* in an attitude
of reverence before the God who could fulfill his promise,
and at the same time *he laughed* at the idea that a couple as
old as he and his wife (v. 17) would become parents. The
aged patriarch had assumed that Ishmael, son of Hagar
(16:15-16), would be his heir, and now he hears the incomprehensible word about a child by Sarah. Small wonder that
the astonished old man prayed on behalf of Ishmael, and
attempted to coax God into accepting him as heir to the
patriarchal promises (v. 18). But that was not God's plan.
Isaac, the child of an extraordinary birth, was to be the child
of promise. He and his offspring would inherit the covenant,
and they would enjoy a special relationship with God that
would distinguish them from all peoples. However, God
would not abandon Ishmael, and he too would prosper and
become the *father of twelve princes* (v. 20, *cf.,* 25:12-16 P).
The Priestly author here wishes us to connect the name
Isaac (v. 19) with the Hebrew verb *yitzhaq, he laughed* (v.
17). The Yahwist (18:12; 21:6b, 7) and the Elohist (21:6a)
will make the same connection later.

Verses 23-27 form the logical sequel to the account of the
giving of the covenant (vv. 1-14), and they simply assure us

that Abraham carried out the command regarding circumcision (vv. 11-14). One notices the redundant style of the passage and the typically Priestly characteristic of repeating the words of the command in the description of its execution.

DESERT HOSPITALITY
18:1-15 (J)

18   And the Lord appeared to him by the oaks of Mamre, as he sat at the door of his tent in the heat of the day. ²He lifted up his eyes and looked, and behold, three men stood in front of him. When he saw them, he ran from the tent door to meet them, and bowed himself to the earth, ³and said, "My lord, if I have found favor in your sight, do not pass by your servant. ⁴Let a little water be brought, and wash your feet, and rest yourselves under the tree, ⁵while I fetch a morsel of bread, that you may refresh yourselves, and after that you may pass on—since you have come to your servant." So they said, "Do as you have said." ⁶And Abraham hastened into the tent to Sarah, and said, "Make ready quickly three measures of fine meal, knead it, and make cakes." ⁷And Abraham ran to the herd, and took a calf, tender and good, and gave it to the servant, who hastened to prepare it. ⁸Then he took curds, and milk, and the calf which he had prepared, and set it before them; and he stood by them under the tree while they ate.

⁹They said to him, "Where is Sarah your wife?" And he said, "She is in the tent." ¹⁰The Lord said, "I will surely return to you in the spring, and Sarah your wife shall have a son." And Sarah was listening at the tent door behind him. ¹¹Now Abraham and Sarah were old, advanced in age; it had ceased to be with Sarah after the manner of women. ¹²So Sarah laughed to herself, saying, "After I have grown old, and my husband is old, shall I have pleasure?" ¹³The Lord said to Abraham, "Why did Sarah laugh, and say, 'Shall I indeed bear a child, now

that I am old?" [14]Is anything too hard for the Lord? At the appointed time I will return to you, in the spring, and Sarah shall have a son." [15]But Sarah denied, saying, "I did not laugh"; for she was afraid. He said, "No, but you did laugh."

In chapters 18-19 we encounter the Yahwist at his best as he presents us with masterpieces of narrative art. *Mamre* (18:1), where we find Abraham, is situated about two miles north of Hebron (*cf.,* 13:18), and some twenty miles south of Jerusalem. Suddenly noticing three men on the horizon, the patriarch ran to meet them and to offer them hospitality. With typical bedouin formality and show, he offered simple refreshment to the weary and dusty travellers (vv. 3-5). The lavish meal which was hurriedly provided (vv. 6-8) was in marked contrast to Abraham's modest proposal, and his standing by to wait on his guests showed his eagerness to ensure that none of the proprieties of hospitality would be neglected.

In vv. 9-15 the interest is clearly in the dialogue between the Lord and Abraham. The prediction that the aging Sarah become a mother evoked in her a laugh that expressed scepticism and incredulity (v. 12). The Lord's reaction to this laugh was a rhetorical question (v. 14), which is a remarkable declaration of God's omnipotence (*cf.,* Jer 32:17-18; Zech 8:6). The stern tone of the question shattered Sarah, caused a sudden change in her mood, and led her to deny that she had laughed at the extraordinary promise she had overheard. Although Sarah's future child is not named here, this passage of the Yahwistic account predicts the birth of Isaac, a prediction which has already been recorded in the Priestly source (*cf.,* 17:16, 19) where it was explicitly associated with the Hebrew word *yitzhaq, he laughed.*

SODOM AND GOMORRAH
18:16-33

[16]Then the men set out from there, and they looked toward Sodom; and Abraham went with them to set them

on their way. [17]The Lord said, "Shall I hide from Abraham what I am about to do, [18]seeing that Abraham shall become a great and mighty nation, and all the nations of the earth shall bless themselves by him? [19]No, for I have chosen him, that he may charge his children and his household after him to keep the way of the Lord by doing righteousness and justice; so that the Lord may bring to Abraham what he has promised him." [20]Then the Lord said, "Because the outcry against Sodom and Gomorrah is great and their sin is very grave, [21]I will go down to see whether they have done altogether according to the outcry which has come to me; and if not, I will know."

[22]So the men turned from there, and went toward Sodom; but Abraham still stood before the Lord. [23]Then Abraham drew near, and said, "Wilt thou indeed destroy the righteous with the wicked? [24]Suppose there are fifty righteous within the city; wilt thou then destroy the place and not spare it for the fifty righteous who are in it? [25]Far be it from thee to do such a thing, to slay the righteous with the wicked, so that the righteous fare as the wicked! Far be that from thee! Shall not the Judge of all the earth do right?" [26]And the Lord said, "If I find at Sodom fifty righteous in the city, I will spare the whole place for their sake." [27]Abraham answered, "Behold, I have taken upon myself to speak to the Lord, I who am but dust and ashes. [28]Suppose five of the fifty righteous are lacking? Wilt thou destroy the whole city for lack of five?" And he said, "I will not destroy it if I find forty-five there." [29]Again he spoke to him, and said, "Suppose forty are found there." He answered, "For the sake of forty I will not do it." [30]Then he said, "Oh let not the Lord be angry, and I will speak. Suppose thirty are found there." He answered, "I will not do it, if I find thirty there." [31]He said, "Behold, I have taken upon myself to speak to the Lord. Suppose twenty are found there." He answered, "For the sake of twenty I will not destroy it." [32]Then he said, "Oh let not the Lord be angry, and I will speak again but this once. Suppose ten are found there." He answered, "For the

sake of ten I will not destroy it." [33]And the Lord went his way, when he had finished speaking to Abraham; and Abraham returned to his place.

Although the events recorded in vv. 9-15 could have left no doubt about the presence of God among Abraham's guests, the story now talks simply about *the men* (v. 16). But as Abraham showed them the courtesy of escorting them a little way on their journey to Sodom, *the Lord* again suddenly takes the centre of the stage and begins a soliloquy (v. 17). In this reflection (vv. 17-19) the Lord reveals his intention to make Abraham privy to his plan (v. 17), celebrates the patriarch's greatness (v. 18) in terms that recall the original blessing of 12:2-3, and proclaims his responsibility as the leader of a chosen family (v. 19). The anthropomorphic terms of vv. 20-21 which portray God as going down to investigate the serious complaints that have come to him about Sodom and Gomorrah remind one of a similar scene in the Tower of Babel story (*cf.,* 11:5-7, J).

Left alone with God (v. 22), Abraham tactfully asked him about the standards and methods of divine judgment. The question, *Wilt thou indeed destroy the righteous with the wicked?* (v. 23), and the following specification in v. 24, presuppose the ancient Israelite concept of corporate personality, according to which the destiny of the individual and that of the community were inseparably linked (*cf.,* 20:9; Josh 7:16-26), so that the wickedness of a few could bring disaster on a city, while the virtue of a handful could merit salvation for a whole community. Abraham asked if a minority of righteous inhabitants should not save the whole city of Sodom, and he engaged in a typically oriental bargaining process to establish the limits to which God's mercy could be pushed. With all due deference this man who knew himself to be but *dust and ashes* (v. 27) dared to approach *the Judge of all the earth* (v. 25), and with increasing audacity attempted to fix the absolute minimum of righteous people whose merit could win divine mercy for all their fellow citizens. There is a certain naivete in the story, and yet there is tremendous tension as the patriarch moves step by step to the limit beyond which he could not dare to go. For Abraham knew that although the Lord recoils from punishing the guilty (*cf.,* Hos 11:8-9), he also knew that the divine justice demands that the Lord's wrath cannot be restrained for ever.

The author of the story of Abraham's urgent pleading with the Lord was not so much interested in the patriarch's effort to save Sodom as in establishing the principle that God judges the world with equity, and that his anger is always tempered by mercy and by a readiness to save. The narrative also shows the beneficent effect of the righteous on the community to which they belong, and thus prepares the way for the teaching about that one servant who would be the source of salvation for many (*cf.,* Isa 53:5, 10).

THE CRIME OF THE SODOMITES
19:1-23

19   The two angels came to Sodom in the evening; and Lot was sitting in the gate of Sodom. When Lot saw them, he rose to meet them, and bowed himself with his face to the earth, ²and said, "My lords, turn aside, I pray you, to your servant's house and spend the night, and wash your feet; then you may rise up early and go on your way." They said, "No; we will spend the night in the street." ³But he urged them strongly; so they turned aside to him and entered his house; and he made them a feast, and baked unleavened bread, and they ate. ⁴But before they lay down, the men of the city, the men of Sodom, both young and old, all the people to the last man, surrounded the house; ⁵and they called to Lot, "Where are the men who came to you tonight? Bring them out to us, that we may know them." ⁶Lot went out of the door to the men, shut the door after him, ⁷and said, "I beg you, my brothers, do not act so wickedly. ⁸Behold, I have two daughters who have not known man; let me bring them out to you, and do to them as you please; only do nothing to these men, for they have come under the shelter of my roof." [9]But they said, "Stand back!" And they said, "This fellow came to sojourn, and he would play the judge! Now we will deal worse with you than with them." Then they pressed hard against the man Lot, and drew near to break the door. [10]But the men put forth their hands and brought Lot into the house to them, and shut the door. [11]And they struck with blindness the men who were at the door of the house, both small and great, so that they wearied themselves groping for the door.

[12]Then the men said to Lot, "Have you any one else here? Sons-in-law, sons, daughters, or any one you have in the city, bring them out of the place; [13]for we are about to destroy this place, because the outcry against its people has become great before the Lord, and the Lord has sent us to destroy it." [14]So Lot went out and said to his sons-in-law, who were to marry his daughters, "Up, get out of this place; for the Lord is about to destroy the city." But he seemed to his sons-in-law to be jesting.

[15]When morning dawned, the angels urged Lot, saying, "Arise, take your wife and your two daughters who are here, lest you be consumed in the punishment of the city." [16]But he lingered; so the men seized him and his wife and his two daughters by the hand, the Lord being merciful to him, and they brought him forth and set him outside the city. [17]And when they had brought them forth, they said, "Flee for your life; do not look back or stop anywhere in the valley; flee to the hills, lest you be consumed." [18]And Lot said to them, "Oh no, my lords; [19]behold, your servant has found favor in your sight, and you have shown me great kindness in saving my life; but I cannot flee to the hills, lest the disaster overtake me, and I die. [20]Behold, yonder city is near enough to flee to, and it is a little one. Let me escape there—is it not a little one?—and my life will be saved!" [21]He said to him, "Behold, I grant you this favor also, that I will not overthrow the city of which you have spoken. [22]Make haste, escape there; for I can do nothing till you arrive there." Therefore the name of the

city was called Zoar. [23]The sun had risen on the earth
when Lot came to Zoar.

The two "angels," or "messengers," as the Hebrew might
also be translated, who are the first subjects mentioned in
this chapter (v. 1), must be identified with "the men" (18:22)
who set out for Sodom, leaving the Lord, the third member
of the original trio (18:2), behind with Abraham. On arrival
at Sodom the two wayfarers, who become "the men" as the
story progresses (*cf.,* vv. 5, 8, 10, etc.), encountered Lot,
whom we last heard of when he was rescued by his uncle
from the pillaging kings (*cf.,* 14:12-16). Lot treated his
unheralded guests to the same kind of hospitality that Abraham had shown to his unexpected visitors (vv. 2-3; *cf.,*
18:2-8). Lot's fellow-citizens, however, in flagrant violation
of the sacred law of hospitality, sought out the new arrivals
in order to *know them* (vv. 4-5). The euphemism "know
them" can, in the context, only refer to homosexual activity
and our present story accounts for the fact that this form of
sexual behavior is known as sodomy. In the many passages,
however, where Sodom and Gomorrah are mentioned as
paradigms of depravity this particular activity is never mentioned as the characteristic vice of the cities, except in our
present text (*cf.,* Isa 1:9-17; Jer 23:14; Ezek 16:48-50). Since,
however, promiscuous homosexual activity was among the
sexual aberrations known among the pre-Israelite occupants of Palestine (*cf.,* Lev 18:22; 20:13; and especially Judg
19:22-26 which has close similarities to our present passage),
one can understand why the Yahwist, who wished to indulge
in a subtle polemic against the Canaanites, identified the sin
of the Sodomites with this form of sexual expression which
was so unacceptable to Israel.

In order to protect the inviolability of hospitality Lot was
even willing to hand over his virgin daughters to the lustful
townsmen (vv. 6-8). Judged by our modern western standards his proposal is outrageous. But although the Yahwist
does not condone it, neither does he condemn it, and his
ancient Israelite readers, for whom the duty of hospitality
was most sacred, would not have found it as reprehensible

as we do. In any case, Lot's efforts were in vain, and the Sodomites not only rudely rejected his offer but also threatened his person. With obvious reference to 13:8-13 they poured scorn on Lot, referring to him as a mere sojourner who had no right whatsoever to judge their conduct (v. 9). In the end it was the guests who saved Lot by striking the violent Sodomites with blindness (vv. 10-11; *cf.*, 2 Kgs 6:18).

The men (v. 12), or *the angels* (v. 15), declare that the outcry against Sodom (*cf.*, 18:20-21) was justified, and that the guilt of the city had been established. God however would not wipe out the innocent with the wicked, and the two visitors urged Lot and his family to escape from the doomed city. But these found it difficult to take the strange message seriously, so that they had to be literally dragged to safety (v. 16) in the little town with the appropriate name of Zoar, which means "little" (*cf.*, vv. 20, 22).

BRIMSTONE AND FIRE
19:24-29

> [24]Then the Lord rained on Sodom and Gomorrah brimstone and fire from the Lord out of heaven; [25]and he overthrew those cities, and all the valley, and all the inhabitants of the cities, and what grew on the ground. [26]But Lot's wife behind him looked back, and she became a pillar of salt. [27]And Abraham went early in the morning to the place where he had stood before the Lord; [28]and he looked down toward Sodom and Gomorrah and toward all the land of the valley, and beheld, and lo, the smoke of the land went up like the smoke of a furnace.
>
> [29]So it was that, when God destroyed the cities of the valley, God remembered Abraham, and sent Lot out of the midst of the overthrow, when he overthrew the cities in which Lot dwelt.

Two short verses (24-25) describe the disaster that spelled the end of Sodom and Gomorrah, a disaster that was to become the paradigm of the judgment of Yahweh (*cf.*, Deut

29:22-23; Jer 20:16; 49:17-18; Amos 4:11). The account of the destruction of the two cities probably retains the distant recollection of an actual disaster. It is possible that an earthquake could have released the natural gases that are present in this area at the southern end of the Dead Sea. When ignited, these gases could have caused a flagration that would explain the "brimstone and fire" (v. 24) and smoke (v. 28). But however the actual event that gave rise to the story may be explained, the author has a theological reason for giving it a place in his narrative. The grim fate of the wicked cities shows that human depravity incurs the divine judgment, and that disregard for God's law inevitably brings retribution on the guilty.

The legend of Lot's wife becoming a pillar of salt (v. 26) may originally have served to explain the salt-rock formations on the mountains along the southern end of the Dead Sea. But the story of the punishment of Lot's wife has more than folkloristic value for the Yahwist. He regards it as a warning to those who disobey the word of God or who hesitate in carrying it out.

MOABITES AND AMMONITES
19:30-38

[30]Now Lot went up out of Zoar, and dwelt in the hills with his two daughters, for he was afraid to dwell in Zoar; so he dwelt in a cave with his two daughters. [31]And the first-born said to the younger, "Our father is old, and there is not a man on earth to come in to us after the manner of all the earth. [32]Come, let us make our father drink wine, and we will lie with him, that we may preserve offspring through our father." [33]So they made their father drink wine that night; and the first-born went in, and lay with her father; he did not know when she lay down or when she arose. [34]And on the next day, the first-born said to the younger, "Behold, I lay last night with my father; let us make him drink wine tonight also; then you go in and lie with him, that we may preserve offspring through

our father." [35]So they made their father drink wine that night also; and the younger arose, and lay with him; and he did not know when she lay down or when she arose. [36]Thus both the daughters of Lot were with child by their father. [37]The first-born bore a son, and called his name Moab; he is the father of the Moabites to this day. [38]The younger also bore a son, and called his name Benammi; he is the father of the Ammonites to this day.

This rather offensive story of Lot's incestuous relationship with his two daughers may have originally been intended to praise the ancestresses of the Moabites and Ammonites, who took desperate measures to fulfill their destiny as women and to save their people from extinction. In its present context, however, the story is meant to heap opprobrium on the Moabites and Ammonites who were traditional enemies of Israel (*cf.,* Judg 10:6-9; 11:4—12:4; 1 Sam 11:1-11; 14:47). By recognizing Lot as the ancestor of the two hated people who dwelt in Transjordan, the writer acknowledged Israel's kinship with them. But by focussing on the disgraceful origins of Moab and Ammon he reveals his deep-seated antipathy towards them. The popular etymology of the names of the two peoples (*cf.,* vv. 37-38) reflects their unnatural parentage, for Moab can be taken to mean "from my father," while Ammon can be understood as "[son of] my kin."

ABRAHAM AT GERAR
20:1-18 (E)

20   From there Abraham journeyed toward the territory of the Negeb, and dwelt between Kadesh and Shur; and he sojourned in Gerar. [2]And Abraham said of Sarah his wife, "She is my sister." And Abimelech king of Gerar sent and took Sarah. [3]But God came to Abimelech in a dream by night, and said to him, "Behold, you are a dead man, because of the woman whom you have taken; for she is a man's wife." [4]Now Abimelech had not approached her; so he said, "Lord, wilt thou slay an innocent people? [5]Did he not himself say to me, 'She is my sister'? And she herself said, 'He is my brother.' In the integrity of my heart and the innocence of my hands I have done this." [6]Then God said to him in the dream, "Yes, I know that you have done this in the integrity of your heart, and it was I who kept you from sinning against me; therefore I did not let you touch her. [7]Now then restore the man's wife; for he is a prophet, and he will pray for you, and you shall live. But if you do not restore her, know that you shall surely die, you, and all that are yours."

[8]So Abimelech rose early in the morning, and called all his servants, and told them all these things; and the men were very much afraid. [9]Then Abimelech called Abraham, and said to him, "What have you done to us? And how have I sinned against you, that you have brought on me and my kingdom a great sin? You have done to me things that ought not to be done." [10]And Abimelech said to Abraham, "What were you thinking of, that you did this thing?" [11]Abraham said, "I did it because I thought, There is no fear of God at all in this place, and they will kill me because of my wife. [12]Besides she is indeed my sister, the daughter of my father but not the daughter of my mother; and she became my wife. [13]And when God caused me to wander from my father's house, I said to her, 'This is the kindness you must do me; at every place to which we come, say of me, He is my brother.'" [14]Then Abimelech took sheep and oxen, and male and female slaves, and gave them to Abraham, and restored Sarah his wife to him. [15]And Abimelech said, "Behold, my land is before you; dwell where it pleases you." [16]To Sarah he said, "Behold, I have given your brother a thousand pieces of silver; it is your vindication in the eyes of all who are with you; and before every one you are righted." [17]Then Abraham prayed to God; and God healed Abimelech, and also healed his wife and female slaves so that they bore children. [18]For the Lord had closed all the

wombs of the house of Abimelech because of Sarah, Abraham's wife.

This is the first complete story we owe to the Elohist, and it repeats the motif of 12:10-20 (J; see above pp. 95-97). This time the episode is located, not in Egypt, but in Gerar, about fifteen miles southeast of Gaza. The royal protagonist is no longer Pharaoh but Abimelech. Here we are informed that God told Abimelech in a dream that Sarah was Abraham's wife (v. 3), whereas in the earlier account we were left wondering how Pharaoh discovered the fact. (In the Elohist tradition the dream is the usual means of communication between God and people; *cf.,* v. 6; 28:12; 31:10-11). In the present story we are told explicitly that *Abimelech had not approached Sarah* (v. 4), while 12:15 does not assure us that her honour was preserved when she was taken into Pharaoh's house. Here we are told that the patriarch had not actually lied when he passed off Sarah as his sister (v. 12), whereas in 12:13 there is no effort made to excuse him of deceit. The Elohist portrays Abraham as a prophet (v. 7), but he seems to understand a prophet to be one who can make effective intercession with God (*cf.,* v. 17; see Num 11:12; 12:13; Deut 9:20, 26, etc.).

In spite of the fact that the Elohist shows a greater sensitivity to moral issues than the Yahwist, and in spite of his minimizing of Abraham's guilt, the patriarch does not emerge from this scene with his honour untarnished. The pagan Abimelech who was genuinely shocked when he discovered how he had been tricked (vv. 4-5, 8-10), shows himself to be more god-fearing than Abraham who had expressed the conviction that there was no fear of God in Gerar (v. 11). The king's generosity was manifested in the rich gifts he gave to Abraham (vv. 14-15), and he reveals his eagerness to make amends for any wrong done when he explains to Sarah that the gifts he had given to Abraham are her vindication in the eyes of all (v. 16). The idea seems to be that the gifts vindicated Sarah's honour and forestalled any suspicions that the episode with Abimelech might arouse.

But whatever may be said about the characters of Abraham and Abimelech, the Elohist has told the story in order to show how God intervened to ensure that his plan for Abraham and Sarah would not be hindered by human weakness. In telling the story he imprints his own theological stamp on it and gives a new flavour to the old material.

VII. ISAAC STORIES
21:1—25:11

THE BIRTH OF ISAAC
21:1-7 (JEP)

21 The Lord visited Sarah as he had said, and the Lord did to Sarah as he had promised. ²And Sarah conceived, and bore Abraham a son in his old age at the time of which God had spoken to him. ³Abraham called the name of his son who was born to him, whom Sarah bore him, Isaac. ⁴And Abraham circumcised his son Isaac when he was eight days old, as God had commanded him. ⁵Abraham was a hundred years old when his son Isaac was born to him. ⁶And Sarah said, "God has made laughter for me; every one who hears will laugh over me." ⁷And she said, "Who would have said to Abraham that Sarah would suckle children? Yet I have borne him a son in his old age."

Sarah's giving birth *at the time of which God had spoken* (v. 2) was a fulfillment of the divine promise that was recorded in 17:21. By calling his new-born son Isaac (v. 3), Abraham fulfilled the directive of 17:19, and by circumcising him when he was eight days old (v. 4) he was obeying the regulation announced in 17:12. The notice that the patriarch was a hundred years old when the child was born (v. 5) tallies with the figures in 17:21, 24.

The Yahwist's birth notice (vv. 1, 6b, 7) also informs us that the Lord fulfilled the promise he had made to Abraham (*cf.*, 18:10, J). Sarah played on the name Isaac, which, as we noted (see the comment on 17:17-19; above 111), can be linked with the Hebrew verb meaning "to laugh," as she applied the theme of laughter to her own situation. In what is apparently the Elohist's only contribution to the story of Isaac's birth (v. 6a) the laughter theme is linked with Sarah's rejoicing at the unexpected blessing of motherhood (*cf.*, 1 Sam 2:5; Ps 113:9).

FLIGHT OF HAGAR
21:8-21 (E)

8And the child grew, and was weaned; and Abraham made a great feast on the day that Isaac was weaned. 9But Sarah saw the son of Hagar the Egyptian, whom she had borne to Abraham, playing with her son Isaac. 10So she said to Abraham, "Cast out this slave woman with her son; for the son of this slave woman shall not be heir with my son Isaac." 11And the thing was very displeasing to Abraham on account of his son. 12But God said to Abraham, "Be not displeased because of the lad and because of your slave woman; whatever Sarah says to you, do as she tells you, for through Isaac shall your descendants be named. 13And I will make a nation of the son of the slave woman also, because he is your offspring." 14So Abraham rose early in the morning, and took bread and a skin of water, and gave it to Hagar, putting it on her shoulder, along with the child, and sent her away. And she departed, and wandered in the wilderness of Beersheba.

15When the water in the skin was gone, she cast the child under one of the bushes. 16Then she went, and sat down over against him a good way off, about the distance of a bowshot; for she said, "Let me not look upon the death of the child." And as she sat over against him, the child lifted up his voice and wept. [17]And God heard the voice of the lad; and the angel of God called to Hagar from heaven, and said to her, "What troubles you, Hagar? Fear not; for God has heard the voice of the lad where he is. [18]Arise, lift up the lad, and hold him fast with your hand; for I will make him a great nation." [19]Then God opened her eyes, and she saw a well of water; and she went, and filled the skin with water, and gave the lad a drink. [20]And God was with the lad, and he grew up; he lived in the wilderness, and became an expert with the bow. [21]He lived in the wilderness of Paran; and his mother took a wife for him from the land of Egypt.

This rather touching passage gives us the Elohist parallel to the Yahwist story of chap. 16. Whereas the Yahwist place the episode before Ishmael's birth, the present story tells us that Hagar's expulsion took place after the weaning of the boy (v. 1). (According to Hebrew custom a child was weaned when it was about three years old; *cf.,* 1 Sam 1:22-28; 2 Macc 7:27.) The Yahwist (16:4-6) told us that it was Hagar's contempt for her barren mistress that occasioned her expulsion from Abraham's household; according to the present story (vv. 9-10) it was Sarah's jealousy of Ishmael, and her fear that he would become joint heir with Isaac of Abraham's property, that decided Hagar's fate. In the earlier version (16:5-6) Abraham seemed passive in the face of Sarah's determination to get rid of Hagar; here (vv. 11-13) he shows great affection for his concubine and her child, and he yields to Sarah's demands only at God's command, and only when God had promised that Ishmael too would be blessed (*cf.,* 17:18, 20, P). Thus the Elohist shows a greater sensitivity to Abraham's feelings, and he presents the patriarch in a more favourable light than did the Yahwist.

The angel of the Lord, who is to be identified with God himself (see the comment on 16:7; above p. 106), came to the assistance of the abandoned Hagar (vv. 17-18). He assured her that her child would become a great nation. The sons of Ishmael were in fact to become mighty nomadic tribes, who, like their ancestor, would be experts with the bow (*cf.,* v. 20b), and who would often live by their skill as hunters and by their ability to make quick raids on settled peoples and on caravans (see comment on 16:12; above p. 107).

The Lord's words to Abraham — *through Isaac shall your children be named* (v. 12b) — point unambiguously to Isaac as the son of the promise. He is to be the transmitter of God's blessings to future generations, and from now on our attention will be focussed on him. With Ishmael's departure from Abraham's house he is excluded from the divine plan, and apart from one brief entry on the occasion of his father's death (*cf.,* 25:9) he will never again make a personal appearance on the stage of sacred history.

A COVENANT WITH ABIMELECH
21:22-34

22At that time Abimelech and Phicol the commander of his army said to Abraham, "God is with you in all that you do; 23now therefore swear to me here by God that you will not deal falsely with me or with my offspring or with my posterity, but as I have dealt loyally with you, you will deal with me and with the land where you have sojourned." 24And Abraham said, "I will swear."

25When Abraham complained to Abimelech about a well of water which Abimelech's servants had seized, 26Abimelech said, "I do not know who has done this thing; you did not tell me, and I have not heard of it until today." 27So Abraham took sheep and oxen and gave them to Abimelech, and the two men made a covenant. 28Abraham set seven ewe lambs of the flock apart. 29And Abimelech said to Abraham, "What is the meaning of these seven ewe lambs which you have set apart?" 30He said, "These seven ewe lambs you will take from my hand, that you may be a witness for me that I dug this well." 31Therefore that place was called Beer-sheba; because there both of them swore an oath. 32So they made a covenant at Beer-sheba. Then Abimelech and Phicol the commander of his army rose up and returned to the land of the Philistines. ³³Abraham planted a tamarisk tree in Beer-sheba, and called there on the name of the Lord, the Everlasting God. ³⁴And Abraham sojourned many days in the land of the Philistines.

This narrative is generally regarded as a combination of two traditions, although critics vary in their apportioning of different verses to different sources. One tradition (vv. 22-24, 27, 31) tells how Abimelech approached Abraham, whom he knew to be under special divine protection (*cf.,* v. 22b), with a view to establishing a covenant with him. Following the pattern of near eastern suzerainty pacts, by which kings and princes ensured mutual loyalty, the astute king invited the blessed newcomer to form an alliance with him. Abraham's gift of sheep and oxen (v. 27) apparently signified his willingness to ratify an agreement with the king, and so a covenant of friendship was sealed. By taking the place-name *Beer-sheba* to mean "the well (*beer*) of the oath (*shaba*)," this tradition links the place with the pact which the ancestor made with a Canaanite king.

The other tradition (vv. 25-26, 28-30, 32) does not describe a treaty of friendship, but rather a pact that settles a dispute over a well. The establishment of rights to sources of water was, of course, of vital importance to nomads in semi-desert areas. This time Abraham took the initiative, and Abimelech, by accepting the seven lambs which the patriarch offered him, acknowledged the latter's rights to the well. The place-name *Beer-sheba* is implicitly linked with the word (*sheba*), seven, which occurs three times in the narrative with reference to the lambs.

Beer-sheba, which was situated about fifty miles southwest of Jerusalem, formed the southern outpost of the Holy Land (*cf.,* Judg 20:1). By planting a tamarisk tree there (v. 33) Abraham symbolically laid claim to the land, and his calling on the name of God there legitimized later Israelite cult at that site (*cf.,* Amos 5:5; 8:14). *Everlasting God* (in Hebrew, *El Olam*) was probably the title of a Canaanite

god. The Hebrews applied this title to their own God, just as
they did in the case of other divine titles like El Elyon (*cf.,*
14:18), El Roi (*cf.,* 16:13), El Shaddai (*cf.,* 17:1) and El
Bethel (35:7).

THE SACRIFICE OF ISAAC
22:1-19 (E)

22 After these things God tested Abraham, and said to
him, "Abraham!" And he said, "Here I am." ²He said,
"Take your son, your only son Isaac, whom you love, and
go to the land of Moriah, and offer him there as a burnt
offering upon one of the mountains of which I shall tell
you." ³So Abraham rose early in the morning, saddled his
ass, and took two of his young men with him, and his son
Isaac; and he cut the wood for the burnt offering, and
arose and went to the place of which God had told him.
⁴On the third day Abraham lifted up his eyes and saw the
place afar off. ⁵Then Abraham said to his young men,
"Stay here with the ass; I and the lad will go yonder and
worship, and come again to you." ⁶And Abraham took
the wood of the burnt offering, and laid it on Isaac his
son; and he took in his hand the fire and the knife. So they
went both of them together. ⁷And Isaac said to his father
Abraham, "My father!" And he said, "Here am I, my
son." He said, "Behold, the fire and the wood; but where
is the lamb for a burnt offering?" ⁸Abraham said, "God
will provide himself the lamb for a burnt offering, my
son." So they went both of them together.

⁹When they came to the place of which God had told
him, Abraham built an altar there, and laid the wood in
order, and bound Isaac his son, and laid him on the altar,
upon the wood. ¹⁰Then Abraham put forth his hand, and
took the knife to slay his son. ¹¹But the angel of the Lord
called to him from heaven, and said, "Abraham, Abraham!" And he said, "Here am I." ¹²He said, "Do not lay
your hand on the lad or do anything to him; for now I
know that you fear God, seeing you have not withheld

your son, your only son, from me." [13] And Abraham lifted up his eyes and looked, and behold, behind him was a ram, caught in a thicket by his horns; and Abraham went and took the ram, and offered it up as a burnt offering instead of his son. [14] So Abraham called the name of that place The Lord will provide; as it is said to this day, "On the mount of the Lord it shall be provided."

[15] And the angel of the Lord called to Abraham a second time from heaven, [16] and said, "By myself I have sworn, says the Lord, because you have done this, and have not withheld your son, your only son, [17] I will indeed bless you, and I will multiply your descendants as the stars of heaven and as the sand which is on the seashore. And your descendants shall possess the gate of their enemies, [18] and by your descendants shall all the nations of the earth bless themselves, because you have obeyed my voice." [19] So Abraham returned to his young men, and they arose and went together to Beer-sheba; and Abraham dwelt at Beer-sheba.

This moving story, which is usually attributed to the Elohist, is full of drama and tension, dignity and reserve. Rich in detail and full of pathos it recounts the harrowing experience of Abraham and his son. The monstrous character of the murder that Abraham feels compelled to commit under divine command (v. 2) cannot escape anyone. But the fact that Isaac is the one on whom the fulfillment of the promise of many descendants of Abraham now depends (*cf.,* 21:12) renders God's order totally incomprehensible. We are shocked by the almost casual way in which Abraham goes about carrying out the extraordinary divine directive. Yet he was obliged to equivocate in order to hide the terrible reality from his companions (v. 5) and even from Isaac (vv. 7-8). Abraham's final preparations for the frightful deed are described in some detail (vv. 9-10), but his feelings, and those of Isaac, are passed over in silence. These are heard between the words! Suddenly the tension is broken by the voice of "the angel of the Lord" (vv. 11-12), who must be identified with Yahweh himself (*cf.,* comment on 16:7; above p. 106). Abraham is dispensed from carrying out the gruesome deed, and his readiness to sacrifice the boy on whom all his hopes rested is applauded in biblical tradition as a proof of his obedience.

The story of the ram (v. 13) is really an addendum to the main story, and it may be noted that the ram was offered not by reason of a divine command, but on Abraham's own initiative. The remark that *Abraham called the name of that place The Lord will provide* (v. 14) obviously refers to the fact that God provided a victim that replaced Isaac (vv. 8, 13), but really does not give us a place-name at all. Actually the location of the land of Moriah where the episode is said to have taken place (vv. 2, 9) is unknown. The author of 2 Chron 3:1 identified Moriah with the site of the temple of Jerusalem in order to link the place of Isaac's near sacrifice with the place where the Israelites offered their sacrifices. His statement is therefore of theological import, but it has no historical value. The blessing already given in 12:2-3 and 15:5-6 is renewed in vv. 15-18, but is now seen as a reward for Abraham's obedience.

The story of the sacrifice of Isaac as it has come down to us is obviously intended to illustrate Abraham's unwavering faith and unflinching obedience in the face of an incomprehensible command (*cf.,* Heb 11: 17-19). But the story existed long before it received its present place and its present interpretation in the Bible. It is possible that it may have developed originally as a repudiation of human sacrifice in Israel, where such sacrifice was not absolutely unknown (*cf.,* Judg 11:30-40; 1 Kgs 16:34).

In rabbinic tradition Isaac was no longer seen as a passive victim, but as one who freely consented to his father's plan to sacrifice him. His self-offering was regarded as a true sacrifice, and the merits of that sacrifice were thought to be available to all his descendants. One notices the similarity between this rabbinic image of Abraham, the loving father, offering a willing son, with the New Testament presentation of God the Father offering his willing beloved Son as a victim for the redemption of humankind (*cf.,* Rom 8:32; Gal 2:20; Eph 5:2, 25; John 3:16).

THE GRAVE AT MACHPELAH
23:1-20 (P)

23 Sarah lived a hundred and twenty-seven years; these were the years of the life of Sarah. ²And Sarah died at Kiriatharba (that is, Hebron) in the land of Canaan; and Abraham went in to mourn for Sarah and to weep for her. ³And Abraham rose up from before his dead, and said to the Hittites, ⁴"I am a stranger and a sojourner among you; give me property among you for a burying place, that I may bury my dead out of my sight." ⁵The Hittites answered Abraham, ⁶"Hear us, my lord; you are a mighty prince among us. Bury your dead in the choicest of our sepulchres; none of us will withhold from you his sepulchre, or hinder you from burying your dead." ⁷Abraham rose and bowed to the Hittites, the people of the land. ⁸And he said to them, "If you are willing that I should bury my dead out of my sight, hear me, and entreat for me Ephron the son of Zohar, ⁹that he may give me the cave of Machpelah, which he owns; it is at the end of his field. For the full price let him give it to me in your presence as a possession for a burying place." ¹⁰Now Ephron was sitting among the Hittites; and Ephron the Hittite answered Abraham in the hearing of the Hittites, of all who went in at the gate of his city, ¹¹"No, my lord, hear me; I give you the field, and I give you the cave that is in it; in the presence of the sons of my people I give it to you; bury your dead." ¹²Then Abraham bowed down before the people of the land. ¹³And he said to Ephron in the hearing of the people of the land, "But if you will, hear me; I will give the price of the field; accept it from me, that I may bury my dead there." ¹⁴Ephron answered Abraham, ¹⁵"My lord, listen to me; a piece of land worth four hundred shekels of silver, what is that between you and me? Bury your dead." ¹⁶Abraham agreed with Ephron;

and Abraham weighed out for Ephron the silver which he had named in the hearing of the Hittites, four hundred sheckels of silver, according to the weights current among the merchants.

[17]So the field of Ephron in Machpelah, which was to the east of Mamre, the field with the cave which was in it and all the trees that were in the field, throughout its whole area, was made over [18]to Abraham as a possession in the presence of the Hittites, before all who went in at the gate of his city. [19]After this, Abraham buried Sarah his wife in the cave of the field of Machpelah east of Mamre (that is, Hebron) in the land of Canaan. [20]The field and the cave that is in it were made over to Abraham as a possession for a burying place by the Hittites.

This narrative which is remarkable for its vitality and freshness is usually attributed to the Priestly author, whom we usually associate with sober and staid accounts. The difference in style may possibly be accounted for by the fact that the author is transmitting an ancient narrative that had already acquired its own character and style before he used it.

The Hittites whom Abraham approached with a view to acquiring a family grave (vv. 3-4) are not to be identified with the people of that name who established a mighty kingdom in Anatolia (modern central Turkey) in the 16th-15th centuries B.C., and again in the 14th-12th centuries B.C. The term "Hittites" in the present context seems to refer to one group of the pre-Israelite inhabitants of Canaan. These natives, "the people of the land" (vv. 7, 12, 13), were unwilling to sell a plot to Abraham, who, as a sojourner (v. 4), was not legally entitled to hold property in the area. Abraham adroitly sidestepped their suggestion that he lay Sarah to rest in their burial ground (v. 6), and bowing down to the community leaders who were gathered at the gate of the city to consider his important request (*cf.,* vv. 10, 18), he urged them to induce a certain Ephron to sell him a particular piece of his property (vv. 8-9). Ephron's willingness to sell not only a burial place, but also the field in which it was located may be accounted for by the fact that ownership of the field carried with it certain feudal obligations which he would be glad to transfer to Abraham. Ephron even volunteered to "give" the field to the patriarch, but Abraham, with due urbanity, declined the offer. These gestures of generosity were merely part of the conventionalized ritual of an oriental transaction, and when it actually came to business, Ephron struck a hard bargain. We cannot estimate the value of four hundred shekels (v. 15), since the weight of the shekel differed according to time and place. But since David bought a threshing floor and oxen for fifty shekels (*cf.*, 2 Sam 24:24), we must regard Ephron's price as exorbitant. Verses 17-18 spell out the details of the sale. The elders acted as witnesses who gave legal authentication to the deal, so that Abraham's ownership of the field was beyond dispute. Thus the patriarch took possession of a little portion of the land that had been promised to him and his descendants. The site that would serve as a burial place for Sarah (v. 19), Abraham (25:9), Isaac (35:29), Rebekah and Leah (49:31), and Jacob (50:13), was the first instalment of an inheritance for which the only pledge was the divine word.

MATCHMAKING
24:1-67 (J)

This matchmaking scene, at once so romantic and so dramatic, is regarded as one of the Yahwist's most superb contributions to the Pentateuch. It is composed of four finely drawn scenes which tell a story of rare charm.

1) The Commission
24:1-9

> **24** Now Abraham was old, well advanced in years; and the Lord had blessed Abraham in all things. ²And Abraham said to his servant, the oldest of his house, who had

charge of all that he had, "Put your hand under my thigh, [3]and I will make you swear by the Lord, the God of heaven and of the earth, that you will not take a wife for my son from the daughters of the Canaanites, among whom I dwell, [4]but will go to my country and to my kindred, and take a wife for my son Isaac." [5]The servant said to him, "Perhaps the woman may not be willing to follow me to this land; must I then take your son back to the land from which you came?" [6]Abraham said to him, "See to it that you do not take my son back there. [7]The Lord, the God of heaven, who took me from my father's house and from the land of my birth, and who spoke to me and swore to me, 'To your descendants I will give this land,' he will send his angel before you, and you shall take a wife for my son from there. [8]But if the woman is not willing to follow you, then you will be free from this oath of mine; only you must not take my son back there." [9]So the servant put his hand under the thigh of Abraham his master, and swore to him concerning this matter.

Following the custom which demanded that a father arrange a marriage for his son, Abraham entrusted the delicate task of finding a suitable wife for Isaac to his most trusted servant. The supreme importance of the mission is indicated by the solemn oath which the patriarch required of the servant. The command *Put your hand under my thigh* (v. 2b) is a euphemism that substitutes the thigh for the genital organs, which were regarded as the source of life, and therefore sacred. The strict prohibition against Isaac's marrying a Canaanite woman (v. 3) was intended to prevent assimilation with the religiously depraved inhabitants of Canaan (*cf.,* Exod 34:15-16; Deut 7:3). Under no circumstances is Isaac to return to his father's homeland (vv. 5-9), since Canaan is the land that is linked with the promise of descendants (*cf.,* 15:7, 18). Abraham's assurance that the Lord would send his angel before the servant (v. 7; see comment on 16:7; above p. 106) expresses the patriarch's unfailing trust in God who could be relied on to provide Isaac with a suitable wife.

2) Encounter At The Well
24:10-27

[10]Then the servant took ten of his master's camels and departed, taking all sorts of choice gifts from his master; and he arose, and went to Mesopotamia, to the city of Nahor. [11]And he made the camels kneel down outside the city by the well of water at the time of evening, the time when women go out to draw water. [12]And he said, "O Lord, God of my master Abraham, grant me success today, I pray thee, and show steadfast love to my master Abraham. [13]Behold, I am standing by the spring of water, and the daughters of the men of the city are coming out to draw water. [14]Let the maiden to whom I shall say, 'Pray let down your jar that I may drink,' and who shall say, 'Drink, and I will water your camels' — let her be the one whom thou hast appointed for thy servant Isaac. By this I shall know that thou hast shown steadfast love to my master."

[15]Before he had done speaking, behold, Rebekah, who was born to Bethuel the son of Milcah, the wife of Nahor, Abraham's brother, came out with her water jar upon her shoulder. [16]The maiden was very fair to look upon, a virgin, whom no man had known. She went down to the spring, and filled her jar, and came up. [17]Then the servant ran to meet her, and said, "Pray give me a little water to drink from your jar." [18]She said, "Drink, my lord"; and she quickly let down her jar upon her hand, and gave him a drink. [19]When she had finished giving him a drink, she said, "I will draw for your camels also, until they have done drinking." [20]So she quickly emptied her jar into the trough and ran again to the well to draw, and she drew for all his camels. [21]The man gazed at her in silence to learn whether the Lord had prospered his journey or not.

[22]When the camels had done drinking, the man took a gold ring weighing a half shekel, and two bracelets for her arms weighing ten gold shekels, [23]and said, "Tell me whose daughter you are. Is there room in your father's house for us to lodge in?" [24]She said to him, "I am the

daughter of Bethuel the son of Milcah, whom she bore to Nahor." 25She added, "We have both straw and provender enough, and room to lodge in." 26The man bowed his head and worshipped the Lord, 27and said, "Blessed be the Lord, the God of my master Abraham, who has not forsaken his steadfast love and his faithfulness toward my master. As for me, the Lord has led me in the way to the house of my master's kinsmen."

Focussing all his attention on the interests of his master (*cf.,* vv. 12, 14, 27), the servant set out for the city of Nahor, which, in the light of 11:31, must be regarded as Haran in northern Mesopotamia. The camels mentioned in vv. 10-11 would seem to be an anachronism (see note on 12:16; above p. 97). but the idea of women coming to draw water at the well is true to life. In this idyllic setting the trusted envoy was to find a wife for Isaac, just as Jacob (29:1-12, J) and Moses (Exod 2:15-21, J) would find the wife of their dreams in similar surroundings. Not relying on his own judgment and shrewdness the servant placed the whole enterprise in God's hand, and asked for a sign by which he would recognize the woman whom the Lord intended to be wife for Isaac (vv. 12-14). Soon his attention was attracted by Rebekah, the daughter of his master's kinsman, and a virgin, who combined good looks with graciousness and a readiness to help (vv. 15-21). Having thoughtfully gazed at her in silence for a while (v. 21) he presented her with valuable gifts (v. 22) which was a proof of his master's wealth, and a sign that a marriage proposal was in the offing. When the beautiful maiden invited him to share her father's hospitality he knew he had met the woman he was looking for, and he offered a prayer of praise and thanks to his God.

3) In Laban's House
24:28-61

28Then the maiden ran and told her mother's household about these things. 29Rebekah had a brother whose name was Laban; and Laban ran out to the man, to the spring. ³⁰When he saw the ring, and the bracelets on his sister's arms, and when he heard the words of Rebekah his sister, "Thus the man spoke to me," he went to the man; and behold, he was standing by the camels at the spring. ³¹He said, "Come in, O blessed of the Lord; why do you stand outside? For I have prepared the house and a place for the camels." ³²So the man came into the house; and Laban ungirded the camels, and gave him straw and provender for the camels, and water to wash his feet and the feet of the men who were with him. ³³Then food was set before him to eat; but he said, "I will not eat until I have told my errand." He said, "Speak on."

³⁴So he said, "I am Abraham's servant. ³⁵The Lord has greatly blessed my master, and he has become great; he has given him flocks and herds, silver and gold, manservants and maidservants, camels and asses. ³⁶And Sarah my master's wife bore a son to my master when she was old; and to him he has given all that he has. ³⁷My master made me swear, saying, 'You shall not take a wife for my son from the daughters of the Canaanites, in whose land I dwell; ³⁸but you shall go to my father's house and to my kindred, and take a wife for my son.' ³⁹I said to my master, 'Perhaps the woman will not follow me.' ⁴⁰But he said to me, 'The Lord, before whom I walk, will send his angel with you and prosper your way; and you shall take a wife for my son from my kindred and from my father's house; ⁴¹then you will be free from my oath, when you come to my kindred; and if they will not give her to you, you will be free from my oath.'

⁴²"I came today to the spring, and said, 'O Lord, the God of my master Abraham, if now thou wilt prosper the way which I go, ⁴³behold, I am standing by the spring of water; let the young woman who comes out to draw, to whom I say, "Pray give me a little water from your jar to drink," ⁴⁴and who will say to me, "Drink, and I will draw for your camels also," let her be the woman whom the Lord has appointed for my master's son.'

⁴⁵"Before I had done speaking in my heart, behold, Rebekah came out with her water jar on her shoulder; and she went down to the spring, and drew. I said to her, 'Pray let me drink.' ⁴⁶She quickly let down her jar from her shoulder, and said, 'Drink, and I will give your camels drink also.' So I drank, and she gave the camels drink also. ⁴⁷Then I asked her, 'Whose daughter are you?' She said, 'The daughter of Bethuel, Nahor's son, whom Milcah bore to him.' So I put the ring on her nose, and the bracelets on her arms. ⁴⁸Then I bowed my head and worshipped the Lord, and blessed the Lord, the God of my master Abraham, who had led me by the right way to take the daughter of my master's kinsman for his son. ⁴⁹Now then, if you deal loyally and truly with my master, tell me; and if not, tell me; that I may turn to the right hand or to the left."

⁵⁰Then Laban and Bethuel answered, "The thing comes from the Lord; we cannot speak to you bad or good. ⁵¹Behold, Rebekah is before you, take her and go, and let her be the wife of your master's son, as the Lord has spoken."

⁵²When Abraham's servant heard their words, he bowed himself to the earth before the Lord. ⁵³And the servant brought forth jewelry of silver and gold, and rainment, and gave them to Rebekah; he also gave her her brother and to her mother costly ornaments. ⁵⁴And he and the men who were with him ate and drank, and they spent the night there. When they arose in the morning, he said, "Send me back to my master." ⁵⁵Her brother and her mother said, "Let the maiden remain with us a while, at least ten days; after that she may go." ⁵⁶But he said to them, "Do not delay me, since the Lord has prospered my way; let me go that I may go to my master." ⁵⁷They said, "We will call the maiden, and ask her." ⁵⁸And they called Rebekah, and said to her, "Will you go with this man?" She said, "I will go." ⁵⁹So they sent away Rebekah their sister and her nurse, and Abraham's servant and his men. ⁶⁰And they blessed Rebekah, and said to her, "Our sister,

be the mother of thousands of ten thousands; and may your descendants possess the gate of those who hate them!" ⁶¹Then Rebekah and her maids arose, and rode upon the camels and followed the man; thus the servant took Rebekah, and went his way.

The fact that Rebekah is said to have run to her mother's house (v. 28) gives the impression that her father was dead, and this is confirmed by the fact that the woman's brother plays a leading role in the negotiations that follow. Having heard Rebekah's story about the well-to-do traveller, and having seen the ring and the bracelets that signalled his wealth, Laban hurried to meet him (vv. 29-30). There is more than a hint of greed in his haste, so that this episode gives us a little insight into the character of this man who will play such a venal part in the Jacob story. The pagan Laban acknowledged that the prosperous stranger was "blessed of the Lord"(v. 31), and he invited him to his home. The servant, without taking time to eat or drink, eloquently outlined the nature of his mission in terms with which we are already familiar (vv. 34-48). However, he tactfully omitted Abraham's refusal to allow Isaac to return to Mesopotamia (*cf.,* vv. 6, 8), since this detail would be offensive to the patriarch's relatives. Seeing the hand of God in the events that brought the servant to their house, Rebekah's family felt they had no choice but to grant his request (vv. 50-51).

Although custom demanded that the servant should celebrate with the girl's kinsfolk for several days, he was eager to return home with the bride-to-be (vv. 54b, 56). Understandably, Rebekah's family objected to such haste, but, having received the young woman's consent to marriage, they allowed her to set out on her journey to her future husband (vv. 55, 57-59). This respect for the lady's feelings about the situation reflects the ancient law which protected a woman's right to refuse to leave her homeland to join a prospective husband. The blessing which the family bestowed on the departing lady (v. 60) echoes the theme of a great progeny that runs through the patriarchal narratives, but ends on a warlike note as it wishes Rebekah's descendants victory over all their enemies.

4) She Became His Wife
24:62-67

> [62]Now Isaac had come from Beerlahairoi, and was dwelling in the Negeb. [63]And Isaac went out to meditate in the field in the evening; and he lifted his eyes and looked, and behold, there were camels coming. [64]And Rebekah lifted up her eyes, and when she saw Isaac, she alighted from the camel, [65]and said to the servant, "Who is the man yonder, walking in the field to meet us?" The servant said, "It is my master." So she took her veil and covered herself. [66]And the servant told Isaac all the things that he had done. [67]Then Isaac brought her into the tent, and took Rebekah and she became his wife; and he loved her. So Isaac was comforted after his mother's death.

The scene suddenly switches from Mesopotamia, and we find Isaac alone in a field in the Negeb. We cannot know what he was doing there, since the Hebrew verb rendered "meditate" in the RSV baffles the translators. In conformity with the custom which forbade a man to see his wife's face before the wedding ceremony, Rebekah "took her veil and covered herself" (v. 65) when she saw Isaac. Isaac now becomes the main actor in our story and takes Rebekah as wife, thus providing a new mother for the blessed progeny of Abraham.

This charming matchmaking story that ends so happily was intended by its author to show how God's hidden hand guided the whole affair in an unsensational way (*cf.,* vv. 7, 12-14, 21, 27, 40, 42, 48, 50, 56). The narrative shows that God never abandons those who, like Abraham and the servant, entrust themselves to him. But it also shows that Abraham and the servant took prudent and courageous measures to reach their goals. From this one may conclude that putting one's trust in God can never be an excuse for neglect of personal responsibility.

ABRAHAM'S DEATH — ISAAC'S ELECTION
25:5-11 (JP)

⁵Abraham gave all he had to Isaac. ⁶But to the sons of his concubines Abraham gave gifts, and while he was still living he sent them away from his son Isaac, eastward to the east country.

⁷These are the days of the years of Abraham's life, a hundred and seventy-five years. ⁸Abraham breathed his last and died in a good old age, an old man and full of years, and was gathered to his people. ⁹Isaac and Ishmael his sons buried him in a the cave of Machpelah, in the field of Ephron the son of Zohar the Hittite, east of Mamre, ¹⁰the field which Abraham purchased from the Hittites. There Abraham was buried, with Sarah his wife. ¹¹After the death of Abraham God blessed Isaac his son. And Isaac dwelt at Beerlahairoi.

Sandwiched between the list of Abraham's sons by Keturah (vv. 1-4) and the roster of the sons of Ishmael (vv. 12-16) this passage records the passing of Abraham, and brings Isaac's privileged place among the patriarch's sons into clear focus. Verses 7-11 (P) describe the death and burial of Abraham which took place exactly one hundred years after he had left Haran (*cf.,* v. 7 and 12:4b, P). "Dying at a ripe old age, grown old after a full life" (v. 8, NAB), he was "gathered to his people" (v. 8b). This latter phrase which will occur later with reference to Isaac and to Jacob (*cf.,* 35:29; 49:29) cannot, of course, be applied in a literal sense to Abraham who had left his homeland and his family. The term suggests the bonds that unite the successive generations that give permanence to a family. Abraham was, however, buried in what was to become the family vault (*cf.,* vv. 9-10, and see above pp. 134-135). In view of the fact that Ishmael had been expelled from his father's household and had gone his own way (*cf.,* 16:1-14; 21:8-21) we are surprised to find him at Abraham's graveside joining his brother in acquitting their last filial duty towards their father. But there the Priestly author leaves him as he gives us our last glimpse of this son of the patriarch who is to have no further part in the patriarchal story.

By giving gifts to his concubine's sons while he was still alive (v. 6) Abraham was not only fulfilling his parental duty towards them, but was also, in effect, getting rid of them. By sending them off "to the east country," that is, to the desert lands east of Canaan, he was separating them physically from Isaac in whose destiny they would have no share. Those who are listed as Ishmael's sons (vv. 12-16) are mostly shadowy figures about whom we have little information. They too seem to have been dwellers of the Syro-Arabian desert, and like the sons of Keturah they do not belong to that line from which Israel descended. Isaac alone was Abraham's legal heir (v. 5), he alone was blessed by God (v. 11), and from this point on (*cf.,* v. 19) he and his descendants become subjects of the Genesis narrative.

VIII. THE STORY OF JACOB
25:19—36:43

STRUGGLE IN THE WOMB
25:19-26 (JP)

[19]These are the descendants of Isaac, Abraham's son: Abraham was the father of Isaac, [20]and Isaac was forty years old when he took to wife Rebekah, the daughter of Bethuel the Aramean of Paddan-aram, the sister of Laban the Aramean. [21]And Isaac prayed to the Lord for his wife, because she was barren; and the Lord granted his prayer, and Rebekah his wife conceived. [22]The children struggled together within her; and she said, "If it is thus, why do I live?" So she went to inquire of the Lord. [23]And the Lord said to her.

"Two nations are in your womb,
   and two peoples, born of you, shall be divided;
the one shall be stronger than the other,
   the elder shall serve the younger."

[24]When her days to be delivered were fulfilled, behold, there were twins in her womb. [25]The first came forth red, all his body like a hairy mantle; so they called his name Esau. [26]Afterward his brother came forth, and his hand had taken hold of Esau's heel; so his name was called Jacob. Isaac was sixty years old when she bore them.

The Priestly author's flair for statistics and his interest in chronology are both apparent in his contribution to this passage (vv. 19-20, 26b). Paddan-aram (v. 20; *cf.,* 28:2-7; 31:18, etc.) is the Priestly designation for the area that is known to the Yahwist as Aram-Naharain (*cf.,* 24:10). This latter place-name which literally means "Aram of two Rivers," remains untranslated in NAB and NEB, but is rendered as Mesopotamia ("Between the Rivers") in RSV. The rest of the passage can be attributed to the Yahwist with reasonable confidence. Like Sarah before her and Rachel after her, (*cf.,* 11:30 and 29:31) Rebekah was barren, and it was only in answer to her husband's prayer that she was blessed with twins. (This recurring theme of barrenness of the ancestresses makes the point that the chosen people exists only as a result of divine intervention.) The struggling of the children in Rebekah's womb caused her such distress that "she went to inquire of the Lord" (v. 22), that is, to consult Yahweh at some unspecified shrine where a priest or prophet would communicate a divine message to her about the meaning of the strange struggle within her (*cf.,* Judg 18:5-6; 1 Sam 9:9; 1 Kgs 22:6). The divine response (v. 23) explained that the struggle between the unborn twins foreshadowed future relations between their descendants. The Israelites, the children of Jacob, and the Edomites, the offspring of Esau, were destined to live in a constant state of enmity. This enmity is reflected in such passages as Num 20:14-21; Ps 137:7, and we know that the children of the older Esau served those of the younger Jacob, when, for a time at least, the Israelites subjugated the Edomites (*cf.,* 2 Sam 8:13-14).

The actual account of the birth of the twins suggests some rather far-fetched etymologies of their names. The fact that Esau "came forth *red*" (*admoni*) points to *Edom*, the place where Esau chose to dwell (*cf.,* 32:3-4; 36:8; Judg 5:4). (In v. 30 the red (*adom*) pottage which Esau enjoyed is explicitly linked with the name *Edom*.) Esau's "mantle of hair" (*se'ar*) suggests *Seir*, the ancient name by which the territory of the Edomites was known (see the texts just referred to). Jacob's name (in Hebrew, *ya'aqob*) is explained from the fact that at his birth "he had taken hold of Esau's *heel* (*'aqeb*)." Esau was later to use this same etymology in order to point to the grasping nature and treachery of his brother (*cf.,* 27:36).

SALE OF A BIRTHRIGHT
25:27-34 (J)

²⁷When the boys grew up, Esau was a skilful hunter, a man of the field, while Jacob was a quiet man, dwelling in tents. ²⁸Isaac loved Esau, because he ate of his game; but Rebekah loved Jacob.

²⁹Once when Jacob was boiling pottage, Esau came in from the field, and he was famished. ³⁰And Esau said to Jacob, "Let me eat some of that red pottage, for I am famished!" (Therefore his name was called Edom.) ³¹Jacob said, "First sell me your birthright." ³²Esau said, "I am about to die; of what use is a birthright to me?" ³³Jacob said, "Swear to me first." So he swore to him, and sold his birthright to Jacob. ³⁴Then Jacob gave Esau bread and pottage of lentils, and he ate and drank, and rose and went his way. Thus Esau despised his birthright.

The grown-up twins personified two typical Palestinian life-styles: the more precarious way of life of the hunter, and the more secure profession of the shepherd. The relations between these two groups were sometimes tense, and it may be that our present story was intended to reflect the animosity that existed between them. The apparently insignificant remark that the father loved Esau more than his brother (v. 28), while the mother's preference was for Jacob, prepares for the dramatic scenes of chap. 27, where the intrigue of the doting mother on behalf of her favourite son figures largely.

Since the firstborn was destined to become the leader of his family or clan, he enjoyed a privileged status within the social group. His position also carried with it certain economic advantages, such as a double share in the father's property (*cf.,* Deut 21:15-17). No one with any sense of values would forfeit such rights. And yet this is what Esau did. The comment that "he despised his birthright" (v. 34b) is an unambiguous censure of his conduct, a censure that is taken up in the New Testament (*cf.,* Heb 12:16). The statement that Esau, having eaten the red pottage that was the miserable price of his precious birthright, "ate and drank, and rose and went his way" (v. 34) suggests that there was something crude about the whole business.

But if the author gives a negative view of Esau he does not exactly idealize Jacob either. This ruthless schemer who took advantage of his starving brother hardly wins our sympathy. His craftiness in exacting an oath from his brother (v. 33) in order to ensure that the sale of the birthright could not be rescinded, shows his determination to turn his brother's distress to his own advantage. It may be, of course, that the Israelite hearers and readers of this story applauded their ancestor who had so effectively outwitted the father of the hated Edomites. Furthermore, we know that what Jacob did was perfectly legal, since the laws of the ancient Middle East allowed one to sell his birthright to a younger brother. Jacob's treatment of his brother, then, would not have appeared as outrageously shabby to them as it does to us.

TRADITIONS ABOUT ISAAC
26:1-35

Chapter 26 collects a series of traditions which have Isaac as their subject. This is the only chapter devoted exclusively to Isaac, perhaps an indication of the shadowy figure of Isaac, lost between the gigantic characters of Abraham and Jacob. Apart from the final verses (34-35) which we owe to the Priestly author, the whole passage stems from the pen of the Yahwist. Most of the material in the chapter is, as we shall notice, closely parallel to narratives we have already read in the Abraham cycle.

Promise And Obedience
26:1-5

26 Now there was a famine in the land, besides the former famine that was in the days of Abraham. And Isaac went to Gerar, to Abimelech king of the Philistines. ²And the Lord appeared to him, and said, "Do not go down to Egypt; dwell in the land of which I shall tell you. ³Sojourn in this land, and I will be with you, and will bless you; for to you and to your descendants I will give all these lands, and I will fulfil the oath which I swore to Abraham your father. ⁴I will multiply your descendants as the stars of heaven, and will give to your descendants all these lands; and by your descendants all the nations of the earth shall bless themselves: ⁵because Abraham obeyed my voice and kept my charge, my commandments, my statutes, and my laws."

The divine command which prevents Isaac from going down to Egypt (v. 2) is a reminder that God's promise is attached to the land and that the bearer of the promise must rely on God to supply all his needs in that land. Later, however, Jacob will go to Egypt with divine approval (*cf.,* 46:2-3), yet even that act leads to Egyptian bondage. The enunciation of the blessings made to Isaac (vv. 3-4) is merely a modified version of those made earlier to Abraham (*cf.,* 12:2-3, 7; 15:5, 7, 18, etc.). New here, and indeed rather surprising, is the connection made between the transmission of the blessings to Isaac and the obedience of Abraham (v. 5). With this one may compare v. 24, where, however, the phrase "for my servant Abraham's sake" may be taken to mean "for the sake of the promise give to Abraham." Later rabbinical tradition was to emphasize Abraham's early goodness in meriting the covenant: "Abraham. . . kept the law of the Most High, and was taken into covenant with him" (Sir 44:20).

Rebekah, Wife Or Sister
26:2-11

⁶So Isaac dwelt in Gerar. ⁷When the men of the place asked him about his wife, he said, "She is my sister"; for he feared to say, "My wife," thinking, "lest the men of the place should kill me for the sake of Rebekah"; because she was fair to look upon. ⁸When he had been there a long time, Abimelech king of the Philistines looked out of a window and saw Isaac fondling Rebekah his wife. ⁹So Abimelech called Isaac, and said, "Behold, she is your wife; how then could you say, 'She is my sister'?" Isaac said to him, "Because I thought, 'Lest I die because of her.'" ¹⁰Abimelech said, "What is this you have done to us? One of the people might easily have lain with your wife, and you would have brought guilt upon us." ¹¹So Abimelech warned all the people, saying, "Whoever touches this man or his wife shall be put to death."

There is little new to us in this third occurrence of the wife-sister motif (*cf.,* 12:10-20; 20:1-18, and see comments above). The statement that no one had lain with Rebekah (v. 10) makes it clear that the ancestress left Gerar with her honour above suspicion (*cf.,* 20:4). The statement that Isaac was "fondling" Rebekah (v. 8) seems to be a euphemism for making love. The Hebrew word for fondling (*sahaq*) sounds somewhat like the name Isaac, and no doubt the author wished his readers to find here yet another pun on that name (*cf.,* 17:17; 18:12-15; 21:6).

Wanderings
26:12-22

¹²And Isaac sowed in that land, and reaped in the same year a hundredfold. The Lord blessed him, ¹³and the man became rich, and gained more and more until he became very wealthy. ¹⁴He had possessions of flocks and herds, and a great household, so that the Philistines envied him. ¹⁵(Now the Philistines had stopped and filled with earth all the wells which his father's servants had dug in the

days of Abraham his father.) ¹⁶And Abimelech said to Isaac, "Go away from us; for you are much mightier than we."

¹⁷So Isaac departed from there, and encamped in the valley of Gerar and dwelt there. ¹⁸And Isaac dug again the wells of water which had been dug in the days of Abraham his father; for the Philistines had stopped them after the death of Abraham; and he gave them the names which his father had given them. ¹⁹But when Isaac's servants dug in the valley and found there a well of springing water, ²⁰the herdsmen of Gerar quarreled with Isaac's herdsmen, saying, "The water is ours." So he called the name of the well Esek, because they contended with him. ²¹Then they dug another well, and they quarreled over that also; so he called its name Sitnah. ²²And he moved from there and dug another well, and over that they did not quarrel; so he called its name Rehoboth, saying "For now the Lord has made room for us, and we shall be fruitful in the land."

Verses 12-14 show that although the patriarchs moved about with their flocks in search of pastures, they could occasionally settle down in one place and practise farming for a time (*cf.,* 27:27-28; 37:7). The signs of the divine blessing as outlined in vv. 13-14 may sound very material to us. But the ancient Hebrews never limited God's gifts to the spiritual, and they sought signs of his favour in the realities of everyday life (*cf.,* Pss 112; 128).

Covenant At Beer-sheba
26:23-33

²³From there he went up to Beer-sheba. ²⁴And the Lord appeared to him the same night and said, "I am the God of Abraham your father; fear not, for I am with you and will bless you and multiply your descendants for my servant Abraham's sake." ²⁵So he built an altar there and called upon the name of the Lord, and pitched his tent there. And there Isaac's servants dug a well.

²⁶Then Abimelech went to him from Gerar with Ahuz-zath his adviser and Phicol the commander of his army. ²⁷Isaac said to them, "Why have you come to me, seeing that you hate me and have sent me away from you?" ²⁸They said, "We see plainly that the Lord is with you; so we say, let there be an oath between you and us, and let us make a covenant with you, ²⁹that you will do us no harm, just as we have not touched you and have done to you nothing but good and have sent you away in peace. You are now blessed of the Lord." ³⁰So he made them a feast, and they ate and drank. ³¹In the morning they rose early and took oath with one another; and Isaac set them on their way, and they departed from him in peace. ³²That same day Isaac's servants came and told him about the well which they had dug, and said to him, "We have found water." ³³He called it Shibah; therefore the name of the city is Beer-sheba to this day.

Leaving vv. 15-22 which tell of Isaac's disputes about watering-places with his neighbors in Gerar, we now rejoin the patriarch in Beer-sheba. (For a note on Beer-sheba see comment on 21:22-34, above pp. 129-130.) Here in a night vision the Lord assured Isaac of his blessing and of his continued presence (v. 24). The title "the God of Abraham your father" identifies Isaac's God as the God who has a special relationship with his family. He is a God whose activity is not limited to shrine or temple, but who accompanies his people wherever they go. By telling us that Isaac built an altar at Beer-sheba the author gives the impression that Isaac was the first to dedicate the place to Yahweh. But we know that Abraham had already claimed the place for his people and their God (*cf.*, 21:33).

The covenant ritual described in vv. 26-31 is another version of the pact that has been recorded in 21:22-34. Here Isaac takes the place of Abraham as partner with Abimelech to the pact. The meal which the covenant partners shared (v. 30) was a sign of reconciliation (*cf.*, v. 27) and friendship, and a solemn ratification of the covenant relationship (*cf.*, 31:54).

IX. JACOB IN EXILE
27:1-32:21

TREACHERY AND DECEIT
27:1-17 (J)

27 When Isaac was old and his eyes were dim so that he could not see, he called Esau his older son, and said to him, "My son"; and he answered, "Here I am." ²He said, "Behold, I am old; I do not know the day of my death. ³Now then, take your weapons, your quiver and your bow, and go out to the field, and hunt game for me, ⁴and prepare for me savory food, such as I love, and bring it to me that I may eat; that I may bless you before I die."

⁵Now Rebekah was listening when Isaac spoke to his son Esau. So when Esau went to the field to hunt for game and bring it, ⁶Rebekah said to her son Jacob, "I heard your father speak to your brother Esau, ⁷'Bring me game, and prepare for me savory food, that I may eat it, and bless you before the Lord before I die.' ⁸Now therefore, my son, obey my word as I command you. ⁹Go to the flock, and fetch me two good kids, that I may prepare from them savory food for your father, such as he loves; ¹⁰and you shall bring it to your father to eat, so that he may bless you before he dies." ¹¹"But Jacob said to Rebekah his mother, "Behold, my brother Esau is a hairy

man, and I am a smooth man. [12]Perhaps my father will feel me, and I shall seem to be mocking him, and bring a curse upon myself and not a blessing." [13]His mother said to him, "Upon me be your curse, my son; only obey my word, and go, fetch them to me." [14]So he went and took them and brought them to his mother; and his mother prepared savory food, such as his father loved. [15]Then Rebekah took the best garments of Esau her older son, which were with her in the house, and put them on Jacob her younger son; [16]and the skins of the kids she put upon his hands and upon the smooth part of his neck; [17]and she gave the savory food and the bread, which she had prepared, into the hand of her son Jacob.

In this chapter of treachery and deceit the Yahwist once again displays his storyteller's talent as he paints a series of dramatic scenes which describe the ruthless exploitation of a helpless old man by his scheming wife and ambitious son. The story is told with such consummate skill that there is little for the commentator to do except to supply some background information that helps one to understand the author's presuppositions and theological stance.

The opening scene which portrays Isaac as an old man who enjoys the results of his favorite son's hunting corresponds to the picture painted in 25:27-28. Realizing that his life was ebbing to its close the old man wished to impart the blessing that was customary at that stage of one's life (*cf.,* 48:9-22; 50:24-25; Deut 33; Josh 23, etc.). Such final blessings were very significant, and were believed to have a decisive effect on the recipient's life. Isaac's words to Esau did not escape the alert Rebekah, who, like Sarah (*cf.,* 18:10), had no scruples about doing a little eavesdropping. The wily woman soon contrived a stratagem that would deceive the doddering Isaac, deprive Esau of his expected blessing, and win a rich heritage for the son whom she loved (vv. 5-17). To us Rebekah's scheme seems naive in the extreme, if not totally ridiculous. How could Issac, who loved the wild meat of the chase, be deceived, even in old age, by goat meat? How could he, even if his eyes were dim, mistake goat's hair for the hair on a man's hands and neck? But we must not expect every element in our story to be perfectly logical. The author is telling of a scheme that had the desired effect, and we must not cross-examine him, and so destroy the beauty and effectiveness of the story.

We notice that Jacob is a mere pawn in the hands of his doting mother, and at the same time we must admire the grim determination which Rebekah shows in the pursuit of her goal. When the hesitant son raises a question about the possible disastrous effects of the plot (vv. 11-12), the resolute mother unhesitatingly takes the consequences of the whole scheme on her own shoulders, and urges the vacillating young man to play his part in the game (v. 13).

JACOB, BLESSED AS FIRST-BORN
27:18-29

18So he went in to his father, and said, "My father"; and he said, "Here I am; who are you, my son?" 19Jacob said to his father, "I am Esau your first-born. I have done as you told me; now sit up and eat of my game, that you may bless me." 20But Isaac said to his son, "How is it that you have found it so quickly, my son?" He answered, "Because the Lord your God granted me success." 21Then Isaac said to Jacob, "Come near, that I may feel you, my son, to know whether you are really my son Esau or not." 22So Jacob went near to Isaac his father, who felt him and said, "The voice is Jacob's voice, but the hands are the hands of Esau." 23And he did not recognize him, because his hands were hairy like his brother Esau's hands; so he blessed him. 24He said, "Are you really my son Esau?" He answered, "I am." 25Then he said, "Bring it to me, that I may eat of my son's game and bless you." So he brought it to him, and he ate; and he brought him wine, and he drank. 26Then his father Isaac said to him, "Come near and kiss me, my son." 27So he came near and kissed him; and he smelled the smell of his garments, and blessed him, and said, "See, the smell of my son is as the smell of a field which the Lord has blessed! [28]May God give you of the dew of heaven, and of the fatness of the earth, and plenty of grain and wine. [29]Let peoples serve you, and nations bow down to you. Be lord over your brothers, and may your mother's sons bow down to you. Cursed be every one who curses you, and blessed be every one who blesses you!"

The author brilliantly succeeds in conveying the tension of the scene in which Jacob approached his aged father on whom he intended to perpetrate a cruel act of deceit (vv. 18-19). In explaining his speedy arrival with the "game," Jacob resorted to hypocritical piety and to blasphemous lying (v. 20). When the aged father was eventually convinced that Esau was in his presence he proceeded to give the all important benediction to the disguised Jacob. The actual blessing (vv. 27b-29) is obviously not addressed to Jacob as an individual, but to the people whom he represents. The first part of the benediction envisages agricultural prosperity (*cf.,* Gen 49:25-26; Deut 33:13-14) for the Israelites, who are seen as a settled agrarian people for whom grain and wine are signs of wealth and ease (*cf.,* Deut 7:13; Hos 2:8,22). The heavy dew (v. 28a) was the only source of moisture in Palestine during the dry season, and was therefore of vital importance for growth. Abundant dew was regarded as a gift from heaven (*cf.,* Mic 5:7), and its absence was regarded as a curse (*cf.,* 2 Sam 1:21). The second part of the blessing (v. 29) foresees the political triumph of Israel, and her domination of the neighboring peoples. It is, in fact, not so much a prayer for the future success of Jacob's descendants, as an echo of the success of the Davidic empire which the author experienced.

ESAU BETRAYED
27:30-45

[30]As soon as Isaac had finished blessing Jacob, when Jacob had scarcely gone out from the presence of Isaac

his father, Esau his brother came in from his hunting. ³¹He also prepared savory food, and brought it to his father. And he said to his father, "Let my father arise, and eat of his son's game, that you may bless me." ³²His father Isaac said to him, "Who are you?" He answered, "I am your son, your first-born, Esau." ³³"Then Isaac trembled violently, and said, "Who was it then that hunted game and brought it to me, and I ate it all before you came, and I have blessed him?—yes, and he shall be blessed." ³⁴When Esau heard the words of his father, he cried out with an exceedingly great and bitter cry, and said to his father, "Bless me, even me also, O my father!" ³⁵But he said, "Your brother came with guile, and he has taken away your blessing." ³⁶Esau said, "Is he not rightly named Jacob? For he has supplanted me these two times. He took away my birthright; and behold, now he has taken away my blessing." Then he said, "Have you not reserved a blessing for me?" ³⁷Isaac answered Esau, "Behold, I have made him your lord, and all his brothers I have given to him for servants, and with grain and wine I have sustained him. What then can I do for you, my son?" ³⁸Esau said to his father, "Have you but one blessing, my father? Bless me, even me also, O my father." And Esau lifted up his voice and wept.

³⁹Then Isaac his father answered him:
"Behold, away from the fatness of the
    earth shall your dwelling be,
    and away from the dew of heaven on high.
⁴⁰By your sword you shall live,
    and you shall serve your brother;
but when you break loose
    you shall break his yoke from your neck."

⁴¹Now Esau hated Jacob because of the blessing with which his father had blessed him, and Esau said to himself, "The days of mourning for my father are approaching; then I will kill my brother Jacob." ⁴²But the words of Esau her older son were told to Rebekah; so she sent and called Jacob her younger son, and said to him, "Behold,

> your brother Esau comforts himself by planning to kill you. 43Now therefore, my son, obey my voice; arise, flee to Laban my brother in Haran, 44and stay with him a while, until your brother's fury turns away, 45until your brother's anger turns away, and he forgets what you have done to him; then I will send, and fetch you from there. Why should I be bereft of you both in one day?"

In this scene, the most tense and emotional of the whole drama, the author brings out the bewilderment of the old man who was asked to grant a blessing he thought he had already given. Isaac's "who are you" (v. 32) and his violent trembling (v. 33) express confusion and shock. As for the unsuspecting Esau, his wild cry and his urgent plea for a blessing (v. 34) proclaim the sense of tragedy and desperation that overwhelmed him on his discovery of the vile deception of which he was victim. His bitter play on Jacob's name, which he derives from *'aqab*, to supplant, allows him to recall how Jacob had already deprived him of his birthright (v. 36; *cf.,* 25:26, 29-34). The distraught father was helpless to right the wrong his favorite son had suffered (v. 37), since a blessing, once given, was irrevocable. The "blessing" which the shattered patriarch gave in response to Esau's pleading (vv. 38-40) is in reality a curse, or at least a condemnation to a life of poverty and subjection. As in the case of Jacob, the "blessing," which is not given in the form of an invocation, envisages, not Esau in person, but his descendants, the Edomites. The first part of Isaac's prediction (v. 39) is the direct opposite of the blessing given to Jacob (*cf.,* v. 28), and it condemns the Edomites to a frugal existence in the arid and infertile regions south of the Dead Sea. The second part of the "blessing" (v. 40) refers to the warlike character of the sons of Esau and to their subjection to Israel (*cf.,* 25:23, and see comment above p. 146). The prediction that Esau would break the yoke of Jacob (v. 40b) may be a late addition to the text which takes into consideration the fact that Edom regained independence from Judah in the ninth century. Or it may be a reference to Edom's attempts to regain her freedom during the reign of Solomon (*cf.,* 1Kgs 11:14-22). The drama ends with an angry Esau declaring murderous designs that precipitated his brother's flight into exile. Rebekah's fear that she should lose both her sons in one day (v. 45) was not without foundation, for if Esau were to murder Jacob he would have to flee to escape the blood vengeance that would surely be exacted for his deed.

As we read this tale of deception we cannot but feel sorry for the hapless Isaac who was so cruelly tricked. Our sympathies also lie with Esau, the innocent victim of a scandalous plot. We cannot approve of Rebekah's part in the drama, but we must admire her resourcefulness and determination. Jacob is the weakest character in the plot, where he appears as the puppet of a domineering mother. Later Hebrew writers referred to his treatment of Esau with obvious disapproval (*cf.,* Hos 12:3; Jer 9:3[4]). Yet it was this reprehensible Jacob who became the bearer of the divine promises. The Lord, who can incorporate ambiguous human conduct into his design for the world, chose to fulfil the blessing that was given to the unworthy twin.

IN SEARCH OF A WIFE
27:46—28:9 (P)

⁴⁶Then Rebekah said to Isaac, "I am weary of my life because of the Hittite women. If Jacob marries one of the Hittite women such as these, one of the women of the land, what good will my life be to me?" **28** Then Isaac called Jacob and blessed him, and charged him, "You shall not marry one of the Canaanite women. ²Arise, go to Paddan-aram to the house of Bethuel your mother's father; and take as wife from there one of the daughters of Laban your mother's brother. ³God Almighty bless you and make you fruitful and multiply you, that you may become a company of peoples. ⁴May he give the blessing of Abraham to you and to your descendants with you, that you may take possession of the land of your sojourn-

ings which God gave to Abraham!" [5]Thus Isaac sent Jacob away; and he went to Paddan-aram to Laban, the son of Bethuel the Aramean, the brother of Rebekah, Jacob's and Esau's mother.

[6]Now Esau saw that Isaac had blessed Jacob and sent him away to Paddan-aram to take a wife from there, and that as he blessed him he charged him, "You shall not marry one of the Canaanite women," [7]and that Jacob had obeyed his father and his mother and gone to Paddan-aram. [8]So when Esau saw that the Canaanite women did not please Isaac his father, [9]Esau went to Ishmael and took to wife, besides the wives he had, Mahalath the daughter of Ishmael Abraham's son, the sister of Nebaioth.

Here the Priestly author takes up the story he had begun at 26:34-35, and goes on to tell how Esau's marriage to Hittite women occasioned Jacob's departure for Mesopotamia. This version of events seems not to have known the Yahwistic account (chap. 27), which informs us that it was Jacob's fear of his brother's wrath that motivated his flight to his mother's homeland. The prohibition against Jacob's marrying a Canaanite woman (28:1) is based on the fact that intermarriage was a threat to Israel's religious distinctiveness and to the purity of the race (see comment on 24:3: above p. 136). During the time of the Babylonian exile (587-539 B.C.) and in the period following the return, that is, during the period that forms the background to the Priestly writers' activity, the Israelites were very sensitive about these matters, and they protected the integrity of the faith and the purity of the race by banning marriages with foreigners (*cf.,* Ezra 9:1-5; 10:1-5; Neh 13:23-29). The blessings (28:3-4) which Isaac gave to his departing son in the name of God Almighty (see comment on 17:1; above p. 108) gave the young man a share in the promise of descendants and of land that had been given to Abraham (*cf.,* 12:2, 7; 13:16-17, etc.). Paddan-aram is the Priestly designation for Mesopotamia (see comment on 25:20; above p. 146).

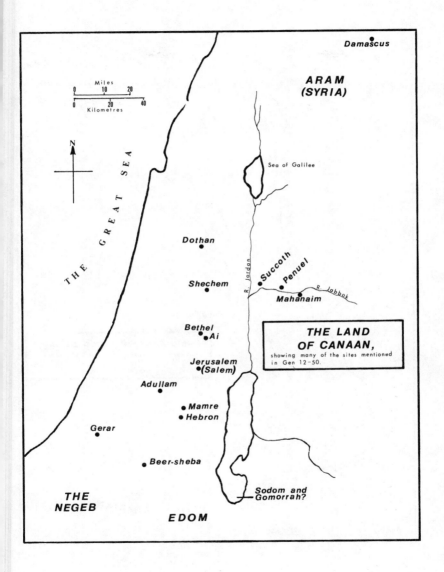

THE LAND
OF CANAAN,
showing many of the sites mentioned
in Gen 12-50.

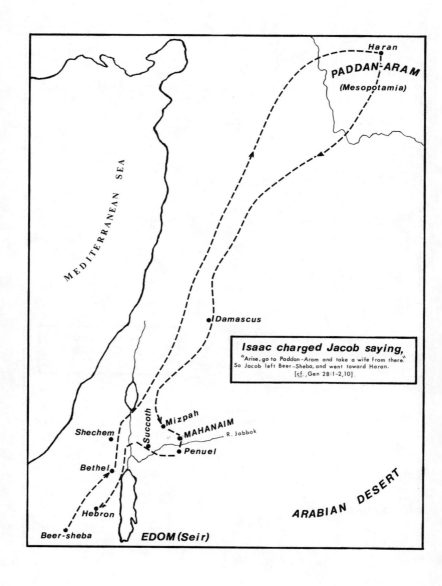

Isaac charged Jacob saying,
"Arise, go to Paddan-Aram and take a wife from there."
So Jacob left Beer-Sheba, and went toward Haran.
[cf., Gen 28:1-2,10]

JACOB'S VISION
28:10-22 (JE)

[10]Jacob left Beer-sheba, and went toward Haran. [11]And he came to a certain place, and stayed there that night, because the sun had set. Taking one of the stones of the place, he put it under his head and lay down in that place to sleep. [12]And he dreamed that there was a ladder set up on the earth, and the top of it reached to heaven; and behold, the angels of God were ascending and descending on it! [13]And behold, the Lord stood above it and said, "I am the Lord, the God of Abraham your father and the God of Isaac; the land on which you lie I will give to you and to your descendants; [14]and your descendants shall be like the dust of the earth, and you shall spread abroad to the west and to the east and to the north and to the south; and by you and your descendants shall all the families of the earth bless themselves. [15]Behold, I am with you and will keep you wherever you go, and will bring you back to this land; for I will not leave you until I have done that of which I have spoken to you." [16]Then Jacob awoke from his sleep and said, "Surely the Lord is in this place; and I did not know it." [17]And he was afraid, and said, "How awesome is this place! This is none other than the house of God, and this is the gate of heaven."

[18]So Jacob rose early in the morning, and he took the stone which he had put under his head and set it up for a pillar and poured oil on the top of it. [19]He called the name of that place Bethel; but the name of the city was Luz at the first. [20]Then Jacob made a vow, saying, "If God will be with me, and will keep me in this way that I go, and will give me bread to eat and clothing to wear, [21]so that I come again to my father's house in peace, then the Lord shall be my God, [22] and this stone, which I have set up for a pillar, shall be God's house; and of all that thou givest me I will give the tenth to thee."

In this passage, which takes up the story that broke off at 27:45, Jacob, the fugitive from his brother's wrath, becomes a visionary and the recipient of divine promises. A dream (v. 12) is the ordinary means of divine communication according to the Elohist tradition (see comment on 20:3; above p. 123). The *ladder*, or perhaps the *ramp*, which Jacob saw in his vision may have been suggested by the ziggurats of Babylonia, which were equipped with ramps that reached to the summit where the god was thought to dwell (see the comment on 11:4; above p. 83). The *angels*, or the *messengers*, as we gather from other Old Testament passages (*e.g.,* Job 1:6-7; Zech 1:8-11), had the task of patrolling the earth and reporting to God about the conduct of humans. However, it was not the angels, but God himself who spoke to Jacob and renewed the promises that had been made to his fathers (vv. 13-14; *cf.,* 12:2-3, 7; 26:2-5, etc.). The God who introduced himself as the God of Abraham and Isaac (*cf.,* 24:12; 26:24) assured Jacob that he would enjoy his protection wherever he went, and that he would eventually return safely to the promised land (v. 15: *cf.,* v. 21). The promise that his God would be with Jacob even in Mesopotamia implies an understanding of God that differed from that held by Israel's neighbors. While these latter believed that each God had its own acknowledged territory to which its activity was limited, the patriarchs' God was not limited to any area or to any shrine, but accompanied his worshippers wherever they went.

This extraordinary experience convinced Jacob of God's immediate presence, and caused him to shudder with reverent awe (vv. 16-17). He recognized the site as "the house of God," the place where Yahweh renders himself present. He saw it also as "the gate of heaven," the place where the messengers of God communicate with humans and from whence they bring human prayers to heaven. The type of "pillar" which Jacob erected (v. 18) was a regular feature of the Canaanite shrines (*cf.,* Exod 23:24; 34:13). These pillars, or cultic monoliths, which were probably regarded as the dwelling place of the god, were severely condemned in later

Israelite tradition (*cf.,* Lev 26:1; Deut 7:5; 12:3, etc.). The author of our present passage would have seen the stone as a memorial of the divine manifestation at the site. Jacob's anointing of the stone symbolized the sacred character of the place and its dedication to Yahweh (*cf.,* Exod 30:25-32; Lev 8:10-12).

Jacob's vow (vv. 20-22) would, on the face of it, seem to involve a primitive type of bartering with God. It seems to imply that Jacob's future loyalty to God depends on whether or not God will fulfil the stipulations laid down by the patriarch. But, like similar vows recorded in the Old Testament (*cf.,* Judg 11:30-31; 1 Sam 1:11; 2 Sam 15:7-12; Ps 66:13-15) Jacob's promise to acknowledge Yahweh as God can be seen as a strengthening of his prayer, and as an expression of his conviction that his prayer would be heard.

The primary purpose of this story of Jacob's vision was to explain the origin of Bethel as a sacred shrine of the Israelites. Bethel was, in fact, one of Israel's chief sanctuaries from very early times (*cf.,* 1 Kgs 12:28-29) until it was destroyed by Josiah at the end of the seventh century B.C. (*cf.,* 2 Kgs 23:15). The fact that Jacob encountered God there, that he anointed a stone on the site, and made a vow to offer tithes there, legitimized Israelite worship at the sanctuary of Bethel. Although Abraham had built an altar there (*cf.,* 12:8; 13:3-4), the present narrative teaches that the sacred place owes it holiness to the vision which Jacob experienced as he set out for Mesopotamia.

JACOB AT HARAN
29:1-20

29 Then Jacob went on his journey, and came to the land of the people of the east. ²As he looked he saw a well in the field, and lo, three flocks of sheep lying beside it; for out of that well the flocks were watered. The stone on the well's mouth was large, ³and when all the flocks were gathered there, the shepherds would roll the stone from the mouth of the well, and water the sheep, and put the stone back in its place upon the mouth of the well.

⁴Jacob said to them, "My brothers, where do you come from?" They said, "We are from Haran." ⁵He said to them, "Do you know Laban the son of Nahor?" They said, "We know him." ⁶He said to them, "Is it well with him?" They said, "It is well; and see, Rachel his daughter is coming with the sheep!" ⁷He said, "Behold, it is still high day, it is not time for the animals to be gathered together; water the sheep, and go, pasture them." ⁸But they said, "We cannot until all the flocks are gathered together, and the stone is rolled from the mouth of the well; then we water the sheep."

⁹While he was still speaking with them, Rachel came with her father's sheep; for she kept them. ¹⁰Now then Jacob saw Rachel the daughter of Laban his mother's brother, and the sheep of Laban his mother's brother, Jacob went up and rolled the stone from the well's mouth, and watered the flock of Laban his mother's brother. ¹¹Then Jacob kissed Rachel, and wept aloud. ¹²And Jacob told Rachel that he was her father's kinsman, and that he was Rebekah's son; and she ran and told her father.

¹³When Laban heard the tidings of Jacob his sister's son, he ran to meet him, and embraced him and kissed him, and brought him to his house. Jacob told Laban all these things, ¹⁴and Laban said to him, "Surely you are my bone and my flesh!" And he stayed with him a month.

¹⁵Then Laban said to Jacob, "Because you are my kinsman, should you therefore serve me for nothing? Tell me, what shall your wages be?" ¹⁶Now Laban had two daughters; the name of the older was Leah, and the name of the younger was Rachel. ¹⁷Leah's eyes were weak, but Rachel was beautiful and lovely. ¹⁸Jacob loved Rachel; and he said, "I will serve you seven years for your younger daughter Rachel." ¹⁹Laban said, "It is better that I give her to you than that I should give her to any other man; stay with me." ²⁰So Jacob served seven years for Rachel, and they seemed to him but a few days because of the love he had for her.

Like chap. 24, this chapter deals with a patriarchal search for a suitable wife from Mesopotamian relatives, and, like that chapter, it is usually assigned to the Yahwist, although it is agreed that it may contain elements from another tradition. Jacob, whom we last encountered at Bethel where he experienced a heavenly vision, is now among "the people of the East" (v. 1). This rather vague phrase usually refers to the nomadic tribes who inhabited the Syrian desert east and northeast of Palestine (*cf.,* Judg 6:3, 33; Isa 11:14; Jer 49:28 etc.), and therefore is not an appropriate designation for Haran (v. 4), the homeland of Jacob's ancestors. Nevertheless, the author clearly visualizes Jacob as encountering his kinsfolk among "the people of the East". The fact that the well at which Jacob found his cousins (*cf.,* 24:11-27) was covered by a large stone which could be moved only by several men (v. 3) shows that it was under communal control, and that it could not be used by any particular individual who might take more than a fair share of the limited supply of water. The statement that Jacob rolled back the huge stone on his own (v. 10) may reflect a tradition that ascribed superhuman strength to him, a tradition which may also be echoed in 28:18 and 32:24-25 where Jacob seems to be portrayed as a man of prodigious stamina.

Jacob's warm inquiries about his relatives (vv. 4-6), and his emotional reaction on meeting Rachel who appeared on the scene at the right moment (vv. 9-11) contrast with the callous and calculating way in which he had dealt with his own brother (*cf.,* 25:29-34; 27). The patriarch's encounter with uncle Laban (vv. 12-14) was also marked by a moving display of family affection, which, however, would soon give way to a prolonged hostility between uncle and nephew. The offer of wages made by Laban (v. 15) seems to suggest that he was not obliged to pay a relative who was willing to contribute his labour to the family concern. Jacob, on his part, was ready to take advantage of the offer, and was quick to specify that he would work for seven years in order to acquire his beautiful cousin Rachel as wife (v. 18). Not being in a position to pay the bride price (*cf.,* 34:12;

Exod 22:16-17) for the girl he loved, he was ready to give his service in lieu of direct payment.

Commentators cannot agree whether the remark that Leah's eyes were weak (v. 17) is complimentary or otherwise. The traditional understanding has been that weakness referred either to defective vision, or to paleness in the colour of the eyes which would be regarded by orientals as a blemish on female beauty. But since the Hebrew word rendered "weak" really means "tender" or "delicate," some modern writers claim that in applying the term to Leah's eyes the biblical writer wished to praise their attractiveness. But even if Leah's eyes had something special about them, her overall loveliness was overshadowed by the outstanding beauty of her younger sister for whom Jacob was willing to wait and work.

MARRIAGE
29:21-30

21Then Jacob said to Laban, "Give me my wife that I may go in to her, for my time is completed." 22So Laban gathered together all the men of the place, and made a feast. 23But in the evening he took his daughter Leah and brought her to Jacob; and he went in to her 24(Laban gave his maid Zilpah to his daughter Leah to be her maid.) 25And in the morning, behold, it was Leah; and Jacob said to Laban, "What is this you have done to me? Did I not serve with you for Rachel? Why then have you deceived me?" 26Laban said, "It is not so done in our country, to give the younger before the first-born. 27Complete the week of this one, and we will give you the other also in return for serving me another seven years." 28Jacob did so, and completed her week; then Laban gave him his daughter Rachel to wife. 29(Laban gave his maid Bilhah to his daughter Rachel to be her maid.) 30So Jacob went in to Rachel also, and he loved Rachel more than Leah, and served Laban for another seven years.

The patient Jacob who had waited so long for the woman of his choice was in for a cruel shock. On the morning after the wedding he found the less favored Leah in the bridal chamber instead of Rachel (vv. 21-25). The Middle Eastern custom of bringing the bride heavily veiled into the marriage chamber made Laban's shameful ruse possible. When Jacob discovered that he was the victim of an unscrupulous trick, his justified indignation (v. 25) was of no avail. The consummated marriage could not be repudiated. Furthermore, the shrewd uncle claimed the sanction of tradition for his behaviour, claiming that local custom did not allow a younger daughter to get married before her older sister (v. 26). Thus the ambitious Jacob, whose chicanery had deprived his brother of his rights as firstborn son (*cf.*, 25:29-34; 27), is now frustrated in his own designs by an outrageous trick that can be defended on the basis of the rights of a firstborn daughter.

However, if Jacob had lost the first round in the battle of wits with his wily uncle, he was not completely vanquished nor totally discouraged. He was willing to accept his new father-in-law's offer to give him Rachel in marriage in return for another seven-year period of service. So having finished the week's festivities that necessarily marked his marriage to Leah (*cf.*, Judg 14:12, 17) Jacob married the bride of his choice (vv. 27-28) and settled down to the seven years of work which he owed her father as her bride-price. Although later Israelite law would prohibit marriage to two sisters (*cf.*, Lev 18:18), the practice must have been acceptable at the time of the Yahwist who records the event without comment. The assignment of a maid each to Leah and Rachel (vv. 24, 29) is in conformity with a custom known to us from Mesopotamian sources.

One notices that this story of Jacob's quest for a wife has nothing explicitly religious about it. The patriarch did not commend his case to God as did Abraham's servant (*cf.*, 24:12-14), and he enjoyed no guarantee of divine assistance as did the pious servant (*cf.*, 24:7, 40). Yet, the hand of God was discreetly at work leading Jacob to his kinspeople in

Mesopotamia, and providing him, not only with the wife of his choice, but also with a second wife from whom the priestly tribe of Levi and the royal family of David would descend (*cf.,* 29:34-35). Jacob, who had robbed his brother, was clearly under the provident care of God, who guided events according to his own plan independently of the merits of his human agent.

JACOB'S CHILDREN
29:31—30:24

[31] When the Lord saw that Leah was hated, he opened her womb; but Rachel was barren. [32] And Leah conceived and bore a son, and she called his name Reuben; for she said, "Because the Lord has looked upon my affliction; surely now my husband will love me." [33] She conceived again and bore a son, and said, "Because the Lord has heard that I am hated, he has given me this son also"; and she called his name Simeon. [34] Again she conceived and bore a son, and said, "Now this time my husband will be joined to me because I have borne him three sons"; therefore his name was called Levi. [35] And she conceived again and bore a son, and said, "This time I will praise the Lord"; therefore she called his name Judah; then she ceased bearing.

30 When Rachel saw that she bore Jacob no children, she envied her sister; and she said to Jacob, "Give me children, or I shall die!" [2] Jacob's anger was kindled against Rachel, and he said, "Am I in the place of God, who has withheld from you the fruit of the womb?" [3] Then she said, "Here is my maid Bilhah; go in to her, that she may bear upon my knees, and even I may have children through her." [4] So she gave him her maid Bilhah as a wife; and Jacob went in to her. [5] And Bilhah conceived and bore Jacob a son. [6] Then Rachel said, "God has judged me, and has also heard my voice and given me a son"; therefore she called his name Dan. Rachel's maid Bilhah conceived again and bore Jacob a second son. [8] Then

Rachel said, "With mighty wrestlings I have wrestled with my sister, and have prevailed"; so she called his name Naphtali.

9When Leah saw that she had ceased bearing children, she took her maid Zilpah and gave her to Jacob as a wife. 10Then Leah's maid Zilpah bore Jacob a son. 11And Leah said, "Good fortune!" so she called his name Gad. 12Leah's maid Zilpah bore Jacob a second son. 13And Leah said, "Happy am I! For the women will call me happy"; so she called his name Asher.

14In the days of wheat harvest Reuben went and found mandrakes in the field, and brought them to his mother Leah. Then Rachel said to Leah, "Give me, I pray, some of your son's mandrakes." 15But she said to her, "Is it a small matter that you have taken away my husband? Would you take away my son's mandrakes also?" Rachel said, "Then he may lie with you tonight for your son's mandrakes." 16When Jacob came from the field in the evening, Leah went out to meet him, and said, "You must come in to me; for I have hired you with my son's mandrakes." So he lay with her that night. 17And God hearkened to Leah, and she conceived and bore Jacob a fifth son. 18Leah said, "God has given me my hire because I gave my maid to my husband"; so she called his name Issachar. 19And Leah conceived again, and she bore Jacob a sixth son. 20Then Leah said, "God has endowed me with a good dowry; now my husband will honor me, because I have borne him six sons"; so she called his name Zebulun. 21Afterwards she bore a daughter, and called her name Dinah. 22Then God remembered Rachel, and God hearkened to her and opened her womb. 23She conceived and bore a son, and said, "God has taken away my reproach"; 24and she called his name Joseph, saying, "May the Lord add to me another son!"

This passage records the birth of eleven sons and a daughter to Jacob in Mesopotamia. With Benjamin, who was to be born in the land of Canaan, (*cf.,* 35:16-20), these eleven sons form the link between the patriarchs and the tribes of Israel. The explanations of the names given in this passage are not etymologies in the strict sense, but rather farfetched puns based on a vague similarity of sound. Thus, for example, the name Joseph is associated with two verbs, *'asaph*, "he has taken away" (30:23, E), and *yasaph* or *yoseph*, "may he add" (30:24, J). The names given to the children either reflect the domestic rivalry that existed between Leah and Rachel, or they bear testimony to the fact that God is the giver of life

In saying that "Leah was hated" by Jacob (29:31) the author wishes us to understand that she was not cherished by her husband (*cf.,* Deut 25:15-16; Matt 6:24) as was the favorite wife, Rachel. But the Lord was on the side of the neglected Leah whom he blessed with children, while the beautiful Rachel remained childless. So once again we encounter the theme of the barren wife (*cf.,* 11:30; 25:21), and once again the Lord will intervene to overcome the natural obstacle and to grant a child to the sterile Rachel (30:22-24). But before the birth of her natural children, Rachel, overcome with envy towards Leah who had already borne four sons (*cf.,* 29:31-35), took steps to acquire children who would be regarded as her own. Following the legal procedure that had enabled Sarah to become a mother (*cf.,* 16:1-3; see comment above p. 105) she acquired two sons by her maid Bilhah (30:1-8). The image of Bilhah giving birth on Rachel's knees (v. 3) refers to an ancient rite of adoption, according to which the child of a substitute wife would be placed on the lap of an adopting woman as a sign that the latter acknowledged the child as her own and laid legal claim to it (comp. 50:23).

While this drastic action is readily understandable in the case of the childless Rachel, it is not easy to see why Leah, who could already boast of four sons, should have recourse to the same expedient (30:9-13). Nothing other than female rivalry and spite seems to have motivated her giving her maid to Jacob in order to acquire two more sons through her.

The peculiar story of the mandrakes (30:14-16) may have originally explained how Rachel eventually became a mother. The mandrake was a plant that was known as an aphrodisiac and as an aid to fertility, and Rachel may have wished to use it as a means of overcoming her humiliating barrenness. However, according to our present version of the story, when she did finally conceive it was not because of the effect of mandrakes, but because God blessed her with a child (vv. 22-24). So the mandrake bargain gained nothing for Rachel, but was the occasion of Leah's bearing two more sons to Jacob (vv. 17-20).

Although Jacob had more daughters than one (*cf.*, 37:35) the biblical narrative only tells of the birth of Dinah (30:21). According to many commentators the mention of the daughter's birth in the context of the birth of Jacob's sons may be a later addition that was introduced as a preparation for the story in chap. 34.

Individuals Or Personifications?

The account of the twelve sons of Jacob (29:31—30:24; 35:16-20) suggests that the tribes of Israel that bear the names of these sons descended from a common ancestor. The twelve-tribal system appears in other lists (*cf.*, chap. 49; Num 26:4-51; Deut 27:12-13), although the order of names may not always be the same. The insistence on the number twelve points to the importance of the twelve-tribal system in the mind of the Israelites and to the antiquity of that system. Nevertheless, the origins and history of Israel's twelve-tribal confederacy are unclear, and the picture of twelve tribes descending from twelve sons of Jacob is an artificial reconstruction from the time of David and Solomon rather than a declaration of fact. The bonds that united the tribes were religious, geographical and political, rather than biological as our present text might give one to understand. The twelve-tribal grouping emerged not by natural increase from twelve individuals, but by the coming together of groups who formed a confederation that had a common religion and culture as its source of unity. According to the custom of the time, genealogies would be constructed for persons or tribes, newly united by treaty or adoption. In other words the bonds must be sanctioned by the deceased ancestors, in order to share mutually in their promises and privileges. Even today among some Arab tribes, the word for "adoption" is to "genealogize": a child is not adopted simply by a couple or a family but by all their forebears.

JACOB'S WEALTH
30:25-43

25When Rachel had borne Joseph, Jacob said to Laban, "Send me away, that I may go to my own home and country. 26Give me my wives and my children for whom I have served you, and let me go; for you know the service which I have given you." 27But Laban said to him, "If you will allow me to say so, I have learned by divination that the Lord has blessed me because of you; 28name your wages, and I will give it." 29Jacob said to him, "you yourself know how I have served you, and how your cattle have fared with me. 30For you had little before I came, and it has increased abundantly; and the Lord has blessed you wherever I turned. But now when shall I provide for my own household also?" 31He said, "What shall I give you?" Jacob said, "You shall not give me anything; if you will do this for me, I will again feed your flock and keep it: 32let me pass through all your flock today, removing from it every speckled and spotted sheep and every black lamb, and the spotted and speckled among the goats; and such shall be my wages. 33So my honesty will answer for me later, when you come to look into my wages with you. Every one that is not speckled and spotted among the goats and black among the lambs, if found with me, shall be counted stolen." 34Laban said, "Good! Let it be as you have said." 35But that day Laban removed the he-goats that were striped and spotted, and all the she-goats that were speckled and spotted, every one that had white on it, and every lamb that was black, and put them in charge of his sons; [36]and he set a distance of three days' journey between himself and Jacob; and Jacob fed the rest of Laban's flock.

[37]Then Jacob took fresh rods of poplar and almond and plane, and peeled white streaks in them, exposing the white of the rods. [38]He set the rods which he had peeled in front of the flocks in the runnels, that is, the watering troughs, where the flocks came to drink. And since they bred when they came to drink, [39]the flocks bred in front of the rods and so the flocks brought forth striped, speckled, and spotted. [40]And Jacob separated the lambs, and set the faces of the flocks toward the striped and all the black in the flock of Laban; and he put his own droves apart, and did not put them with Laban's flock. [41]Whenever the stronger of the flock were breeding Jacob laid the rods in the runnels before the eyes of the flock, that they might breed among the rods, [42]but for the feebler of the flock he did not lay them there; so the feebler were Laban's and the stronger Jacob's. [43]Thus the man grew exceedingly rich, and had large flocks, maidservants and men-servants, and camels and asses.

When Jacob grew weary of what was in effect a servant status in Laban's household, his request to return home to Canaan (vv. 25-26, 30) did not please his father-in-law. Nevertheless, the latter, who had learned by the use of omens (v. 27; *cf.,* 44:5, 15) that he had profited greatly by Jacob's service, agreed to the departure of the shepherd who had been such a valuable asset to him. Jacob's readiness to cede any claim to recompense for work done for his father-in-law (v. 31a) must be seen as an example of oriental courtesy, as is indicated by the fact that he goes on immediately to determine what his wages should be (vv. 32-33). To understand Jacob's proposal we must keep in mind that sheep were usually white (*cf.,* Isa 1:18; Cant 4:2), and that goats were normally black (Cant 4:1). Speckled sheep or goats and black sheep were rare, so that Jacob's request to receive only these exceptional types of animals as a reward for his work was very modest indeed. Not surprisingly, Laban was eager to accept these terms that seemed so favorable to him (v. 34). By removing the speckled and white goats and the black lambs (vv. 35-36), which alone could be expected to produce similar offspring, the greedy uncle deprived Jacob of every hope of multiplying the number of abnormally colored animals that would eventually be his.

Nevertheless, Jacob was not to be outdone by his cunning uncle. The stratagem he used to produce many of the strangely colored animals he wanted (vv. 37-42) is based on an ancient belief that the nature of animal offspring can be determined by what the females see at the time of conception. Although the details of Jacob's breeding procedure are difficult to follow, we are assured that he acquired many unusually coloured animals that would be his own (v. 39). Then by a process of selective breeding he was able to produce a sturdy type of animal for his own flock, while leaving his greedy employer with a flock of weaklings (vv. 41-42). The list in v. 43 is a typical description of a semi-nomad's wealth (*cf.,* 12:16; 24:35).

Although both Laban and Jacob attribute the former's prosperity to the Lord (30:27,30), the story of Jacob's acquisition of wealth is totally lacking in religious content. It is a story of questionable dealing, and it makes no attempt to excuse or to moralize. Yet, the author very probably intended his readers to see in Jacob's wealth a proof that God was on his side in the battle of wits with his scheming uncle. The whole episode shows that God can write straight with crooked lines, and that he can incorporate even the scheming of men and women into the divine scheme of things.

DECISION TO LEAVE
31:1-16

31 Now Jacob heard that the sons of Laban were saying, "Jacob has taken all that was our father's; and from what was our father's he has gained all this wealth." ²And Jacob saw that Laban did not regard him with favor as before. ³Then the Lord said to Jacob, "Return to the land of your fathers and to your kindred, and I will be with you." ⁴So Jacob sent and called Rachel and Leah into the field where his flock was, ⁵and said to them, "I see that your father does not regard me with favor as he did before. But the God of my father has been with me. ⁶You know that I have served your father with all my strength; ⁷yet your father has cheated me and changed my wages ten times, but God did not permit him to harm me. ⁸If he said, 'The spotted shall be your wages,' then all the flock bore spotted; and if he said, 'The striped shall be your wages,' then all the flock bore striped. ⁹Thus God has taken away the cattle of your father, and given them to me. ¹⁰In the mating season of the flock I lifted up my eyes, and saw in a dream that the he-goats which leaped upon the flock were striped, spotted, and mottled. ¹¹Then the angel of God said to me in the dream, 'Jacob,' and I said, 'Here I am!' ¹²And he said, 'Lift up your eyes and see, all the goats that leap upon the flock are striped, spotted, and mottled; for I have seen all that Laban is doing to you. ¹³I am the God of Bethel, where you anointed a pillar and made a vow to me. Now arise, go forth from this land, and return to the land of your birth.'" ¹⁴Then Rachel and Leah answered him, "Is there any portion or inheritance left to us in our father's house? ¹⁵Are we not regarded by him as foreigners? For he has sold us, and he has been using up the money given for us. ¹⁶All the property which God has taken away from our father belongs to us and to our children; now then, whatever God has said to you, do."

The story of Jacob's preparation to depart from Mesopotamia (vv. 1-18) comes to us mainly from the Elohist, with minor contributions from the Yahwist (vv. 1 and 3) and from the Priestly authors (v. 18). According to the Yahwist, Jacob's decision to part company with his father-in-law was prompted both by the hostility and jealousy of Laban's sons (v. 1), and by an explicit divine command (v. 3). The Lord who had promised Jacob at Bethel that he would bring him back safely to his homeland (*cf.,* 28:15, J) now assures him that he will be with him on his homeward journey.

The Elohist also gives two reasons for Jacob's decision to leave Mesopotamia. Laban's unfriendly attitude (v. 2) and a clear direction from God (v. 13b) convince Jacob that he should put an end to his stay with his kinspeople. In justifying his decision to set out for Canaan to his wives, Jacob recalls the shabby way in which his bullying father-in-law had treated him (vv. 4-12). This Elohist account of the negotiations between employer and employee differs considerably from the Yahwist's story in 30:25-43, even though both narratives tell of breeding animals and of trickery. In the Elohist version of the story Jacob appears as a conscientious shepherd while Laban is portrayed as a shady dealer who modifies the terms of his agreement with his son-in-law at his whim. This account not only frees Jacob of all moral blame, but also makes it clear that God was on his side (vv. 5b, 7b, 9, 12) to frustrate the machinations of the wily herdowner. As is usual in the Elohist tradition, God does not appear directly to Jacob, but communicates with him in a dream or through an angel (vv. 10-11; *cf.,* 20:3, 6; 28:12, etc.).

Rachel and Leah agree that their husband's decision to leave their father was totally justifiable. They even declare that they too have been badly treated in their paternal home (vv. 14-16). The women's claim that their father had used up the money, that is, the bridal price, given for them, strikes a jarring note in the context of the whole Jacob story. Jacob had in fact paid no money for his wives, but had worked to acquire them (*cf.,* 29:20, 27).

FLIGHT
31:17-42

17So Jacob arose, and set his sons and his wives on camels; 18and he drove away all his cattle, all his livestock which he had gained, the cattle in his possession which he had acquired in Paddan-aram, to go to the land of Canaan to his father Isaac. 19Laban had gone to shear his sheep, and Rachel stole her father's household gods. 20And Jacob outwitted Laban the Aramaean, in that he did not tell him that he intended to flee. 21He fled with all that he had, and arose and crossed the Euphrates, and set his face toward the hill country of Gilead.

22When it was told to Laban on the third day that Jacob had fled, 23he took the kinsmen with him and pursued him for seven days and followed close after him into the hill country of Gilead. 24But God came to Laban the Aramaean in a dream by night, and said to him, "Take heed that you say not a word to Jacob, either good or bad."

25And Laban overtook Jacob. Now Jacob had pitched his tent in the hill country, and Laban with his kinsmen encamped in the hill country of Gilead. 26And Laban said to Jacob, "What have you done, that you have cheated me, and carried away my daughters like captives of the sword? 27Why did you flee secretly, and cheat me, and did not tell me, so that I might have sent you away with mirth and songs, with tambourine and lyre? 28And why did you not permit me to kiss my sons and my daughters farewell? Now you have done foolishly. 29It is in my power to do you harm; but the God of your father spoke to me last night, saying, "Take heed that you speak to Jacob neither good nor bad.' 30And now you have gone away because you longed greatly for your father's house, but why did you steal my gods?" 31Jacob answered Laban, "Because I was afraid, for I thought that you would take your daughters from me by force. 32Any one with whom you find your gods shall not live. In the presence of our kinsmen point out what I have that is yours, and take it." Now Jacob did not know that Rachel had stolen them.

³³So Laban went into Jacob's tent, and into Leah's tent, and into the tent of the two maidservants, but he did not find them. And he went out of Leah's tent, and entered Rachel's. ³⁴Now Rachel had taken the household gods and put them in the camel's saddle, and sat upon them. Laban felt all about the tent, but did not find them. ³⁵And she said to her father, "Let not my lord be angry that I cannot rise before you, for the way of women is upon me." So he searched, but did not find the household gods.

³⁶Then Jacob became angry, and upbraided Laban; Jacob said to Laban, "What is my offence? What is my sin, that you have hotly pursued me? ³⁷Although you have felt through all my goods, what have you found of all your household goods? Set it here before my kinsmen and your kinsmen, that they may decide between us two. ³⁸These twenty years I have been with you; your ewes and your she-goats have not miscarried, and I have not eaten the rams of your flocks. ³⁹That which was torn by wild beasts I did not bring to you; I bore the loss of it myself; of my hand you required it, whether stolen by day or stolen by night. ⁴⁰Thus I was; by day the heat consumed me, and the cold by night, and my sleep fled from my eyes. ⁴¹These twenty years I have been in your house; I served you fourteen years for your two daughters, and six years for your flock, and you have changed my wages ten times. ⁴²If the God of my father, the God of Abraham and the Fear of Isaac, had not been on my side, surely now you would have sent me away empty-handed. God saw my affliction and the labor of my hands, and rebuked you last night."

While Laban and his men were busy at the sheepshearing, and when they were distracted by the festivities that accompanied it (*cf.,* 1 Sam 25:4, 8, 11, 36; 2 Sam 13:23-28), Jacob took the opportunity to flee with his family and flocks (vv. 19-21). The notice that Rachel stole her father's household gods (v. 19) is far from clear. It has been claimed that according to Mesopotamian law the possessor of such domestic idols had a right to the family property. Rachel's purpose, then, in taking the gods would be to ensure that her husband would inherit her father's wealth. But there is no suggestion in the story that Jacob had a claim to his father-in-law's property. In fact, Laban states to the contrary (v. 43). Furthermore, when Jacob discovers the theft, he seems to regard the idols simply as family cult-objects in which he has no interest (vv. 30-31). Yet he did not regard the theft of the idols as a trivial matter, as is shown by the fact that he was ready to condemn to death anyone who might be found guilty of stealing them (v. 32). The biblical author, however, seems to ridicule Laban's feverish search for the gods when he tells how Rachel sat upon the precious idols during her menstrual period (v. 35), thus violating a taboo and rendering them unsuitable for purposes of worship (*cf.,* Lev 15:19-24).

The idea that Jacob could cross the Euphrates and come to the hill country of Gilead in a matter of ten days (vv. 21-23) is rather surprising. Since Gilead is an area immediately east of the Jordan this would imply that the patriarch covered a distance of about four hundred miles with his family and with all his flocks in this short space of time. It is possible that the Elohist situated Laban's homeland not in Haran, but in northwestern Arabia, and therefore relatively close to Gilead (*cf.,* 29:1, and comment above p. 167). The wealthy flock-owner, highly offended by the fact that his shepherd should run off with his daughters and with some of his possessions, was quick to set out in pursuit of the fleeing Jacob. The pursuing father-in-law's anger was cooled somewhat when God warned him in a dream not to say anything to Jacob (vv. 24, 29). When the aggrieved old man overtook his son-in-law his accusations against him were couched in very moderate language (vv. 26-30). He played the role of the injured partner, accused Jacob of wrongfully taking away his daughters, and gave the impression that he would have agreed to their departure if Jacob had approached the whole matter decently and fairly. In his excuse for running away with Laban's daughters Jacob seems to imply that their father could have prevented the women's departure for a foreign land (v. 31). But when Laban failed to find his idols among the possessions of Jacob's family, Jacob's apologetic tone gave way to indignation. In a speech that is full of passion (v. 36-42) the escaping shepherd accused his master of having treated him shamefully and of showing no appreciation of his diligent service. The honest shepherd had even gone beyond the call of duty in that he had not taken advantage of the legal stipulation which would free him from the obligation of making restitution for animals that had been killed by wild beasts (v. 39; *cf.,* Exod 22:13; Amos 3:12). Yet, were it not for the protection of the God of his ancestors Jacob would have left the service of his mean father-in-law in a state of utter poverty (v. 42). The title "Fear of Isaac," which occurs only here and in v. 53, seems to be simply a title for the God whom Isaac worshipped with fear and reverence.

In the Yahwist's story (30:25-43) Jacob was portrayed as an able schemer who used his wits to outdo his cunning master. In the present narrative he appears as the honest shepherd who was tricked by a ruthless employer (31:6-8, 36-42) and who owed anything he had to the protection of his God (vv. 7, 9, 16, 24, 29, 42). Thus the Elohist, as is his wont (see comments on chap. 20; above pp. 123-124), portrays his hero in a favorable light, and, at the same time, shows that God never abandons his chosen ones.

AGREEMENT AND SEPARATION
31:43—32:2 (JE)

> [43]Then Laban answered and said to Jacob, "The daughters are my daughters, the children are my children, the flocks are my flocks, and all that you see is mine. But what can I do this day to these my daughters, or to their children whom they have borne? [44]Come now, let us make a covenant, you and I; and let it be a witness between you and me." [45]So Jacob took a stone, and set it up as a pillar. [46]And Jacob said to his kinsmen, "Gather stones," and

they took stones, and made a heap; and they ate there by the heap. [47]Laban called it Jegarsahadutha: but Jacob called it Galeed. [48]Laban said, "This heap is a witness between you and me today." Therefore he named it Galeed, [49]and the pillar Mizpah, for he said, "The Lord watch between you and me, when we are absent one from the other. [50]If you ill-treat my daughters, or if you take wives besides my daughters, although no man is with us, remember, God is witness between you and me."

[51]Then Laban said to Jacob, "See this heap and the pillar, which I have set between you and me. [52]This heap is a witness, and the pillar is a witness, that I will not pass over this heap to you, and you will not pass over this heap and this pillar to me, for harm. [53]The God of Abraham and the God of Nahor, the God of their father, judge between us." So Jacob swore by the Fear of his father Isaac, [54]and Jacob offered a sacrifice on the mountain and called his kinsmen to eat bread; and they ate bread and tarried all night on the mountain.

[55]Early in the morning Laban arose, and kissed his grandchildren and his daughters and blessed them; then he departed and returned home.

32 Jacob went on his way and the angels of God met him; [2]and when Jacob saw them he said, "This is God's army!" So he called the name of that place Mahanaim.

Finally admitting that he was beaten by his son-in-law, Laban resigned himself to letting his daughters depart with their husband (v. 43). Wishing to ensure their status in their new home he proposed to establish a covenant with Jacob concerning them (vv. 44, 50). The account of the covenant (vv. 44-54) is complicated by the fact that two versions of the story (JE) are fused in the present narrative. In one version we are told of a standing stone or pillar that served as a sign of the covenant (vv. 45, 51-52), and in the other we are informed that a heap of stones served the same purpose (vv. 46, 48, 51-52). We read twice about a shared meal (vv. 46, 54); we have two reports of the content of the covenant (vv.

50, 52), and we hear of two place-names, Galeed and Mizpah, in connection with the covenant (vv. 47, 49).

Our understanding of the narrative is further complicated by the fact that we cannot read the story in purely personal terms. The authors, while apparently describing a pact between individuals, actually echo an ancient tradition about a covenant between the Israelites, represented by Jacob, and their Aramaean neighbors in Transjordan, who are represented by Laban the Aramaean (vv. 20, 24). The text as it now stands personalizes the agreement, and the only direct echo of the boundary pact is the mention of the pillar or the heap of stones that marked the dividing line beyond which the contracting parties would not pass in the future. The God of each of the contracting parties was invoked as a witness to the pact (v. 53), and the new agreement was sealed by a shared meal (*cf.,* vv. 46, 54). According to the Elohistic version of events the covenant was also ratified by a sacrifice (v. 54; *cf.,* Exod 24:3-8, E).

Thus, in the amicable atmosphere of a shared meal, the story of intrigue and trickery that goes to make up the Jacob-Laban saga ends. Here Laban fades from the pages of the Bible. Jacob continued his journey to the land of Canaan only to encounter "the angels of God" (32:1; *cf.,* 28:12 and comments above p. 164), whom he identifies as "God's army." Why the place where this encounter took place is called "Mahanaim" is not clear. The word means "two armies," and the reference may be to "God's army" and Jacob's company.

ANXIOUS MOMENTS
32:3-21 (JE)

> ³And Jacob sent messengers before him to Esau his brother in the land of Seir, the country of Edom, ⁴instructing them, "Thus you shall say to my lord Esau: Thus says your servant Jacob, 'I have sojourned with Laban, and stayed until now; ⁵and I have oxen, asses, flocks, menservants, and maidservants; and I have sent to

tell my lord, in order that I may find favor in your sight.'"

⁶And the messengers returned to Jacob, saying, "We came to your brother Esau, and he is coming to meet you, and four hundred men with him." ⁷Then Jacob was greatly afraid and distressed; and he divided the people that were with him, and the flocks and herds and camels, into two companies, ⁸thinking, "If Esau comes to the one company and destroys it, then the company which is left will escape."

⁹And Jacob said, "O God of my father Abraham and God of my father Isaac, O Lord who didst say to me, 'Return to your country and to your kindred, and I will do you good,' ¹⁰I am not worthy of the least of all the steadfast love and all the faithfulness which thou hast shown to thy servant, for with only my staff I crossed this Jordan; and now I have become two companies. ¹¹Deliver me, I pray thee, from the hand of my brother, from the hand of Esau, for I fear him, lest he come and slay us all, the mothers with the children. ¹²But thou didst say, 'I will do you good, and make your descendants as the sand of the sea, which cannot be numbered for multitude.'"

¹³So he lodged there that night, and took from what he had with him a present for his brother Esau, ¹⁴two hundred she-goats and twenty he-goats, two hundred ewes and twenty rams, ¹⁵thirty milch camels and their colts, forty cows and ten bulls, twenty she-asses and ten he-asses. ¹⁶These he delivered into the hand of his servants, every drove by itself, and said to his servants, "Pass on before me, and put a space between drove and drove." ¹⁷He instructed the foremost, "When Esau my brother meets you, and asks you, 'To whom do you belong? Where are you going? And whose are these before you?' ¹⁸then you shall say, 'They belong to your servant Jacob; they are a present sent to my lord Esau; and moreover he is behind us.'" ¹⁹He likewise instructed the second and the third and all who followed the droves, "You shall say the same thing to Esau when you meet him, ²⁰and you shall

say, 'Moreover your servant Jacob is behind us.'" For he
thought, "I may appease him with the present that goes
before me, and afterwards I shall see his face; perhaps he
will accept me." [21]So the present passed on before him;
and he himself lodged that night in the camp.

When Jacob was about to reenter the promised land his
guilty past caught up with him. The prospect of meeting the
brother whom he had robbed of the blessing that was rightly
his (*cf.,* 25:21-34) filled him with a sense of foreboding. Our
present passage combines two very different accounts of the
stratagem which the resourceful Jacob devised in order to
ensure that his encounter with Esau would not have totally
disastrous consequences for him.

The Yahwist (vv. 3-13a) tells how Jacob sent messengers
to "Seir, the country of Edom" (v. 3; *cf.,* 25:25, and see
comment above p. 146), that is, to the territory of Esau. In a
speech that is redolent of the language of diplomacy, the
messengers acknowledge Jacob's dependence on Esau's
favour, and by describing the returning brother's wealth
they drop a hint to Esau that Jacob would shower gifts on
him if normal brotherly relations were restored (vv. 4-5).
Hearing that Esau was coming toward him with four
hundred men, Jacob took practical steps to avoid total
disaster (vv. 6-9). Having taken this precautionary measure,
Jacob, in what was for him an unusual gesture of piety,
turned in prayer to the God of his ancestors (vv. 9-12). By
recalling the divine command that set him on his journey
home, and by appealing to God's promise to grant him
continued protection (vv. 9-10; *cf.,* 31:3), he established a
basis for confidence that his prayer would be heard. He
knew that his God was bound to him by bonds of steadfast
love and faithfulness (v. 10; *cf.,* Exod 34:6; Pss 25:10; 40:11;
57:3, etc.); the Lord's dealings with him, therefore, would be
motivated by these qualities rather than by any merit on
Jacob's part. In spite of the threatening situation of the
moment Jacob could hope for a favorable outcome, since
the God who promised to multiply his seed would not
abandon him now (v. 12; *cf.,* 28:14).

The Elohist account of Jacob's strategy to dispel his brother's anger centres on the giving of lavish gifts (vv. 13-21). In order to increase the impact of his generous gesture he sent his gifts in instalments, and continued to surprise Esau with new additions to the presents which, he hoped, would prepare the way for fraternal reconciliation.

X. RETURN TO THE PROMISED LAND 32:22—35:29

WRESTLING AT PENIEL
32:22-32 (J)

²²The same night he arose and took his two wives, his two maids, and his eleven children, and crossed the ford of the Jabbok. ²³He took them and sent them across the stream, and likewise everything that he had. ²⁴And Jacob was left alone; and a man wrestled with him until the breaking of the day. ²⁵When the man saw that he did not prevail against Jacob, he touched the hollow of his thigh; and Jacob's thigh was put out of joint as he wrestled with him. ²⁶Then he said, "Let me go, for the day is breaking." But Jacob said, "I will not let you go, unless you bless me." ²⁷And he said to him, "What is your name?" And he said, "Jacob." ²⁸Then he said, "Your name shall no more be called Jacob, but Israel, for you have striven with God and with men, and have prevailed." ²⁹Then Jacob asked him, "Tell me, I pray, your name." But he said, "Why is it that you ask my name?" And there he blessed him. ³⁰So Jacob called the name of the place Peniel, saying, "For I have seen God face to face, and yet my life is preserved." ³¹The sun rose upon him as he passed Penuel, limping because of his thigh. ³²Therefore to this day the Israelites do not eat the sinew of the hip which is upon the hollow of the thigh, because he touched the hollow of Jacob's thigh on the sinew of the hip.

Having sent his whole retinue across the Jabbok, which flows westward through Gilead (*cf.,* 31:21-23) to join the Jordan about thirty miles north of the Dead Sea, Jacob alone remained behind (vv. 22-23). The text mentions only eleven children, doubtless because Dinah is omitted from the count according to the regular practice of excluding women from family lists.

The theme of a protecting spirit who guards the passage of a river and who assails those who attempt to cross it, is well-known from ancient folklore. The present narrative applies this folkloristic theme to Jacob, and portrays him as locked in indecisive battle with a mysterious assailant until the latter magically lamed him by touching "the hollow of his thigh" (vv. 24-25). When, according to the folkloristic pattern, the unidentified adversary had to depart at break of day, Jacob refused to let him go, and by asking for a blessing gives us a first hint about the supernatural identity of "the man" who attacked him (v. 26). The nocturnal visitor, however, did not give a blessing immediately, but instead, proceeded to give Jacob a new name (vv. 27-28). The real meaning of the new name, Israel, is unknown, but the author links it, rather implausibly, with the verb *saritha,* "you have striven," and with the divine name *El,* God. (The Priestly author, without explaining the new name, will later tell us that God himself personally changed Jacob's name to Israel; *cf.,* 35:9-10.) In the explanation "you have striven with God" the identity of the mysterious antagonist is at last revealed. What is meant by saying that Jacob strove "with men" is not at all clear in the context. Perhaps the author is referring to his earlier skirmishes with Esau, Isaac and Laban. Having received a blessing from the visitor (v. 29b) Jacob clearly recognized him as God, and called the place *Peniel,* or "the face of God" (v. 30). Since, however, no one can see God and live (*cf.,* Exod 33:20; Judg 6:22-23; 13:22), the patriarch expressed surprise that he had lived through the experience.of such a close encounter with God.

Three different elements can easily be distinguished in the present narrative. We are given, first of all, an etymology of the name Israel (v. 28). Then the place-name Peniel (v. 30), or Penuel as it is called in v. 31, is explained. Thirdly, a dietary prescription which forbade the eating of the "sinew of the hip," or the sciatic muscle, is linked with the night wrestler who injured Jacob's thigh (vv. 25, 31-32). Incidentally, we may note that this prescription was not observed in later Israel, and we find no mention of it outside this passage.

However, when the Yahwist gave this story a place in the Jacob saga, he was not primarily interested in these points. He identified the strange wrestler with Yahweh who blessed Jacob and gave him a new name. The change of name signified a change in status. He, who up to this point was known mainly as an able deceiver, is now given the name that shows that he was the ancestor of the chosen race that was to bear the name Israel. When Jacob was about to leave the promised land he received a promise of divine protection (*cf.,* 28:10-17); now, as he returns, he receives a blessing that will affect him and all his descendants. Furthermore, the Yahwist probably saw Jacob as an embodiment of the people of Israel, and he wished to make the point that just as Jacob, who was heir to the divine promises, had to strive with God, so would Israel have to strive and suffer in its role as bearer of the divine promises.

RECONCILED WITH ESAU
33:1-20

33   And Jacob lifted up his eyes and looked, and behold, Esau was coming, and four hundred men with him. So he divided the children among Leah and Rachel and the two maids. ²And he put the maids with their children in front, then Leah with her children, and Rachel and Joseph last of all. ³He himself went on before them, bowing himself to the ground seven times, until he came near to his brother.

⁴But Esau ran to meet him, and embraced him, and fell on his neck and kissed him, and they wept. ⁵And when Esau raised his eyes and saw the women and children, he

said, "Who are these with you?" Jacob said, "The children whom God has graciously given your servant." [6]Then the maids drew near, they and their children, and bowed down; [7]Leah likewise and her children drew near and bowed down; and last Joseph and Rachel drew near, and they bowed down. [8]Esau said, "What do you mean by all this company which I met?" Jacob answered, "To find favor in the sight of my lord." [9]But Esau said, "I have enough, my brother; keep what you have for yourself." [10]Jacob said, "No, I pray you, if I have found favor in your sight, then accept my present from my hand; for truly to see your face is like seeing the face of God, with such favor have you received me. [11]Accept, I pray you, my gift that is brought to you, because God has dealt graciously with me, and because I have enough." Thus he urged him, and he took it.

[12]Then Esau said, "Let us journey on our way, and I will go before you." [13]But Jacob said to him, "My lord knows that the children are frail, and that the flocks and herds giving suck are a care to me; and if they are overdriven for one day, all the flocks will die. [14]Let my lord pass on before his servant, and I will lead on slowly, according to the pace of the children, until I come to my lord in Seir."

[15]So Esau said, "Let me leave with you some of the men who are with me." But he said, "What need is there? Let me find favor in the sight of my lord." [16]So Esau returned that day on his way to Seir. [17]But Jacob journeyed to Succoth, and built himself a house, and made booths for his cattle; therefore the name of the place is called Succoth.

[18]And Jacob came safely to the city of Shechem, which is in the land of Canaan, on his way from Paddan-aram; and he camped before the city. [19]And from the sons of Hamor, Shechem's father, he bought for a hundred pieces of money the piece of land on which he had pitched his tent. [20]There he erected an altar and called it El-Elohe-Israel.

This mainly Yahwistic story presumes the preparations described in 32:4-21. The thought of Esau coming towards him with four hundred men (*cf.,* 32:6) filled Jacob with anxiety. He arranged his retinue in such a way that his favorite wife Rachel, with her son Joseph, would bring up the rear, and thus have a better chance of surviving Esau's expected angry attack (33:1-2). Jacob himself led the procession, and greeted the approaching Esau with an extreme gesture of servility (v. 3). When Esau arrived, however, his mood was not one of anger or revenge. Overcome with joy at the return of his brother, he greeted him with deep emotion (v. 4). No explanation is given of the change of heart that had overcome Esau whose murderous plans (*cf.,* 27:41) had occasioned Jacob's long exile. But the author surely wishes us to understand that God was at work, ordering circumstances so that Jacob would come to no harm at his brother's hand. Jacob himself makes the point that his large family is a sign of God's favor that had accompanied him in his wanderings (vv. 5-7). Esau's question about the company he had met (v. 8) seems to refer to the gifts Jacob had sent ahead with a view to appeasing his brother (*cf.,* 32:13-21). Esau's conventional demonstration of reluctance to accept the gifts (v. 9) was silenced by Jacob's expected insistence (vv. 10-11). So overjoyed was Jacob with the unexpected outcome of his encounter with Esau that he compared the experience to a meeting with God himself (v. 10).

In vv. 12-17 Jacob again appears as the crafty dealer, who, by his shrewd playing of his cards, could frustrate the intentions of his brother. Without doubt Esau believed that his returning brother, who had made obeisance to him, called himself servant, and addressed Esau as lord (vv. 3, 5, 8), would become a submissive vassal (v. 12). Jacob, however, had other ideas. Pleading his inability to journey with Esau at a pace suitable to the latter, he convinced his brother to leave him behind (vv. 13-14). When Esau set out for his homeland in Seir (*cf.,* 32:4; 25:25; see comment on this latter text, above p. 146), Jacob secretly waved him goodbye, and blithely went off in the other direction to settle at Succoth, which is situated north of the Jabbok (*cf.*, 32:22). But his stay at Succoth was not prolonged, and he soon made his way across the Jordan and into the promised land. There, at Shechem, he erected an altar, which he consecrated to El-Elohe-Israel, that is, to "God, the God of Israel" (v. 20). Abraham had earlier built an altar on the site, thus consecrating it to Yahweh (*cf.*, 12:6-7; see comment above p. 92). Jacob, however, went a step further, and bought a piece of land at Shechem, as Abraham had done at Machpelah (*cf.*, chap. 23).

RAPE OF DINAH
34:1-31 (JE)

34 Now Dinah the daughter of Leah, whom she had borne to Jacob, went out to visit the women of the land; [2]and when Shechem the son of Hamor the Hivite, the prince of the land, saw her, he seized her and lay with her and humbled her. [3]And his soul was drawn to Dinah the daughter of Jacob; he loved the maiden and spoke tenderly to her. [4]So Shechem spoke to his father Hamor, saying, "Get me this maiden for my wife." [5]Now Jacob heard that he had defiled his daughter Dinah; but his sons were with his cattle in the field, so Jacob held his peace until they came. [6]And Hamor the father of Shechem went out to Jacob to speak with him. [7]The sons of Jacob came in from the field when they heard of it; and the men were indignant and very angry, because he had wrought folly in Israel by lying with Jacob's daughter, for such a thing ought not to be done.

[8]But Hamor spoke with them, saying, "The soul of my son Shechem longs for your daughter; I pray you, give her to him in marriage. [9]Make marriages with us; give your daughters to us, and take our daughters for yourselves. [10]You shall dwell with us; and the land shall be open to you; dwell and trade in it, and get property in it." [11]Shechem also said to her father and to her brothers,

"Let me find favor in your eyes, and whatever you say to me I will give. [12]Ask of me ever so much as marriage present and gift, and I will give according as you say to me; only give me the maiden to be my wife."

[13]The sons of Jacob answered Shechem and his father Hamor deceitfully, because he had defiled their sister Dinah. [14]They said to them, "We cannot do this thing, to give our sister to one who is uncircumcised, for that would be a disgrace to us. [15]Only on this condition will we consent to you: that you will become as we are and every male of you be circumcised. [16]Then we will give our daughters to you, and we will take your daughters to ourselves, and we will dwell with you and become one people. [17]But if you will not listen to us and be circumcised, then we will take our daughter, and we will be gone."

[18]Their words pleased Hamor and Hamor's son Shechem. [19]And the young man did not delay to do the thing, because he had delight in Jacob's daughter. Now he was the most honored of all his family. [20]So Hamor and his son Shechem came to the gate of their city and spoke to the men of their city, saying, [21]"These men are friendly with us; let them dwell in the land and trade in it, for behold, the land is large enough for them; let us take their daughters in marriage, and let us give them our daughters. [22]Only on this condition will the men agree to dwell with us, to become one people: that every male among us be circumcised as they are circumcised. [23]Will not their cattle, their property and all their beasts be ours? Only let us agree with them, and they will dwell with us." [24]And all who went out of the gate of his city hearkened to Hamor and his son Shechem; and every male was circumcised, all who went out of the gate of his city.

[25]On the third day, when they were sore, two of the sons of Jacob, Simeon and Levi, Dinah's brothers, took their swords and came upon the city unawares, and killed all the males. [26]They slew Hamor and his son Shechem with the sword, and took Dinah out of Shechem's house, and

went away. [27]And the sons of Jacob came upon the slain, and plundered the city, because their sister had been defiled; [28]they took their flocks and their herds, their asses, and whatever was in the city and in the field; [29]all their wealth, all their little ones and their wives, all that was in the houses, they captured and made their prey. [30]Then Jacob said to Simeon and Levi, "You have brought trouble on me by making me odious to the inhabitants of the land, the Canaanites and the Perizzites; my numbers are few, and if they gather themselves against me and attack me, I shall be destroyed, both I and my household [31]But they said, "Should he treat our sister as a harlot?"

When Shechem's violation of Dinah (vv. 1-3) became known to her brothers, they were "indignant and very angry, because he had wrought folly in Israel" (v. 7). Although Shechem had only asked his father to arrange his marriage to Dinah (v. 4), Hamor went much further and proposed that the Shechemites and Israelites enter into a close relationship involving intermarriage and commerce (vv. 8-10). Shechem's own request to Dinah's family was purely personal, and he was ready to pay whatever bridal price her family might demand (vv. 11-12). In response to the sincere proposals of Shechem and Hamor, Jacob's sons "answered deceitfully" (v. 13). Under the pretext of piety they claimed that they could not allow Dinah to marry one who is uncircumcised (v. 14), and at the same time they were hatching a treacherous plan against the unsuspecting Shechemites. Since the inhabitants of Canaan practised circumcision it is surprising to hear that the inhabitants of Shechem were uncircumcised. But it may be that certain tribes did not follow the general practice. Hamor and Shechem had no difficulty in accepting circumcision as a condition for intermarriage between two peoples, and they persuaded their fellow citizens to accept the painful rite, assuring them that intermarriage with the tribe of Jacob would be economically advantageous (vv. 15-24). The actual circumcision, performed with primitive instruments and with minimal hygiene, had very painful and debilitating effects, so that when Simeon and Levi came to attack the city they found it practically undefended (vv. 25-26). Nevertheless the idea that two men could slaughter all the males in the city, incapacitated though they might be, is rather far-fetched, and indicates that we should not take the story literally. When Jacob's other sons had plundered the city (vv. 27-29), Jacob appeared on the scene for the first time. His disapproval of his two sons' violent action was motivated more by fear of possible reprisal by the local population that by any moral considerations (v. 30). In any case, the reaction of the two young men to their father's rather mild protest was one of proud defiance rather than of remorse. They felt, as all their contemporaries would have felt, that the honor of their sister, and their own pride, demanded that the Shechemites be taught an unforgettable lesson (v. 31).

Modern commentators believe that there is more to this curious narrative than the story of individuals who got caught up in the unfortunate consequences of a young man's amorous folly. It seems that Hamor and his son Shechem embody the city of Shechem and its inhabitants, while Simeon and Levi represent the tribes that bear their names.

It is very probable that the story echoes the memory of a time when Simeon and Levi were quite powerful tribes who attempted to settle in the central highlands of Palestine long before the time of the conquest of Joshua. Jacob's disapproval of the two sons' ruthless action (vv. 30-31) may be taken as an explanation of the decline of the tribes of Simeon and Levi (*cf.,* 49:5-7). In later sources (*e.g.,* Josh 19:1-9) Simeon appears as a diminished tribe settled in Judah and absorbed by the tribe of that name. The tribe of Levi is said in some sources to have had no territory in Israel (*cf.,* Deut 18:1; Josh 13:14), although other texts assign certain cities to that clan (*cf.,* Num 35:2-8; Josh 21).

END OF JACOB'S WANDERING
35:1-8 (E)

35 God said to Jacob, "Arise, go up to Bethel, and dwell there; and make there an altar to the God who appeared to you when you fled from your brother Esau." [2]So Jacob said to his household and to all who were with him, "Put away the foreign gods that are among you, and purify yourselves, and change your garments; [3]then let us arise and go up to Bethel, that I may make there an altar to the God who answered me in the day of my distress and has been with me wherever I have gone." [4]So they gave to Jacob all the foreign gods that they had, and the rings that were in their ears; and Jacob hid them under the oak which was near Shechem.

[5]And as they journeyed, a terror from God fell upon the cities that were round about them, so that they did not pursue the sons of Jacob. [6]And Jacob came to Luz (that is, Bethel), which is in the land of Canaan, he and all the people who were with him, [7]and there he built an altar, and called the place El-bethel, because there God had revealed himself to him when he fled from his brother. [8]And Deborah, Rebekah's nurse, died, and she was buried under an oak below Bethel; so the name of it was called Allon-bacuth.

A divine command brought Jacob back to Bethel, where the Lord had appeared to him some twenty years earlier (*cf.,* 28:12ff). The earrings which the patriarch's followers cast away (v. 4) were not simply ornaments, but amulets or cultic symbols. By abandoning their "foreign gods," by casting away the earrings, and by purifying themselves (vv. 2-4), Jacob's retinue declared their total allegiance to Yahweh. Verse 5 seems to link the present story with the preceding chapter. The "terror from God" that fell upon the cities probably refers to a kind of inexplicable paralysis or panic (*cf.,* Exod 23:27; 1 Sam 14:15 etc.) that rendered the Shechemites incapable of molesting Jacob (*cf.,* 34:30). Having arrived at Bethel, Jacob, who had formerly erected a pillar on the spot (*cf.,* 28:18), built an altar there in obedience to a divine command (vv. 2, 7). Thus the consecration of the sacred shrine of Bethel is attributed to both Abraham (*cf.,* 12:8; see comment above, p. 93) and Jacob by the biblical tradition.

ISRAEL SHALL BE YOUR NAME
35:9-15 (P)

> [9]God appeared to Jacob again, when he came from Paddan-aram, and blessed him. [10]And God said to him, "Your name is Jacob; no longer shall your name be called Jacob, but Israel shall be your name." So his name was called Israel. [11]And God said to him, "I am God Almighty: be fruitful and multiply; a nation and a company of nations shall come from you, and kings shall spring from you. [12]The land which I gave to Abraham and Isaac I will give to you, and I will give the land to your descendants after you." [13]Then God went up from him in the place where he had spoken with him. [14]And Jacob set up a pillar in the place where he had spoken with him, a pillar of stone; and he poured out a drink offering on it, and poured oil on it. [15]So Jacob called the name of the place where God had spoken with him, Bethel.

The place-name Paddan-aram (v. 9; see comment on 28:2; above p. 160), the divine title "God Almighty" (v. 11; see comment on 17:1; above p. 108), and the formula "be fruitful and multiply" (v. 11; see comment on 1:22; above p. 27), all show that we owe this passage to the Priestly author. Recording the change in Jacob's name (v. 10; *cf.,* 32:28, J) this writer offers no explanation of the change, and is satisfied with the bland comment, "So his name was called Israel." The command or blessing "be fruitful and multiply" (v. 11) is rather out of place at this stage in the story of Jacob who is already the father of eleven sons (*cf.,* 30:1-24). The promise of numerous descendants and of land, a promise that had been already made to Abraham (*cf.,* 17:3-8, P), is now renewed to Jacob-Israel (vv. 11b-12). The erection and consecration of a pillar which has been recorded at 28:18

(E), and the naming of the sanctuary which had been noted at 28:19 (J), are both recalled here by the Priestly author (vv. 14-15).

THE BIRTH OF BENJAMIN
35:16-21 (E)

> [16]Then they journeyed from Bethel; and when they were still some distance from Ephrath, Rachel travailed, and she had hard labor. [17]And when she was in her hard labor, the midwife said to her, "Fear not; for now you will have another son." [18]And as her soul was departing (for she died), she called his name Benoni, but his father called his name Benjamin. [19]So Rachel died, and she was buried on the way to Ephrath [that is, Bethlehem], [20]and Jacob set up a pillar upon her grave; it is the pillar of Rachel's tomb, which is there to this day. [21]Israel journeyed on, and pitched his tent beyond the tower of Eder.

At the birth of Benjamin, the only one of the ancestors of the twelve tribes to be born in the land of Canaan, Jacob's favorite wife died. The birth of Benjamin was for his mother the fulfilment of a prayer she had made when her only other son was born (*cf.,* 30:24). The name *Benoni,* "son of my sorrow," recalls the pain which marked the child's birth. But such an ill-starred name boded evil, and the child's father had it changed to *Benjamin,* "son of the right hand." Since the right hand is the place of honour and esteem, this new name foreshadowed good fortune and success for its bearer.

By placing the words "that is, Bethlehem" (v. 19), in brackets, the RSV indicates that they are probably a late gloss to the text. In fact the birthplace of Benjamin and the burial place of Rachel are not to be situated at Bethlehem which is in the territory of Judah, but rather in the territory of Benjamin which lies north of Jerusalem (*cf.,* 1 Sam 10:2; Jer 31:15). We do not know where Rachel's burial place is to be found, but we can be sure that she was not buried in the tomb near Bethlehem, which is pointed out to visitors to the Holy Land as the matriarch's grave. The location of "the tower of Eder" (v. 21) is also unknown.

REUBEN'S INCEST
35:22a (J)

> [22]While Israel dwelt in that land Reuben went and lay with Bilhah his father's concubine; and Israel heard of it.

This short notice comes to us from the Yahwist, who, from this point on, calls Jacob by his new name Israel. Commentators agree that the story is a mere fragment of an account that must originally have told of Jacob's reaction to Reuben's outrageous act, and of the consequences for Reuben. Perhaps the Yahwist recorded the story to explain why Reuben, the eldest son of Jacob (*cf.,* 29:31-32) did not obtain primacy in Israel. Like Simeon and Levi, Jacob's second and third sons (*cf.,* 29:33-34), who rendered themselves unworthy of supremacy (*cf.,* 34:30-31), Reuben was deprived of his birthright because of his sin, and the right of the firstborn passed on to Judah, the fourth of Jacob's sons (*cf.,* 29:35). Reuben's offence is referred to again in 49:4, but without the addition of any information that might give us a better understanding of the episode.

DEATH OF ISAAC
35:22b-29 (P)

> Now the sons of Jacob were twelve. [23]The sons of Leah: Reuben (Jacob's first-born), Simeon, Levi, Judah, Issachar, and Zebulun. [24]The sons of Rachel: Joseph and Benjamin. [25]The sons of Bilhah, Rachel's maid: Dan and Naphtali. [26]The sons of Zilpah, Leah's maid: Gad and Asher. These were the sons of Jacob who were born to him in Paddan-aram.
>
> [27]And Jacob came to his father Isaac at Mamre, or Kiriath-arba (that is, Hebron), where Abraham and Isaac had sojourned. [28]Now the days of Isaac were a hundred and eighty years. [29]And Isaac breathed his last; and he died and was gathered to his people, old and full of days; and his sons Esau and Jacob buried him.

The Priestly list of the sons of Jacob (vv. 22b-26) follows essentially the same order that we found in 29:31-30:24 (JE). Dinah is not mentioned in the present roster, and v. 24 leads us to believe that Benjamin was born in Mesopotamia (*cf.,* vv. 16-18, E).

According to 27:41 (J) Isaac was approaching the end of his life when Jacob set out on his wanderings to Mesopotamia. We are now surprised to read (vv. 27-29) that well over twenty years later (*cf.,* 31:38, 41, JE) Jacob returned to find his father alive. But the Priestly author follows his own chronology, and he does not strive for consistency with other contributors to the Genesis narrative. Jacob met his aged father at the place where Abraham had bought a tomb and where he had buried Sarah (v. 27; *cf.,* 23:2, 17, 19, P). The Priestly author doesn't seem to know of the enmity that existed between Jacob and Esau (*cf.,* chap. 27, J), nor of the fact that Esau dwelt in the south, away from Hebron (*cf.,* 25:25, and see comment above p. 146; 32:3; 33:16). In any case, he represents the two brothers as dutifully performing the burial rites of their father, just as Isaac and Ishmael had buried their father at the same spot (cf., 25:8-9, P).

The Schemer Who Was Chosen

From now on in the Genesis narrative Jacob's story will be intimately bound up with that of his son Joseph, so that this may be an appropriate place for us to pause briefly to reflect on Jacob's life and on his role in God's plan. We have seen this patriarch to have been a man of greed and ambition who could stoop to the meanest tricks to reach his selfish goals. His unscrupulous trickery almost cost him his life, and involved him in a painful exile of twenty years duration. Even in exile he remained a crafty schemer who met crookedness with sharp practice. Up to the incident at Peniel we hear of no piety in his life, and we hear little enough about the direct action of God in his career. In short, we don't see much in Jacob that would suggest that he was a divinely chosen agent who had an important part to play in furthering God's plan for the world. Yet this unlikely candidate was the recipient of a divine promise (*cf.*, 28:13-15), and he whose life of sojourning was continually marked by insecurity, came safely from all hazards, because the Lord protected him in all his wanderings (*cf.*, 31:7; 32:10).

XI. THE JOSEPH STORY
37:1—50:26

Literary Background

The Priestly author who inserted a list of the descendants of Ishmael after his account of the death of Abraham (*cf.,* 25:7-18) also added a genealogy of the family of Esau (chap. 36) after his story of the death of Jacob (35:27-29). Thus, although Ishmael and Esau were not destined to play a part in God's plan of salvation, the Priestly author does not exclude them from his horizon. After chap. 36, however, Esau's descendants disappear from the Genesis saga, and the remaining chapters of the book, except chaps. 38 and 49, tell the intriguing tale of Joseph, son of Jacob.

The Joseph story is remarkably different in structure and style from the patriarchal stories in chaps. 12-36. Whereas the earlier stories can be broken down into individual units that once had an independent existence, the Joseph story is a much more consecutive narrative in which the separate incidents are constructed into a biographic sequence, so that each element in the story derives its meaning from its relation to the whole. In chaps. 12-36 the J,E, and P sources were often simply placed side by side, so that they can be rather easily distinguished; in the Joseph story the J and E sources, with a few minor contributions from P, have been moulded into a consistent and free-flowing plot with such skill that the average reader is unaware that the story is a combination of originally independent sources. Indeed there are many recent writers who claim that one cannot identify two continuous sources in the Joseph story at all. However, as we shall note, scholars have detected a few clues that often help to identify the authors of individual passages. Unlike the earlier patriarchal narratives the Joseph story, apart from 46:1-5, tells of no theophanies, and it describes no direct divine interventions in the lives of the protagonists. We do of course hear of dreams and their interpretation, but belief in dreams as a means of divine communication was widespread in the contemporary Middle East and not something specific to the faith of Israel. Again, unlike the earlier chapters which contain several cult-legends (*cf.,* 12:7-8; 28:16-22), the Joseph story shows no interest in cult centres and shrines.

It has been pointed out in recent years that the Joseph story has many points of contact with the Wisdom Literature of Israel, which was practical and secular, rather than theological or cultic. It is true, of course, that Joseph is described as a young man, who by virtue of his force of character and of his wise decisions, climbed from the lowest rung in the social ladder to the highest office in Egypt. While it is also true that Joseph appears as the model courtier, discreet and wise (*cf.,* 41:33, 39), who has the natural talent to advise rulers and to guide the affairs of the state, he is also portrayed as a man who feared the Lord (*cf.,* 42:18; 39:9), who enjoyed God's continued assistance (*cf.,* 39:2-3, 21, 23), and who attributed his personal talents to God (*cf.,* 40:8; 41:16, 39). Joseph believed that his coming to Egypt was divinely ordained (*cf.,* 45:5-8), and he acknowledged that God could use the evil he suffered to bring about good (*cf.,* 50:20). So although the Joseph story may have points of similarity with Wisdom Literature it is not totally lacking in theological motifs and religious background.

Historical Background

Although the casual reader of Genesis might regard the Joseph story as a factual account of events that explain the presence of the Israelites in Egypt, it is generally accepted that the authors of the story were not primarily interested in history. We certainly cannot hope to reconstruct a biography of Joseph from the data supplied in the narrative, and scholars cannot even agree on the question of what period of Egyptian history might form the most plausible setting for the adventures described in the story. Many writers maintain that the age of the *Hyksos* is the most likely period for Joseph's rise to power. The *Hyksos* were Asiatic invaders who controlled the Delta and Upper Egypt from about 1720-1550 B.C. These conquerors included Semitic elements, who would probably give a good reception to fellow Semites like Jacob and his family who came to the Nile valley in search of food. The Hyksos regime would also have afforded opportunities for young Semites like Joseph to gain positions of power in Egypt. What is certain is that during the Hyksos rule the movement of people from Syria and Palestine to Egypt was relatively easy, and during that time the migration of Jacob's family to Egyptian territory would not have been an extraordinary happening. Since the Hyksos era is approximately four hundred years before the probable date of the Exodus (c. 1250 B.C.) a Hyksos date for the descent of Jacob's family to Egypt would fit in with the biblical tradition which teaches that the stay in Egypt lasted four hundred years (*cf.,* Gen 15:13; Exod 12:40-41).

However, we know from extra-biblical records that Semites were allowed into Egypt at all times, and that some among them attained high offices at different periods in Egypt's history. Therefore, it cannot be said that the Hyksos era is the only period that provides a congenial background for the Joseph story. In fact, some writers claim that the so-called Amarna period (1370-1353 B.C.) supplies an appropriate setting for the story. But to whatever historical period we assign the events recorded in the Joseph story, our knowledge of Egypt and of the incursions of Semites into that country assure us that Joseph need not be regarded as a purely fictional character. It may well be that the biblical narrative oversimplifies complex historical events, and that Joseph's connection with the twelve tribes is not as clear as the story suggests. It may be too that the tradition of the descent of Jacob's sons into Egypt telescopes into one story the movement of different groups of Asiatics into the Nile valley at different times. In any case, the Joseph story represents a historical tradition that records the arrival of Israel's ancestors in what was to become for them a land of bondage. However, we must not be tempted to regard that story as raw source-material for the modern historian.

A FATHER'S FAVORITE
37:1-4 (PJ)

> **37** Jacob dwelt in the land of his father's sojournings, in the land of Canaan. ²This is the history of the family of Jacob.
>
> Joseph, being seventeen years old, was shepherding the flock with his brothers; he was a lad with the sons of Bilhah and Zilpah, his father's wives; and Joseph brought an ill report of them to their father. ³Now Israel loved Joseph more than any other of his children, because he was the son of his old age; and he made him a long robe with sleeves. ⁴But when his brothers saw that their father loved him more than all his brothers, they hated him, and could not speak peaceably to him.

Verses 1-2, which we owe to the Priestly author, form a transition from a story centred on Jacob to one that has Joseph as its subject. With v. 1 we leave Jacob dwelling in the land of Canaan—in Hebron, according to the Priestly author's notation in 35:27-29—and in v. 2 our attention is directed to Joseph. The typically Priestly formula *This is the history* (Hebrew *toledoth*) *of the family of Jacob* (v. 2; *cf.*, 2:4a; see comment above p. 32) forms a title for the complex series of events that make up the story of Jacob and his family. Verse 2b associates Joseph only with the sons of Bilhah and Zilpah, the handmaids of Rachel and Leah respectively (*cf.,* 29:31—30:24). This is rather surprising, since Dan and Naphtali, Gad and Asher, the sons of the handmaids (*cf.,* 30:11-13), play no part in the following drama of Joseph's life. The "ill report" which Joseph brought to Jacob is not explained, and the alleged misdemeanours of his brothers remain unspecified. Although the Priestly author does not explicitly link the tale-bearing episode with the brothers' later antipathy toward Joseph, we can readily see how the informer would become the object of his brothers' hatred and scorn.

Verses 3-4 (J) raise a few problems for the commentator. In view of the fact that Jacob was in the prime of life when Joseph was born (*cf.,* 29:31—30:24, JE), the latter can hardly be called the son of his father's old age. There may be here an indication that the Joseph story was once independent of the Jacob Saga. The meaning of the phrase *a long robe with sleeves* is far from clear. It is generally agreed that the traditional rendering, *a coat of many colours,* which is based on the Greek and Latin versions of the Bible, is incorrect. The phrase occurs in 2 Sam 13:18 to describe the garments worn by royalty. Whatever the nature of the garment, whether, as some claim, it was a long garment with sleeves such as ordinary laborers would not wear, or, as others would have it, a richly ornamented robe that would befit a king, it was a symbol of the preferential treatment which Joseph received, and it provoked the envy and hatred of his brothers.

JOSEPH HAD A DREAM
37:5-11 (E)

⁵Now Joseph had a dream, and when he told it to his brothers they only hated him the more. ⁶He said to them, "Hear this dream which I have dreamed: ⁷behold, we were binding sheaves in the field, and lo, my sheaf arose

and stood upright; and behold, your sheaves gathered round it, and bowed down to my sheaf." [8]His brothers said to him, "Are you indeed to reign over us? Or are you indeed to have dominion over us?" So they hated him yet more for his dreams and for his words. [9]Then he dreamed another dream, and told it to his brothers, and said, "Behold, I have dreamed another dream; and behold the sun, the moon, and eleven stars were bowing down to me." [10]But when he told it to his father and to his brothers, his father rebuked him, and said to him, "What is this dream that you have dreamed? Shall I and your mother and your brothers indeed come to bow ourselves to the ground before you?" [11]And his brothers were jealous of him, but his father kept the saying in mind.

Unlike earlier Elohist passages which say that God or his angels appeared in dreams (*cf.,* 20:3-7; 28:10-12; 31:11, 24), the present dream accounts mention neither God nor angels. This is in harmony with the general tenor of the Joseph story which allows events to develop without overt supernatural intervention, and in which dreams are simply cryptic communications that require interpretation. We notice too that the present passage tells of two dreams, one about sheaves (vv. 6-8), and one about the heavenly bodies (v. 9). This coupling of dreams is also characteristic of the Joseph story, which tells us that the head butler, the head baker, and Pharaoh each had two dreams (*cf.,* 40:5-19; 41:1-7). The ancients regarded dreams as means of divine communication, and as prefigurations of events to come. The interpretation of dreams was a science, and whole treatises were written on the subject. Like all their contemporaries, Joseph's father and brothers took dreams very seriously, and they were greatly disturbed by what Joseph had seen in his dreams. For the dreams clearly conveyed the message that Joseph was destined to take precedence over his brothers, and even over his father and mother. Joseph's family immediately saw the implications of the dreams. His father sternly rebuked him for his visions of grandeur, and, clearly worried by the troublesome affair, he kept his son's strange dream in mind. Joseph's brothers were obviously annoyed by his pretensions, and they cordially detested the ambitious dreamer.

We may note in passing that the vision of the family work-force binding sheaves (v. 7) corresponds to other passages (*cf.*, 26:12; 27:27-28) which show that semi-nomads semetimes settled down for a sufficiently long period to engage in agriculture. Another interesting fact is that v. 10 implies that Joseph's mother is still alive. Obviously, then, the present tradition knew nothing about the death of Rachel (*cf.*, 35:16-18), and we may have here another indication that the Joseph story was once independent of the other patriarchal narratives.

HERE COMES THE DREAMER
37:12-36 (JE)

12Now his brothers went to pasture their father's flock near Shechem. 13And Israel said to Joseph, "Are not your brothers pasturing the flock at Shechem? Come, I will send you to them." And he said to him, "Here I am." 14So he said to him, "Go now, see if it is well with your brothers, and with the flock; and bring me word again." So he sent him from the valley of Hebron, and he came to Shechem. 15And a man found him wandering in the fields; and the man asked him, "What are you seeking?" 16"I am seeking my brothers," he said, "tell me, I pray you, where they are pasturing the flock." 17And the man said, "They have gone away, for I heard them say, 'Let us go to Dothan.'" So Joseph went after his brothers, and found them at Dothan. 18They saw him afar off, and before he came near to them they conspired against him to kill him. 19They said to one another, "Here comes this dreamer. 20Come now, let us kill him and throw him into one of the pits; then we shall say that a wild beast has devoured him, and we shall see what will become of his dreams." 21But when Reuben heard it, he delivered him out of their hands, saying, "Let us not take his life." ²² And Reuben said to them, "Shed no blood; cast him into this pit here in the wilderness, but lay no hand upon him"— that he might rescue him out of their hand, to restore him to his father. ²³So when Joseph came to his brothers, they stripped him of his robe, the long robe with sleeves that he wore; ²⁴and they took him and cast him into a pit. The pit was empty, there was no water in it.

²⁵Then they sat down to eat; and looking up they saw a caravan of Ishmaelites coming from Gilead, with their camels bearing gum, balm, and myrrh, on their way to carry it down to Egypt. ²⁶Then Judah said to his brothers, "What profit is it if we slay our brother and conceal his blood? ²⁷Come, let us sell him to the Ishmaelites, and let not our hand be upon him, for he is our brother, our own flesh." And his brothers heeded him. ²⁸Then Midianite traders passed by; and they drew Joseph up and lifted him out of the pit, and sold him to the Ishmaelites for twenty shekels of silver; and they took Joseph to Egypt.

²⁹When Reuben returned to the pit and saw that Joseph was not in the pit, he rent his clothes ³⁰and returned to his brothers, and said, "The lad is gone; and I, where shall I go?" ³¹Then they took Joseph's robe, and killed a goat, and dipped the robe in the blood; ³²and they sent the long robe with sleeves and brought it to their father, and said, "This we have found; see now whether it is your son's robe or not." ³³And he recognized it, and said, "It is my son's robe; a wild beast has devoured him; Joseph is without doubt torn to pieces." ³⁴Then Jacob rent his garments, and put sackcloth upon his loins, and mourned for his son many days. ³⁵All his sons and all his daughters rose up to comfort him; but he refused to be comforted, and said, "No, I shall go down to Sheol to my son, mourning." Thus his father wept for him. ³⁶Meanwhile the Midianites had sold him in Egypt to Potiphar, an officer of Pharaoh, the captain of the guard.

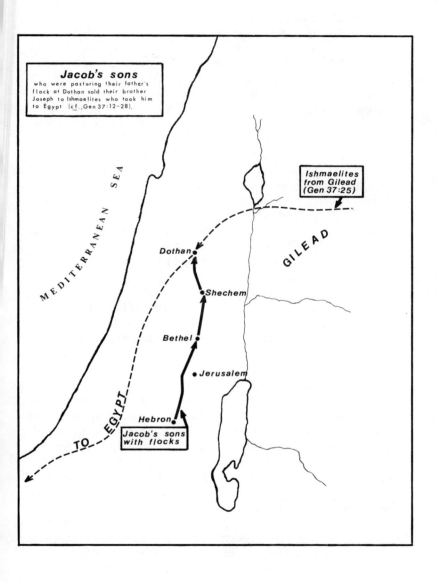

Jacob's sons
who were pasturing their father's
flock at Dothan sold their brother
Joseph to Ishmaelites who took him
to Egypt (cf.,Gen 37:12-28).

MEDITERRANEAN SEA

Ishmaelites
from Gilead
(Gen 37:25)

GILEAD

Dothan

Shechem

Bethel

Jerusalem

Hebron

Jacob's sons
with flocks

TO EGYPT

In much of this passage the Yahwist and Elohist sources are so closely interwoven that it is at times difficult to separate them. The Yahwist sets the scene for the ensuing dreams by describing the events that brought Joseph face to face with his brothers at Dothan (vv. 12-17). Since Jacob seems to have been in Hebron at this time (v. 14b), and Shechem (*ib*) is over fifty miles away to the north, with Dothan another fifteen miles further north, one is surprised to learn that Jacob's sons were pasturing their father's flocks so far away from the paternal dwelling place. It is also surprising to find that Jacob should send his favourite son, seemingly alone, on such a long and hazardous journey over difficult terrain where he was often in danger from predatory animals. Dothan was a very ancient city which was situated right on the caravan route that led from Mesopotamia, through Gilead, and via the coast road to Egypt.

From the point in the story where the brothers see Joseph (v. 18) we have two more or less complete accounts (JE) of the events that led to Joseph's transfer to Egypt. According to the Yahwist the brothers conspired to kill Joseph as soon as they saw him coming toward them at Dothan (18b). When Joseph actually reached them they stripped him of the robe that had made him so obnoxious to them (v. 23; *cf.,* vv. 3-4, J). They then sat down to a meal and discussed the best way of getting rid of their hated brother (vv. 25-28). Their murderous deliberations were interrupted when there arrived on the scene a caravan of Ishmaelites who provided Judah with an opportunity to save Joseph from death. Selling their brother to slave-dealers seemed a preferable alternative to murder, which, even if concealed, would cry out from the ground for vengeance (*cf.,* 4:10 J). The Ishmaelite traders were, of course, cousins of Jacob's sons, since they were descendants of Abraham by Hagar (*cf.,* 16:11-12, 15; 25:12-18; see comment to 16:12, above p. 107). The "gum, balm, and myrrh" (v. 25) which the Ishmaelites took to Egypt were aromatic, resinous products, that were used for medicinal purposes, as incense, and in embalming. We have no way of establishing the value of the "twenty shekels of silver" which the traders paid for Joseph (v. 28b), but Lev 27:5-6, basing, as it seems, a man's value on his capacity to work, determined that a male under twenty years of age was worth this sum. Having sold Joseph the brothers took his robe, dipped it in goat's blood, and took it to Jacob as a proof that the favourite son had been killed by wild animals (vv. 31-33). The thought that Joseph was dead caused Jacob such grief that his mourning would continue until he would rejoin his beloved son in Sheol (v. 35). This is the first mention of Sheol in the Bible, and it tells us nothing about the nature of the place, not about the kind of existence that is the lot of the dead. Certainly the Yahwist did not visualize Sheol as a place where Jacob would enjoy reunion with Joseph, but rather as a place of grim silence (*cf.,* Ps 94:17), where one has no communication with God (*cf.,* Ps 6:5), and where there is only gloom, inactivity, and powerlessness (*cf.,* Isa 14:9-11).

According to the Elohist's story also, the brothers decided to kill Joseph when they saw him coming toward them (vv. 19-20). Having earlier recorded Joseph's dreams (vv. 5-11), the Elohist now has the brothers refer to him as *this dreamer*, literally, *this master of dreams*. Whereas the Yahwist had told us that it was Judah who dissuaded his brothers from killing Joseph (vv. 26-27), the Elohist assures us that it was Reuben who intervened to save his brother's life (vv. 21-22). Reuben figures several times in the Elohist tradition, and he is generally shown in a favorable light (*cf.,* 42:22, 37). Reuben's counsel prevailed, and Joseph was thrown into an empty cistern (v. 24). Such cisterns collected the winter rains, but were dry in summer, and could be used as prisons from which one could not escape (*cf.,* Jer 38:6f., 9f). At the opportune time Midianites, who, like the Ishmaelites of v. 25, were cousins of the Hebrews (*cf.,* 25:1-2), passed by, and unnoticed by the brothers, kidnapped Joseph, and took him to Egypt (v. 28b). When Reuben discovered the empty cistern he was utterly shocked, and displayed his grief with the traditional gesture of tearing his clothes (vv. 29-30). The Elohist version of the story doesn't tell how the brothers communicated the dreadful news to the father, but the latter's rending of his garments (v. 34a) expressed his horror on realizing the fate of his son. Wearing sackcloth (v. 34a), and weeping bitterly (v. 35c), the bereaved father pondered on the tragedy that had come upon him. The Elohist ends this episode with the statement that the Midianites sold Joseph in Egypt, and thus sets the scene for a new act on a new stage.

JUDAH AND TAMAR
38:1-11 (J)

38 It happened at that time that Judah went down from his brothers, and turned in to a certain Adullamite, whose name was Hirah. ²There Judah saw the daughter of a certain Canaanite whose name was Shua; he married her and went in to her, ³and she conceived and bore a son, and he called his name Er. ⁴Again she conceived and bore a son, and she called his name Onan. ⁵Yet again she bore a son, and she called his name Shelah. She was in Chezib when she bore him. ⁶And Judah took a wife for Er his first-born, and her name was Tamar. ⁷But Er, Judah's first-born, was wicked in the sight of the Lord; and the Lord slew him. ⁸Then Judah said to Onan, "Go in to your brother's wife, and perform the duty of a brother-in-law to her, and raise up offspring for your brother." ⁹But Onan knew that the offspring would not be his; so when he went in to his brother's wife he spilled the semen on the ground, lest he should give offspring to his brother. ¹⁰And what he did was displeasing in the sight of the Lord, and he slew him also. ¹¹Then Judah said to Tamar his daughter-in-law, "Remain a widow in your father's house, till Shelah my son grows up"—for he feared that he would die, like his brothers. So Tamar went and dwelt in her father's house.

This rather unedifying narrative abruptly interrupts the Joseph story, and must be regarded as an originally independent tradition which the Yahwist incorporated into his narrative. The statement that "Judah went down from his brothers" (v. 1) means that he left them in the central highlands where they tended their flocks, and went to the plain southwest of Jerusalem where the Canaanites dwelt. The author records Judah's marriage to the Canaanite woman (v. 2) without adding any note of condemnation such as we found in 24:3 (J) and 28:1 (P). In due course Judah married his firstborn son, Er, to a woman who bore the typically Canaanite name Tamar, meaning "palm-tree" (v. 6). Upon Er's untimely death (v. 7) Judah called on his second son, Onan, to "perform the duty of brother-in-law" to his brother's widow (v. 8). This command presupposes an ancient custom according to which the brother of a deceased man was obliged to raise a family for the latter through his widow. According to this custom, which was known as levirate, and which was later enshrined in Israel's law (*cf.,* Deut 25:5-10), the children whom the widow bore to her new husband were considered the children and heirs of her first husband. Onan, for some reason about which our story remains silent, refused to satisfy his levirate obligation to his brother (v. 9). While pretending to perform his sacred duty he ensured that his action would not have its natural effect, and he thus merited a place for his name in the vocabulary of the moral theologians. The biblical author passes no moral judgment on his incomplete sexual act, but informs us that because of his failure to do what custom demanded of him he came to an untimely end (v. 10). Having seen the fate of his two elder sons, Judah came to the conclusion that Tamar was ill-omened, and he hesitated to give her yet a third son as the law of levirate prescribed (v. 11).

LEVIRATE FULFILLMENT BY RUSE
38:12-23

[12]In course of time the wife of Judah, Shua's daughter, died; and when Judah was comforted, he went up to Timnah to his sheepshearers, he and his friend Hirah the

Adullamite. ¹³And when Tamar was told, "Your father-in-law is going up to Timnah to shear his sheep," ¹⁴she put off her widow's garments, and put on a veil, wrapping herself up, and sat at the entrance to Enaim, which is on the road to Timnah; for she saw that Shelah was grown up, and she had not been given to him in marriage. ¹⁵When Judah saw her, he thought her to be a harlot, for she had covered her face. ¹⁶He went over to her at the road side, and said, "Come let me come in to you," for he did not know that she was his daughter-in-law. She said, "What will you give me, that you may come in to me?" ¹⁷He answered, "I will send you a kid from the flock." And she said, "Will you give me a pledge, till you send it?" ¹⁸He said, "What pledge shall I give you?" She replied, "Your signet and your cord, and your staff that is in your hand." So he gave them to her, and went in to her, and she conceived by him. ¹⁹Then she arose and went away, and taking off her veil she put on the garments of her widowhood.

²⁰When Judah sent the kid by his friend the Adullamite, to receive the pledge from the woman's hand, he could not find her. ²¹And he asked the men of the place, "Where is the harlot who was at Enaim by the wayside?" And they said, "No harlot has been here." ²²So he returned to Judah, and said, "I have not found her; and also the men of the place said, 'No harlot has been here.'" ²³And Judah replied, "Let her keep the things as her own, lest we be laughed at; you see, I sent this kid, and you could not find her."

After some time it became obvious to Tamar that Judah had no intention of giving Shelah to her as husband (v. 14), and that her desire to continue her first husband's line was being frustrated. So the resourceful lady devised a plot which would bring Judah himself to fulfil the levirate obligation. On the occasion of the sheep-shearing festivities (*cf.*, 31:19, and see comment above p. 180) she disguised herself as a harlot and seated herself in a strategic place, hoping to attract the attentions of her father-in-law, who was now a widower (vv. 12-14). Harlots who paraded their readiness to do business with passers-by were not unknown in ancient Palestine (*cf.,* Jer 3:2; Ezek 16:25), and the author of our present passage takes no offence at Tamar's ruse. The bargaining between Judah and Tamar (vv. 16-18) sounds squalid to us, but it shows how the clever Tamar ensured that her plan would have the desired effect of giving her a son who would be recognized as the legitimate child of her dead husband. When she possessed Judah's signet, cord, and staff as a pledge of his willingness to pay her what he regarded as her harlot's hire, she had positive proof of his identity. The *signet,* or more correctly, the *seal,* as the Hebrew word is rendered in NAB and NEB, was a little cylinder of ivory, stone or wood, which when rolled across the wet surface of a clay tablet reproduced the distinctive pattern which was incised on the seal. The owner of such a seal wore it on a *cord* around his neck, so that when required he could use it to stamp freshly moulded tablets. The *staff* which Tamar demanded would also bear a distinctive design that would identify its owner. No wonder, then, that the far-seeing widow was anxious to possess the seal and staff with a view to playing them as her trumps at the appropriate time. She was in no hurry to exchange these precious items for the kid that had been promised to her, and when Judah sent a deputy to reclaim the seal and staff that served as his identity cards, his "harlot" was nowhere to be found (vv. 20-23).

CANAANITE ANCESTRESS AND FIRST-BORN
38:24-30 (J)

²⁴About three months later Judah was told, "Tamar your daughter-in-law has played the harlot; and moreover she is with child by harlotry." And Judah said, "Bring her out and let her be burned." ²⁵As she was being brought out, she sent word to her father-in-law, "By the man to whom these belong, I am with child." And she said," Mark, I pray you, whose these are, the signet and

the cord and the staff." 26Then Judah acknowledged them and said, "She is more righteous than I, inasmuch as I did not give her to my son Shelah." And he did not lie with her again.

27When the time of her delivery came, there were twins in her womb. 28And when she was in labor, one put out a hand; and the midwife took and bound on his hand a scarlet thread, saying, "This came out first." 29But as he drew back his hand, behold, his brother came out; and she said, "What a breach you have made for yourself!" Therefore his name was called Perez. 30Afterward his brother came out with the scarlet thread upon his hand; and his name was called Zerah.

When Tamar's pregnancy became known, Judah, who had earlier got rid of her by sending her to her father's house (v. 11), proceeded to treat her as one of his own family, and to act as judge over her (vv. 24-25). Since, according to the levirate custom, Tamar was regarded as betrothed to her brother-in-law, the intercourse which brought about her pregnancy was considered adultery. According to later Israelite law the punishment for adultery was death by stoning (*cf.,* Deut 22:22-24), while death by burning was reserved for the daughter of a priest who became a harlot (*cf.,* Lev 21:9). Judah's sentence of death by burning on Tamar thus seems to reflect an older legal custom.

When Tamar produced the seal and staff to prove that Judah was the father of her unborn child (vv. 25-26) the patriarch was quickly convinced by the evidence. He not only admitted his responsibility, but absolved Tamar of all guilt, and acknowledged his failure to give his third son to her in marriage as the customary law stipulated. The statement "he did not lie with her again" suggests that from then on he treated her as his daughter-in-law. However, the text fails to tell us if Shelah ever took Tamar to wife.

The story of the pre-natal competition between Tamar's twins (vv. 27-30) reminds one immediately of the intra-uterine jostling described in 25:21-26. The struggle between the unborn twins, and Perez' acquisition of the rights of the firstborn, foreshadows the precedence of the tribe of Perez over that of Zerah. In fact, David, whose tribe was to dominate much of the early history of Israel, was descended from Perez (*cf.,* 1 Chron 2:5-15; Ruth 4:18-22).

The story of Judah and Tamar which may sound somewhat scandalous to us, was taken over by the Yahwist from some pre-existing source. In its present form the story portrays Tamar, the Canaanite woman, as the innocent partner, while Judah stands condemned for his failure to comply with traditional law. The dramatic episode shows that in spite of Judah's weakness God's plan for his people was not frustrated. Judah's line was not extinguished, because God chose to use the stratagem of a pagan woman as a means of fulfilling his plan of salvation. The woman whom Judah would have put to death was destined to become the ancestress of the royal tribe to which David belonged, and her name would figure in the genealogy of Jesus (*cf.,* Matt 1:3).

THE RISE OF JOSEPH
39:1-6a

39 Now Joseph was taken down to Egypt, and Potiphar, an officer of Pharaoh, the captain of the guard, an Egyptian, bought him from the Ishmaelites who had brought him down there. ²The Lord was with Joseph, and he became a successful man; and he was in the house of his master the Egyptian, ³and his master saw that the Lord was with him, and that the Lord caused all that he did to prosper in his hands. ⁴So Joseph found favor in his sight and attended him, and he made him overseer of his house and put him in charge of all that he had. ⁵From the time that he made him overseer in his house and over all that he had the Lord blessed the Egyptian's house for Joseph's sake; the blessing of the Lord was upon all that he had, in house and field. ⁶So he left all that he had in Joseph's charge; and having him he had no concern for anything but the food which he ate.

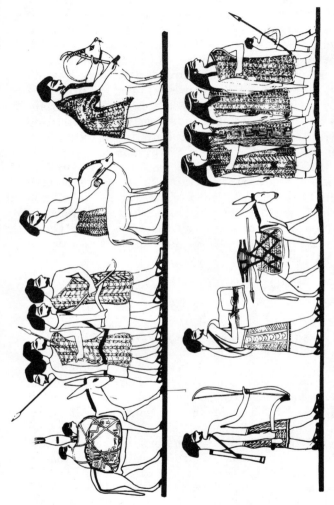

This tomb painting from Beni Hasan in Middle Egypt dates from 1892 B.C., that is, from approximately the time of Abraham. The beasts of burden are donkeys, not camels. The men have cut their hair and beards and wear short skirts and sandals. The women have long hair, and wear long dresses and shoes. The men carry bows and spears, water-skins, a lyre and bellows. (Courtesy of American Schools of Oriental Research)

After the digression of chap. 38 the Yahwist again takes up the story of Joseph whom he had left in the hands of Ishmaelite traders (*cf.,* 37:26-27, 28b). Joseph was rapidly promoted from the position of slave to that of personal attendant to his master. But if fortune smiled on him so that "he became a successful man" (v. 2), this was not entirely due to Joseph's intelligence or to his industry. The Yahwist attributes the young man's meteoric rise to an elevated position to the fact that God was with him (vv. 2, 5). Even his pagan master saw that the Lord caused all that Joseph did to prosper (vv. 3, 5). The statement that Joseph's master "had no concern for anything but the food which he ate" (v. 6b) may simply mean that he had such confidence in his capable servant that he could hand over all responsibility to him (*cf.,* v. 6a). Or it may mean that because of the dietary laws which he as an Egyptian had to observe, the master did not wish to entrust the preparation of his meals to a foreigner (*cf.,* 43:32, J).

THE FALL OF JOSEPH
39:6b-23

Now Joseph was handsome and goodlooking. [7]And after a time his master's wife cast her eyes upon Joseph, and said, "Lie with me." [8]But he refused and said to his master's wife, "Lo, having me my master has no concern about anything in the house, and he has put everything that he has in my hand; [9]he is not greater in this house than I am; nor has he kept back anything from me except yourself, because you are his wife; how then can I do this great wickedness, and sin against God?" [10]And although she spoke to Joseph day after day, he would not listen to her, to lie with her or to be with her. [11]But one day, when he went into the house to do his work and none of the men of the house was there in the house, [12]she caught him by his garment, saying, "Lie with me." But he left his garment in her hand, and fled and got out of the house. [13]And when she saw that he had left his garment in her hand, and had fled out of the house, ¹⁴she called to the men of her household and said to them, "See, he has brought among us a Hebrew to insult us; he came in to me to lie with me, and I cried out with a loud voice; ¹⁵and when he heard that I lifted up my voice and cried, he left his garment with me, and fled and got out of the house." ¹⁶Then she laid up his garment by her until his master came home, ¹⁷and she told him the same story, saying, "The Hebrew servant, whom you have brought among us, came in to me to insult me; ¹⁸but as soon as I lifted up my voice and cried, he left his garment with me, and fled out of the house."

¹⁹When his master heard the words which his wife spoke to him, "This is the way your servant treated me," his anger was kindled. ²⁰And Joseph's master took him and put him into the prison, the place where the king's prisoners were confined, and he was there in prison. ²¹But the Lord was with Joseph and showed him steadfast love, and gave him favor in the sight of the keeper of the prison. ²²And the keeper of the prison committed to Joseph's care all the prisoners who were in the prison; and whatever was done there, he was the doer of it; ²³the keeper of the prison paid no heed to anything that was in Joseph's care, because the Lord was with him; and whatever he did, the Lord made it prosper.

The story of how Joseph's youthful good looks caused his temporary fall from power is one of the most brilliant passages in the Yahwist's narrative. When the lady of the house attempted to seduce the handsome Joseph, he not only rejected her advance but chided her in measured and dignified terms (vv. 7-9). Loyalty to his employer who had placed such trust in him, and fear of God before whom adultery would be an abomination, strengthened the young servant to resist temptation. Joseph's moral stance was closely linked to his religious conviction, and his motivation to resist the temptress was based on both ethics and piety. However, the lusty Egyptian lady did not easily take "no" for an answer, and she persisted "day after day" to pester Joseph. When coaxing failed, the frustrated woman physically seized Joseph, who, however, escaped her unwelcome embrace (vv. 11-12). Then the lust of the would-be seductress turned to hatred and to thoughts of revenge. She had the presence of mind to call the servants to see Joseph's abandoned garment which she intended to use as evidence against him (vv. 13-14). The term "Hebrew" which the angry lady used to describe Joseph occurs five times in the Joseph story (see besides the present text v. 17; 40:15; 41:12; 43:32). It refers, not to Joseph's ethnic origins but to the low social status to which he belonged. Like a related term, "Habiru," which occurs frequently in the literature of the ancient Near East, the word, "Hebrew," primarily designated a social rather than a national group. When Joseph's master heard his wife's story saw the garment which seemed to prove the truth of her claims, "his anger was kindled" (v. 19). But the punishment he meted out to Joseph is most surprising. Just as the Israelites regarded adultery as punishable by death (*cf.,* Deut 22:22), so did the Egyptians deal severely with adulterers or those who attempted adultery. That Joseph, a foreign servant, should have escaped with his life and got off with a prison sentence when a free-born Egyptian for the same crime could have expected death, is truly astonishing. We have no explanation for the lenient sentence imposed on Joseph except to say that God was on his side. Even in prison the Lord favored Joseph, so that the unfortunate servant who had been brought low by female treachery soon became unofficial head of the jail (vv. 21-23).

The story of the attempted seduction of an innocent young man occurs elsewhere in ancient literature. By far the closest parallel to the Joseph episode is the Egyptian *Tale of Two Brothers* which is known from a papyrus dating back to the thirteenth century B.C. According to this tale a frustrated wife sought unsuccessfully to seduce her husband's younger unmarried brother. When the latter nobly refused to respond, the angry wife accused him of trying to rape her. The gallant young brother, by means of miracles and self-castration succeeded in proving his innocence, and the husband proceeded to murder his slanderous wife. Commentators do not claim that the biblical story is directly dependent on the Egyptian tale, but they admit that the Hebrew writer used the same widely diffused folkloristic motif.

INTERPRETER OF DREAMS
40:1-23

The Elohist author of Chap. 40 seems not to have known about the ups and downs of Joseph's career as recorded by the Yahwist in chap. 39. He takes up the story which he left off at 37:36 with the statement that the Midianites sold Joseph in Egypt to "the captain of the guard." In 40:3-4 this same captain now appoints Joseph as servant of the royal prisoners. The Elohist picture of Joseph as menial servant of the prisoners (40:4) forms quite a contrast with the Yahwist image of the young Hebrew holding a position of highest responsibility in the prison (*cf.,* 39:22-23).

40:1-8

40 Some time after this, the butler of the king of Egypt and his baker offended their lord the king of Egypt. ²And Pharaoh was angry with his two officers, the chief butler and the chief baker, ³and he put them in custody in the house of the captain of the guard, in the prison where Joseph was confined. ⁴The captain of the guard charged Joseph with them, and he waited on them: and they continued for some time in custody. ⁵And one night they both dreamed—the butler and the baker of the king of Egypt, who were confined in the prison—each his own dream, and each dream with its own meaning. ⁶When Joseph came to them in the morning and saw them, they were troubled. ⁷So he asked Pharaoh's officers who were with him in custody in his master's house, "Why are your faces downcast today?" ⁸They said to him, "We have had dreams, and there is no one to interpret them." And

Joseph said to them, "Do not interpretations belong to God? Tell them to me, I pray you."

The butler, or cupbearer (NAB), was keeper and taster of the royal wines (*cf.*, vv. 11, 13, 21) and held a high position at court. Since the king's wine would be a powerful instrument in the hands of his enemies, the butler's role could be entrusted only to one whose loyalty was above suspicion. Such a trusted official who had access to the king had considerable influence at court, and could obtain favors for his friends. Joseph, for example, hoped that the butler, when set free from prison, would speak on his behalf (v. 14), and the butler did eventually make the representation that won Joseph his freedom and set him on the road to glory (*cf.*, 41:9-14). The royal baker would have had a somewhat similar position of trust and influence at court.

When the imprisoned butler and baker expressed their distress at having no one to interpret their dreams, Joseph, whom the Elohist has already associated with dreams and their interpretation (*cf.*, 37:5-11), confidently assured them that their problem was not beyond solution (v. 8). His claim that interpretation belongs to God takes dreams and their interpretation out of the sphere of superstition and magic and places them in God's control. God alone knows the future, and he alone directs human destiny.

40:9-23

⁹So the chief butler told his dream to Joseph, and said to him, "In my dream there was a vine before me, ¹⁰and on the vine there were three branches; as soon as it budded, its blossoms shot forth, and the clusters ripened into grapes. ¹¹Pharaoh's cup was in my hand; and I took the grapes and pressed them into Pharaoh's cup, and placed the cup in Pharaoh's hand." ¹²Then Joseph said to him, "This is its interpretation: the three branches are three days; ¹³within three days Pharaoh will lift up your head and restore you to your office; and you shall place Pharaoh's cup in his hand as formerly, when you were his

butler. [14]But remember me, when it is well with you, and do me the kindness, I pray you, to make mention of me to Pharaoh, and so get me out of this house. [15]For I was indeed stolen out of the land of the Hebrews; and here also I have done nothing that they should put me into the dungeon."

[16]When the chief baker saw that the interpretation was favorable, he said to Joseph, "I also had a dream: there were three cake baskets on my head, [17]and in the uppermost basket there were all sorts of baked food for Pharaoh, but the birds were eating it out of the basket on my head." [18]And Joseph answered, "This is its interpretation: the three baskets are three days; [19]within three days Pharaoh will lift up your head—from you!—and hang you on a tree; and the birds will eat the flesh from you."

[20]On the third day, which was Pharaoh's birthday, he made a feast for all his servants, and lifted up the head of the chief butler and the head of the chief baker among his servants. [21]He restored the chief butler to his butlership, and he placed the cup in Pharaoh's hand; [22]but he hanged the chief baker, as Joseph had interpreted to them. [23]Yet the chief butler did not remember Joseph, but forgot him.

The symbolism of the butler's dream (vv. 9-11) was not difficult to discover. Joseph confidently interpreted the image of the butler's pressing grapes into the Pharaoh's cup and giving the cup to the king as a prediction of the butler's restoration to his former post (vv. 12-13). Joseph's claim that he was stolen from his fatherland (v. 15) tallies with the data given in 37:28a, 36(E). To call Palestine of Joseph's time "the land of the Hebrews" (v. 15) is an obvious anachronism, since it was to remain the land of the Canaanites until after the Exodus.

In deciphering the baker's dream Joseph again used the image of "lifting the head" (v. 19) which he had used when acting as interpreter for the butler (v. 13). But the image that conveyed a joyful message to the butler spelled doom for the unfortunate baker. The idea of hanging a criminal's corpse on a tree, or on a stake (NAB), was not unknown in Israel (*cf.,* Deut 21:22; Josh 8:29, etc.), but such a violation of a corpse would have been particularly shocking among the Egyptians who had special reverence for the dead.

Joseph's interpretations proved correct (vv. 20-22). The butler was pardoned, and the baker hanged. But the butler forgot the request Joseph had made (v. 14), and left the servant who had befriended him to spend two more years (*cf.,* 41:1) in his prison surroundings.

SUDDEN RISE TO POWER
41:1-57

41 After two whole years, Pharaoh dreamed that he was standing by the Nile, ²and behold, there came up out of the Nile seven cows sleek and fat, and they fed in the reed grass. ³And behold, seven other cows, gaunt and thin, came up out of the Nile after them, and stood by the other cows on the bank of the Nile. ⁴And the gaunt and thin cows ate up the seven sleek and fat cows. And Pharaoh awoke. ⁵And he fell asleep and dreamed a second time; and behold, seven ears of grain, plump and good, were growing on one stalk. ⁶And behold, after them sprouted seven ears, thin and blighted by the east wind. ⁷And the thin ears swallowed up the seven plump and full ears. And Pharaoh awoke, and behold, it was a dream. ⁸So in the morning his spirit was troubled; and he sent and called for all the magicians of Egypt and all its wise men; and Pharaoh told them his dream, but there was none who could interpret it to Pharaoh.

Cows formed an important element in the economy of Egypt, so that cows coming up from the Nile where they went to drink, or where they stood in water to counteract the heat and the flies, fit well into the Egyptian background to the Pharaoh's dream. Ears of corn blighted by the east wind (*cf.,* Ezek 17:10; Hos 13:15), that is, by the *sirroco,* or *hamsin* as it is known in Egypt, also form part of the Egyptian landscape. The impression made on the Pharaoh by the dreams was so real that on awakening he had to convince himself that they were only dreams (v. 7b). The royal dreamer was greatly disturbed by his experience, and he lost no time in consulting experts in the science of dream interpretation who might discover the meaning of his cryptic visions. The obvious exaggeration involved in the statement that *all the magicians of Egypt* (v. 8) were baffled by the royal dreams serves to bring out the obvious superiority of Joseph who will interpret the dreams without any difficulty. Just as the Hebrew Moses will later outshine the Egyptians in performing marvellous signs (*cf.,* Exod 7-9), so does the Hebrew youth Joseph now put the experts in the science of dreams in the shade.

41:9-24

⁹Then the chief butler said to Pharaoh, "I remember my faults today. ¹⁰When Pharaoh was angry with his servants, and put me and the chief baker in custody in the house of the captain of the guard, ¹¹we dreamed on the same night, he and I, each having a dream with its own meaning. ¹²A young Hebrew was there with us, a servant of the captain of the guard; and when we told him, he interpreted our dreams to us, giving an interpretation to each man according to his dream. ¹³And as he interpreted to us, so it came to pass; I was restored to my office, and the baker was hanged."

¹⁴Then Pharaoh sent and called Joseph, and they brought him hastily out of the dungeon; and when he had shaved himself and changed his clothes, he came in before Pharaoh. ¹⁵And Pharaoh said to Joseph, "I have had a dream, and there is no one who can interpret it; and I have heard it said of you that when you hear a dream you can interpret it." ¹⁶Joseph answered Pharaoh, "It is not in me; God will give Pharaoh a favorable answer." ¹⁷Then Pharaoh said to Joseph, "Behold, in my dream I was

standing on the banks of the Nile; [18]and seven cows, fat and sleek came up out of the Nile and fed in the reed grass; [19]and seven other cows came up after them, poor and very gaunt and thin, such as I had never seen in all the land of Egypt. [20]And the thin and gaunt cows ate up the first seven fat cows, [21]but when they had eaten them no one would have known that they had eaten them, for they were still as gaunt as at the beginning. Then I awoke. [22]I also saw in my dream seven ears growing on one stalk, full and good; [23]and seven ears, withered, thin, and blighted by the east wind, sprouted after them, [24]and the thin ears swallowed up the seven good ears. And I told it to the magicians, but there was no one who could explain it to me."

The failure of the court sages to interpret Pharaoh's dream jogged the memory of the chief butler. His confession of his faults (v. 9) may refer to the offences that had occasioned his imprisonment, or, more probably, it may mean that his conscience pricked him because of his failure to come to the aid of Joseph who had helped him and who had asked for a favour in return (*cf.,* 40:9-15). In any case, he told the Pharaoh of the gifted young Hebrew who had proved his ability as an interpreter of dreams (vv. 10-13). As one would expect, Joseph was rushed to court (v. 14). The prisoner, who until now had continued to follow the Semite custom of wearing a beard, shaved himself as the Egyptians were wont to do, and dressed in a fashion befitting one who was to present himself before the Pharaoh. When the Pharaoh complimented the newly arrived young Hebrew on his talent as an interpreter of dreams (v. 15), Joseph disclaimed all professional skill in this area and attributed his ability to discover the meaning of dreams to divine enlightenment (v. 16). The royal dreamer was not interested in theological discussion about the source of Joseph's talent, and he proceeded to describe his dream to the newcomer (vv. 17-24).

41:25-45

²⁵Then Joseph said to Pharaoh, "The dream of Pharaoh is one; God has revealed to Pharaoh what he is about to do. ²⁶The seven good cows are seven years, and the seven good ears are seven years; the dream is one. ²⁷The seven lean and gaunt cows that came up after them are seven years, and the seven empty ears blighted by the east wind are also seven years of famine. ²⁸It is as I told Pharaoh, God has shown to Pharaoh what he is about to do. ²⁹There will come seven years of great plenty throughout all the land of Egypt, ³⁰but after them there will arise seven years of famine, and all the plenty will be forgotten in the land of Egypt; the famine will consume the land, ³¹and the plenty will be unknown in the land by reason of that famine which will follow, for it will be very grievous. ³²And the doubling of Pharaoh's dream means that the thing is fixed by God, and God will shortly bring it to pass. ³³Now therefore let Pharaoh select a man discreet and wise, and set him over the land of Egypt. ³⁴Let Pharaoh proceed to appoint overseers over the land, and take the fifth part of the produce of the land of Egypt during the seven plenteous years. ³⁵And let them gather all the food of these good years that are coming, and lay up grain under the authority of Pharaoh for food in the cities, and let them keep it. ³⁶That food shall be a reserve for the land against the seven years of famine which are to befall the land of Egypt, so that the land may not perish through the famine."

³⁷This proposal seemed good to Pharaoh and to all his servants. ³⁸And Pharaoh said to his servants, "Can we find such a man as this, in whom is the Spirit of God?" ³⁹So Pharaoh said to Joseph, "Since God has shown you all this, there is none so discreet and wise as you are; ⁴⁰you shall be over my house, and all my people shall order themselves as you command, only as regards the throne will I be greater than you." ⁴¹And Pharaoh said to Joseph, "Behold, I have set you over all the land of Egypt." ⁴²Then Pharaoh took his signet ring from his hand and put it on

Joseph's hand, and arrayed him in garments of fine linen,
and put a gold chain about his neck; [43]and he made him to
ride in his second chariot; and they cried before him, "Bow
the knee!" Thus he set him over all the land of Egypt.
[44]Moreover Pharaoh said to Joseph, "I am Pharaoh, and
without your consent no man shall lift up hand or foot in
all the land of Egypt." [45]And Pharaoh called Joseph's
name Zaphenathpaneah; and he gave him in marriage
Asenath, the daughter of Potiphera priest of On. So
Joseph went out over the land of Egypt.

The imagery involved in Pharaoh's dream was not very
mysterious, and Joseph had no problem in deciphering it. In
an agricultural society sleek cattle and plump ears of corn
were natural symbols of prosperity and plenty, while lean
cattle and withered corn augured scarcity and hunger. A
dream that showed the signs of scarcity devouring tokens of
plenty was a clear indication that famine would take the
place of abundance in the land. Famines which resulted
from the Nile's failure to inundate were not unknown in
Egypt. But a seven-year stretch of infertility must have been
extremely rare. Perhaps the author of the story does not
intend us to take the seven years literally, but wishes us to
see in the seven-year figure the symbol of a prolonged
famine that would grip the whole land. Joseph's assurance
to Pharaoh that God had shown the king what he was about
to do (v. 28), left no doubt about the inevitability of famine.
The fact that the dream was twofold provided Joseph with a
sign that the divine decree to send a famine was irrevocable
(v. 32).

Having interpreted the dreams Joseph took on the role of
counsellor and advised the king about the best procedure to
adopt in order to minimize the effects of the famine that
loomed ahead. Verses 33-36 give the impression that Joseph
was the first to propose the idea of storing grain as a
measure against possible future scarcity. Egyptian texts
show that in fact this policy had long been in operation in

the Nile valley. However that may be, the story tells us that the Pharaoh was so impressed by Joseph's counsel that he acknowledged his wisdom to be divinely bestowed (v. 39). He gave the young foreigner the task of putting into operation the scheme he had proposed, and he appointed him second-in-command, or vizier, over all the land of Egypt, so that he would have full power to implement his plans (vv. 40-41). By giving Joseph the royal signet ring (v. 42), which served the same purpose as the signet mentioned in 38:18 (see comment above p. 217), the Pharaoh appointed him as his own official representative and as executor of the royal decrees. Joseph's status was also symbolized by the fact that he rode in the king's "second chariot" (v. 43), that is, in the chariot immediately after that of the Pharaoh. Those who ran before Joseph's chariot to clear a way for him in the crowded streets cried out "Bow the knee" (v. 43, RSV). The meaning of the verb thus translated is not clear, and the Hebrew verb may be based on an Egyptian word meaning something like "make way" (NEB), or "Attention."

The giving of an Egyptian name to Joseph (v. 45) symbolized his official acceptance into the court of Pharaoh. His marriage to an Egyptian woman was fitting for one who held such a high position in Egypt; it would also strengthen his bonds with the people who had adopted him. Just as the Yahwist passed no moral judgment on Judah's marriage to a Canaanite woman (*cf.*, 38:2; see comment above p. 215), so the author of v. 45, who may also be the Yahwist, takes no exception to Joseph's marriage to an Egyptian. *On*, where Joseph's father-in-law functioned as a priest, was the city which the Greeks knew as Heliopolis, "the city of the sun," and it was situated a short distance northeast of Cairo. As its Greek name indicates the city was a centre of worship of the sun-god Re.

41:46-57

46Joseph was thirty years old when he entered the service of Pharaoh king of Egypt. And Joseph went out from the presence of Pharaoh, and went through all the land of Egypt. ⁴⁷During the seven plenteous years the earth brought forth abundantly, ⁴⁸and he gathered up all the food of the seven years when there was plenty in the land of Egypt, and stored up food in the cities; he stored up in every city the food from the fields around it. ⁴⁹And Joseph stored up grain in great abundance, like the sand of the sea, until he ceased to measure it, for it could not be measured.

⁵⁰Before the year of famine came, Joseph had two sons, whom Asenath, the daughter of Potiphera, priest of On, bore to him. ⁵¹Joseph called the name of the first-born Manasseh, "For," he said, "God has made me forget all my hardship and all my father's house." ⁵²The name of the second he called Ephraim, "For God has made me fruitful in the land of my affliction."

⁵³The seven years of plenty that prevailed in the land of Egypt came to an end; ⁵⁴and the seven years of famine began to come, as Joseph had said. There was famine in all lands; but in all the land of Egypt there was bread. ⁵⁵When all the land of Egypt was famished, the people cried to Pharaoh for bread; and Pharaoh said to all the Egyptians, "Go to Joseph; what he says to you, do." ⁵⁶So when the famine had spread over all the land, Joseph opened all the storehouses, and sold to the Egyptians, for the famine was severe in the land of Egypt. ⁵⁷Moreover, all the earth came to Egypt to Joseph to buy grain, because the famine was severe over all the earth.

The half verse (46a) which represents the Priestly author's sole contribution to this chapter, leads us to conclude that this source allowed thirteen years to pass between Joseph's descent into Egypt (37:2, P) and his rise to power. The birth of Joseph's sons, to whom he gave symbolic names, took place during the years of plenty (vv. 50-52). When the predicted famine came, disaster struck "all lands" (v. 54) except Egypt, where the provident Joseph was able to cater for the needs of his people.

THE BROTHERS AND THE VIZIER
42:1-38 (E)

42:1-17

42   When Jacob learned that there was grain in Egypt, he said to his sons, "Why do you look at one another?" ²And he said, "Behold, I have heard that there is grain in Egypt; go down and buy grain for us there, that we may live, and not die." ³So ten of Joseph's brothers went down to buy grain in Egypt. ⁴But Jacob did not send Benjamin, Joseph's brother, with his brothers, for he feared that harm might befall him. ⁵Thus the sons of Israel came to buy among the others who came, for the famine was in the land of Canaan.

⁶Now Joseph was governor over the land; he it was who sold to all the people of the land. And Joseph's brothers came, and bowed themselves before him with their faces to the ground. ⁷Joseph saw his brothers, and knew them, but he treated them like strangers and spoke roughly to them. "Where do you come from?" he said. They said, "From the land of Canaan, to buy food." ⁸Thus Joseph knew his brothers, but they did not know him. ⁹And Joseph remembered the dreams which he had dreamed of them; and he said to them, "You are spies, you have come to see the weakness of the land." ¹⁰They said to him, "No, my lord, but to buy food have your servants come. ¹¹We are all sons of one man, we are honest men, your servants are not spies." ¹²He said to them, "No, it is the weakness of the land that you have come to see." ¹³And they said, "We, your servants, are twelve brothers, the sons of one man in the land of Canaan; and behold, the youngest is this day with our father, and one is no more." ¹⁴But Joseph said to them, "It is as I said to you, you are spies. ¹⁵By this you shall be tested: by the life of Pharaoh, you shall not go from this place unless your youngest brother comes here. ¹⁶Send one of you, and let him bring your brother, while you remain in prison, that your words may be tested, whether there is truth in you; or else, by the life

of Pharaoh, surely you are spies." [17]And he put them all together in prison for three days.

The famine that affected all the earth (*cf.*, 41:54, 57) forced Jacob to allow his sons to join the caravans setting out for Egypt to buy food (vv. 1-3; *cf.*, 12:10; 26:1). Only Benjamin, the youngest brother, and, as Jacob believed, the only surviving son of the beloved Rachel (*cf.*, 30:23; 35:16-19), was kept behind lest anything should befall him on the precarious journey.

In making a subservient bow to the governor (v. 6b) the ten brothers were observing a ceremonial custom. But Joseph could see more than a ritual gesture in their prostration. He remembered the dream that his brothers would bow down before him (v. 9; *cf.*, 37:5-11, E), and he now saw the dream fulfilled. It is psychologically plausible that Joseph would recognize the brothers, while they would not see their brother whom they presumed dead (*cf.*, vv. 13, 22) in the "lord of the land" (v. 30), who shaved and dressed like an Egyptian (*cf.*, 41:14, 42), spoke in a language they did not understand (*cf.*, v. 23), and who even swore Egyptian oaths (*cf.*, vv. 15-16). The accusation of spying fits well into the Egyptian background of the story, since the Egyptians seem to have had an obsession about spies who, as Joseph said, might come "to see the weakness of the land," or "the weak points in our defences," as the NEB puts it (v. 9). In defending their innocence the brothers revealed details that must have pleased Joseph (vv. 10-13). His father was still alive, and his youngest brother was safe in the parental home. However, this good news did not soften his attitude to the panic-stricken brothers. He wished to test the truth of their protestations, and he insisted that one of them journey to Canaan and bring back Benjamin as a proof of the integrity of their intentions (vv. 15-16). As if giving the shattered brothers time to consider their dreary fate he had them locked in prison for three days (v. 17).

42:18-25

¹⁸On the third day Joseph said to them, "Do this and you will live, for I fear God: ¹⁹if you are honest men, let one of your brothers remain confined in your prison, and let the rest go and carry grain for the famine of your households, ²⁰and bring your youngest brother to me; so your words will be verified, and you shall not die." And they did so. ²¹Then they said to one another, "In truth we are guilty concerning our brother, in that we saw the distress of his soul, when he besought us and we would not listen; therefore is this distress come upon us." ²²And Reuben answered them, "Did I not tell you not to sin against the lad? But you would not listen. So now there comes a reckoning for his blood." ²³They did not know that Joseph understood them, for there was an interpretor between them. ²⁴Then he turned away from them and wept; and he returned to them and spoke to them. And he took Simeon from them and bound him before their eyes. ²⁵And Joseph gave orders to fill their bags with grain, and to replace every man's money in his sack, and to give them provisions for the journey. This was done for them.

On the third day of their imprisonment Joseph approached the brothers in a somewhat more conciliatory mood, and he spoke to them in a less intimidating manner (vv. 18-20). He made a new proposal, and instead of keeping nine brothers in prison while one went to fetch Benjamin, he kept one hostage and ordered the others to go to Canaan and to return with their youngest brother. Faced with the depressing prospect of having to tell their father that yet another member of the family was at least temporarily separated from the group, the anguished brothers saw their unhappy lot as a punishment for past wickedness (vv. 21-22; *cf.,* 37:18-36).

42:26-38

²⁶Then they loaded their asses with their grain, and departed. ²⁷And as one of them opened his sack to give his ass provender at the lodging place, he saw his money in the mouth of his sack; ²⁸and he said to his brothers, "My money has been put back; here it is in the mouth of my sack!" At this their hearts failed them and they turned trembling to one another, saying, "What is this that God has done to us?"

²⁹When they came to Jacob their father in the land of Canaan, they told him all that had befallen them, saying, ³⁰"The man, the lord of the land, spoke roughly to us, and took us to be spies of the land. ³¹But we said to him, 'We are honest men, we are not spies; ³²we are twelve brothers, sons of our father; one is no more, and the youngest is this day with our father in the land of Canaan.' ³³Then the man, the lord of the land, said to us, 'By this I shall know that you are honest men: leave one of your brothers with me, and take grain for the famine of your households, and go your way. ³⁴Bring your youngest brother to me; then I shall know that you are not spies but honest men, and I will deliver to you your brother, and you shall trade in the land.'"

³⁵As they emptied their sacks, behold, every man's bundle of money was in his sack; and when they and their father saw their bundles of money, they were dismayed. ³⁶And Jacob their father said to them, "You have bereaved me of my children: Joseph is no more, and Simeon is no more, and now you would take Benjamin; all this has come upon me." ³⁷Then Reuben said to his father, "Slay my two sons if I do not bring him back to you; put him in my hands, and I will bring him back to you." ³⁸But he said, "My son shall not go down with you, for his brother is dead, and he only is left. If harm should befall him on the journey you are to make, you would bring down my gray hairs with sorrow to Sheol."

When, on their way home (vv. 27-28, J), or on their arrival home (v. 35, E), the brothers discovered the money which Joseph had planted in their sacks (*cf.,* v. 25), they were aghast. They had no reason to think that the vizier intended the money as a gift. Perhaps the money was intended as a trap, so that the brothers could later be accused of theft (*cf.,* 43:18, J) and cast into prison. The brothers were totally disoriented by the whole confusing issue which they attributed to divine intervention (v. 28c). They were faced with a frightening dilemma: if they did not return to Egypt Simeon was doomed to languish in prison until death should deliver him; if they did return they might all end up in prison or in slavery.

When Jacob heard his sons' tragic tale (vv. 29-34), it was his turn to express consternation and grief (v. 36). Reuben, the Elohist's hero (*cf.,* v. 22; 37:21), once again plays the hero's part, and vouches for Benjamin's safe return (v. 37). Jacob's response to Reuben's offer is rather surprising. He seems to have been ready to sacrifice Simeon in order to ensure Benjamin's safety (v. 38). Some authors explain this apparent callousness by attributing v. 38 to the Yahwist who does not mention Simeon's imprisonment. On the biblical author's image of Sheol see the comment on 37:35, J (see above, p. 213).

SECOND TRIP TO EGYPT
43:1-34 (J)

43:1-15 (J)

43 Now the famine was severe in the land. ²And when they had eaten the grain which they had brought from Egypt, their father said to them, "Go again, buy us a little food." ³But Judah said to him, "The man solemnly warned us, saying, 'You shall not see my face unless your brother is with you.' ⁴If you will send our brother with us, we will go down and buy you food; ⁵but if you will not send him, we will not go down, for the man said to us, 'You shall not see my face, unless your brother is with you.'" ⁶Israel said, "Why did you treat me so ill as to tell the man that you had another brother?" ⁷They replied, "The man questioned us carefully about ourselves and our kindred, saying, 'Is your brother still alive? Have you another brother?' What we told him was in answer to these questions; could we in any way know that he would say, 'Bring your brother down'?" ⁸And Judah said to Israel his father, "Send the lad with me, and we will arise and go, that we may live and not die, both we and you and also our little ones. ⁹I will be surety for him; of my hand you shall require him. If I do not bring him back to you and set him before you, then let me bear the blame for ever; ¹⁰for if we had not delayed, we would now have returned twice."

¹¹Then their father Israel said to them, "If it must be so, then do this: take some of the choice fruits of the land in your bags, and carry down to the man a present, a little balm and a little honey, gum, myrrh, pistachio nuts, and almonds. ¹²Take double the money with you; carry back with you the money of your sacks; perhaps it was an oversight. ¹³Take also your brother, and arise, go again to the man; ¹⁴may God Almighty grant you mercy before the man, that he may send back your other brother and Benjamin. If I am bereaved of my children, I am bereaved." ¹⁵So the men took the present, and they took double the money with them, and Benjamin; and they arose and went down to Egypt, and stood before Joseph.

In permitting his sons to return to Egypt for more food (vv. 1-2) Jacob makes no mention of a hostage who lay in an Egyptian prison awaiting rescue by his brothers. In his reply to his father (vv. 3-5) Judah also fails to mention Simeon, and leaves us with the impression that the only reason for taking Benjamin to Egypt was to ensure that Joseph would sell more grain to the brothers (*cf.,* 42:19-20, 34, E). In explaining to Jacob why they had ever mentioned their younger brother to "the man," the brothers said that a series of direct questions had elicited the information from them (v. 7). They had in fact volunteered the information to Joseph in an effort to prove that they were not spies (*cf.,* 42:9-13, E). In order to persuade his father to allow Benjamin to go to Egypt, Judah, to whom the Yahwist gives a prominent role (*cf.,* 37:26-27), offered to accept responsibility for anything that might happen to him on the way (v. 9). Jacob reluctantly took the decision that circumstances forced upon him (v. 11a). But once again the patriarch appears as the shrewd dealer as he takes practical steps to ensure that things will turn out to his advantage. By sending generous gifts to the Pharaoh and by returning the money which his sons had found in their bags, he hoped to convince the king of his family's integrity and to win his benevolence (vv. 11b-15).

43:16-34

16When Joseph saw Benjamin with them, he said to the steward of his house, "Bring the men into the house, and slaughter an animal and make ready, for the men are to dine with me at noon." 17The man did as Joseph bade him, and brought the men to Joseph's house. 18And the men were afraid because they were brought to Joseph's house, and they said, "It is because of the money, which was replaced in our sacks the first time, that we are brought in, so that he may seek occasion against us and fall upon us, to make slaves of us and seize our asses." 19So they went up to the steward of Joseph's house, and spoke with him at the door of the house, 20and said, "Oh, my lord, we came down the first time to buy food; 21and when we came to the lodging place we opened our sacks, and there was every man's money in the mouth of his sack, our money in full weight; so we have brought it again with us, ²²and we have brought other money down in our hand to buy food. We do not know who put our money in our sacks." ²³He replied, "Rest assured, do not be afraid; your God and the God of your father must have put treasure in your sacks for you; I received your money." Then he brought Simeon out to them. ²⁴And when the man had brought the men into Joseph's house, and given them water, and they had washed their feet, and when he had given their asses provender, ²⁵they made ready the present for Joseph's coming at noon, for they heard that they should eat bread there.

²⁶When Joseph came home, they brought into the house to him the present which they had with them, and bowed down to him to the ground. ²⁷And he inquired about their welfare, and said, "Is your father well, the old man of whom you spoke? Is he still alive?" ²⁸They said, "Your servant our father is well, he is still alive." And they bowed their heads and made obeisance. ²⁹And he lifted up his eyes, and saw his brother Benjamin, his mother's son, and said, "Is this your youngest brother, of whom you spoke to me? God be gracious to you, my son!" ³⁰Then Joseph made haste, for his heart yearned for his brother, and he sought a place to weep. And he entered his chamber and wept there. ³¹Then he washed his face and came out; and controlling himself he said, "Let food be served." ³²They served him by himself and them by themselves, and the Egyptians who ate with him by them-selves, because the Egyptians might not eat bread with the Hebrews, for that is an abomination to the Egyptians. ³³And they sat before him, the first-born according to his birthright and the youngest according to his youth; and the men looked at one another in amazement. ³⁴Portions were taken to them from Joseph's table, but Benjamin's

portion was five times as much as any of theirs. So they drank and were merry with him.

An invitation to dine at the vizier's house (v. 16) was something the brothers could not possibly have foreseen, and the idea filled them with anxiety. The thought that the money they had found in their sacks (cf., 42:27-28, J) had been a trap filled them with foreboding, and they were quick to explain the whole situation to the steward (vv. 18-22). The steward expressed no surprise at their story, and calmed their fears by explaining that God's unseen hand had guided the whole affair (v. 23).

The brothers' repeated obeisance before the vizier and their generally obsequious approach (vv. 26, 28) reflect the confusion and awkwardness which the humble shepherd folk from Canaan must have felt in the elegant Egyptian court. The reader easily becomes involved in the moving story of Joseph's encounter with the full complement of his brothers, and one senses the emotion that overcame the vizier as he inquired about his aging father (vv. 29-31). Finally convinced that Joseph had no sinister motives in bringing them into his house, the brothers could relax and enjoy the meal which was served to them. Joseph, as befitted his dignity, dined separately, while his retinue ate at their own table, and the Hebrew family ate by themselves. This segregation was based on social and ritual taboos which established what a person might eat and with whom one might share a meal. The brothers were baffled, and perhaps somewhat worried, by Joseph's ability to seat them according to seniority (v. 33). The ritual of sending a choice portion of food from the host's table to his guests was an accepted sign of friendship (cf., John 13:26).

A FINAL TEST
44:1-34

44:1-13

44 Then he commanded the steward of his house, "Fill the men's sacks with food, as much as they can carry, and put each man's money in the mouth of his sack, ²and put my cup, the silver cup, in the mouth of the sack of the youngest, with his money for the grain." And he did as Joseph told him. ³As soon as the morning was light, the men were sent away with their asses. ⁴When they had gone but a short distance from the city, Joseph said to his steward, "Up, follow after the man; and when you overtake them, say to them, 'Why have you returned evil for good? Why have you stolen my silver cup? ⁵Is it not from this that my lord drinks, and by this that he divines? You have done wrong in so doing.'"

⁶When he overtook them, he spoke to them these words. ⁷They said to him, "Why does my lord speak such words as these? Far be it from your servants that they should do such a thing! ⁸Behold, the money which we found in the mouth of our sacks, we brought back to you from the land of Canaan; how then should we steal silver or gold from your lord's house? ⁹With whomever of your servants it be found, let him die, and we also will be my lord's slaves." ¹⁰He said, "Let it be as you say: he with whom it is found shall be my slave, and the rest of you shall be blameless." ¹¹Then every man quickly lowered his sack to the ground and every man opened his sack. ¹²And he searched, beginning with the eldest and ending with the youngest; and the cup was found in Benjamin's sack. ¹³Then they rent their clothes, and every man loaded his ass, and they returned to the city.

The sense of well-being which the meal in Joseph's house had generated in the brothers (*cf.*, 43:34c) was short-lived. Joseph appears to have played a malicious game as he contrived a scheme that would leave his innocent brothers open to the charge of theft (vv. 1-5). The money that was placed in the sacks is not mentioned again in the story, and the cup that was placed in Benjamin's bag was the only object that was later regarded as incriminating evidence (*cf.*, vv. 8, 12, 16f.). Since the cup was used for divination (*cf.*, vv. 5b, 15) it was a sacred object, and its theft would have constituted a very serious crime. The precise way in which Joseph might have used the cup for divination is not known. It is possible that signs of the future were discovered in the ripples when small objects were dropped into water or oil which were in the cup. Or perhaps oil and water may have been mixed, and some meaning found in the patterns which the oil might take on the surface of the water. Since divination of any kind was strictly forbidden in Israel (*cf.*, Lev 19:31; Deut 18:10-11, etc.) it may seem surprising that the biblical author records Joseph's divining activity without stricture. The Joseph story seems to have allowed its central character to follow Egyptian ways, and to have found nothing objectionable in his marriage to an Egyptian (*cf.*, 41:45), or in his role as an interpreter of dreams (*cf.*, 40; 41:9-33), or, in the present case, in his divination.

When the brothers were accused of theft, so certain were they of their innocence that they were ready to pronounce death on the thief, and to accept collective responsibility for the theft if one of them were found to have the cup (v. 9). The steward who had pursued the brothers rejected the idea of corporate liability, as Joseph was to do later (v. 17), and declared that the culprit alone would be punished (v. 10). The brothers were stunned when the fatal cup was found in Benjamin's sack (v. 12), and they prepared to retrace their steps to Joseph's court where they could only expect humiliation and severe punishment.

44:14-17

¹⁴When Judah and his brothers came to Joseph's house, he was still there; and they fell before him to the ground. ¹⁵Joseph said to them, "What deed is this that you have done? Do you now know that such a man as I can indeed divine?" ¹⁶And Judah said, "What shall we say to my lord? What shall we speak? Or how can we clear ourselves? God has found out the guilt of your servants; behold, we are my lord's slaves, both we and he also in whose hand the cup has been found." ¹⁷But he said, "Far be it from me that I should do so! Only the man in whose hand the cup was found shall be my slave; but as for you, go up in peace to your father."

When they arrived back at court, the anguished brothers received a stinging rebuke from Joseph (15a). As is usual in the Yahwistic tradition (*cf.,* 37:26-27; 43:3, 8-10) Judah is portrayed as the spokesman of the brothers, and it is he who gives stammering expression to their consternation (v. 16). We can understand his inability to say anything in defence of the group, since the cup spoke volumes against them. What surprises us is his readiness to confess to a crime which none of the brothers had committed. We must see Judah's admission of guilt as referring to the earlier crime of their getting rid of Joseph (*cf.,* 37:25-28), a crime which had finally caught up with them. God himself seemed to have pronounced judgment on them, and they had no option but to place themselves in Joseph's hands. In deciding that only the thief should be punished Joseph gives the impression of magnanimity (v. 17). But to the reader who knows the devious plot the vizier had hatched, his words sound cynical in the extreme.

44:18-34

¹⁸Then Judah went up to him and said, "O my lord, let your servant, I pray you, speak a word in my lord's ears, and let not your anger burn against your servant; for you

are like Pharaoh himself. [19] My lord asked his servants, saying, 'Have you a father, or a brother?' [20] And we said to my lord, 'We have a father, an old man, and a young brother, the child of his old age; and his brother is dead, and he alone is left of his mother's children; and his father loves him.' [21] Then you said to your servants, 'Bring him down to me, that I may set my eyes upon him.' [22] We said to my lord, 'The lad cannot leave his father, for if he should leave his father, his father would die.' [23] Then you said to your servants, 'Unless your youngest brother comes down with you, you shall see my face no more.' [24] When we went back to your servant my father we told him the words of my lord. [25] And when our father said, 'Go again, buy us a little food,' [26] we said, 'We cannot go down. If our youngest brother goes with us, then we will go down; for we cannot see the man's face unless our youngest brother is with us.' [27] Then your servant my father said to us, 'You know that my wife bore me two sons; [28] one left me, and I said, Surely he has been torn to pieces; and I have never seen him since. [29] If you take this one also from me, and harm befalls him, you will bring down my gray hairs in sorrow to Sheol.' [30] Now therefore, when I come to your servant my father, and the lad is not with us, then, as his life is bound up in the lad's life, [31] when he sees that the lad is not with us, he will die; and your servants will bring down the gray hairs of your servant our father with sorrow to Sheol. [32] For your servant became surety for the lad to my father, saying, 'If I do not bring him back to you, then I shall bear the blame in the sight of my father all my life.' [33] Now therefore, let your servant, I pray you, remain instead of the lad as a slave to my lord; and let the lad go back with his brothers. [34] For how can I go back to my father if the lad is not with me? I fear to see the evil that would come upon my father."

Foreseeing the unspeakable anguish that would overcome his father if Benjamin were to be left behind in Egypt,

Judah launched into an urgent appeal to Joseph (vv. 18-34). In a speech that was at once impassioned and dignified, emotional and noble, he made no reference to the guilt or otherwise of the brothers, but urged Joseph to spare Jacob the grief which the loss of Benjamin would bring upon him. Having recapitulated the events that brought about the present crisis, Judah unhesitatingly offered to become a substitute for his brother and to bear the burden of slavery in his stead (v. 33). Judah's moving speech proved both his selfless concern for Benjamin and his filial solicitude toward his father. It showed that the brothers had experienced a change of heart. Callousness had given way to feeling; fratricidal intentions had been replaced by self-sarificing concern for a brother's life; and indifference to a father's grief changed into solicitude for an old man's tears. The sin of the past had been atoned for through the anguish endured in Egypt; the brothers had passed the final test, and the way to reconciliation was open.

RECONCILIATION
45:1-28 (E)

45 Then Joseph could not control himself before all those who stood by him; and he cried, "Make every one go out from me." So no one stayed with him when Joseph made himself known to his brothers. ²And he wept aloud, so that the Egyptians heard it, and the household of Pharaoh heard it. ³And Joseph said to his brothers, "I am Joseph; is my father still alive?" But his brothers could not answer him, for they were dismayed at his presence.

⁴So Joseph said to his brothers, "Come near to me, I pray you." And they came near. And he said, "I am your brother, Joseph, whom you sold into Egypt. ⁵And now do not be distressed, or angry with yourselves, because you sold me here; for God sent me before you to preserve life. ⁶For the famine has been in the land these two years; and there are yet five years in which there will be neither plowing no harvest. ⁷And God sent me before you to

preserve for you a remnant on earth, and to keep alive for you many survivors. [8]So it was not you who sent me here, but God; and he has made me a father to Pharaoh, and lord of all his house and ruler over all the land of Egypt. [9]Make haste and go up to my father and say to him, 'Thus says your son Joseph, God has made me lord of all Egypt; come down to me, do not tarry; [10]you shall dwell in the land of Goshen, and you shall be near me, you and your children and your children's children, and your flocks, your herds, and all that you have; [11]and there I will provide for you, for there are yet five years of famine to come; lest you and your household, and all that you have, come to poverty.' [12]And now your eyes see, and the eyes of my brother Benjamin see, that it is my mouth that speaks to you. [13]You must tell my father of all my splendor in Egypt, and of all that you have seen. Make haste and bring my father down here." [14]Then he fell upon his brother Benjamin's neck and wept; and Benjamin wept on his neck. [15]And he kissed all his brothers and wept upon them; and after that his brothers walked with him.

[16]When the report was heard in Pharaoh's house, "Joseph's brothers have come," it pleased Pharaoh and his servants well. [17]And Pharaoh said to Joseph, "Say to your brothers, 'Do this: load your beasts and go back to the land of Canaan; [18]and take your father and your households, and come to me, and I will give you the best of the land of Egypt, and you shall eat the fat of the land. [19]Command them also, 'Do this: take wagons from the land of Egypt for your little ones and for your wives, and bring your father, and come. [20]Give no thought to your goods, for the best of all the land of Egypt is yours.'"

[21]The sons of Israel did so; and Joseph gave them wagons, according to the command of Pharaoh, and gave them provisions for the journey. [22]To each and all of them he gave festal garments; but to Benjamin he gave three hundred shekels of silver and five festal garments. [23]To his father he sent as follows: ten asses loaded with the

good things of Egypt, and ten she-asses loaded with grain, bread, and provision for his father on the journey. [24]Then he sent his brothers away, and as they departed, he said to them, "Do not quarrel on the way." [25]So they went up out of Egypt, and came to the land of Canaan to their father Jacob. [26]And they told him, "Joseph is still alive, and he is ruler over all the land of Egypt." And his heart fainted, for he did not believe them. [27]But when they told him all the words of Joseph, which he had said to them, and when he saw the wagons which Joseph had sent to carry him, the spirit of their father Jacob revived; [28]and Israel said, "It is enough; Joseph my son is still alive; I will go and see him before I die."

Judah's moving speech (44:18-34) had such a shattering effect on Joseph that he broke down in the presence of his courtiers, and now that he was convinced of the changed dispositions of his brothers, he did not need to wear his mask any longer (vv. 1-2). Joseph's question, "is my father still alive?" (v. 3) has meaning only in an Elohist passage, since according to the Yahwist Joseph has already been informed about Jacob's well-being (*cf.*, 43:26-28; 44:24-34).

If the brothers were dumbfounded on hearing the vizier's self-revelation, Joseph set them at ease by showing that God had been secretly at work in all that had happened (vv. 5-8). These verses, which give the key to the whole Joseph story, form one of the few passages in that story where theological reflection becomes explicit (see also 50:20, 24). Joseph declared repeatedly that it was God, and not the brothers, who had taken him to Egypt (vv. 5, 7, 8). He was convinced that it was God who made him "father to Pharaoh" (v. 8). This title was actually one that designated the vizier as early as the third millennium B.C. The term "remnant" which Joseph applied to his family (v. 7) was to become a technical biblical term for the portion of a community that escaped an overwhelming calamity and made possible the future exist-ence of the community (*cf.*, Amos 5:15; Isa 7:3; 37:4, etc.).

The concept of a remnant, if not the word, has already appeared in the Genesis story, when Noah was presented as sole survivor of the Flood (*cf.,* 6:5-8; 7:23). Jacob's family is a "remnant," which, through the intervention of God who sent Joseph to Egypt, survived the disastrous famine to become the ancestors of the people of Israel.

Having clarified the divine dimension in the events that had taken place, Joseph went on to plan for the future. He urged his brothers to go quickly to their father and to bring him and his whole family to Egypt where they would enjoy security during the remaining years of the famine (vv. 9-11, 13). *Goshen* (v. 10), which is the Yahwist's term for the area where the Israelites settled in Egypt, is a name that has not occurred in Egyptian sources. It is generally identified with modern *Wadi Tumilat* at the north-eastern end of the Nile Delta.

Joseph's uninhibited display of affection for his brothers (vv. 14-15) expressed his complete reconciliation with them. The lavish gifts which he showered on them as they set out for the land of Canaan (vv. 21-23) revealed both his generosity and his desire to make amends for the anguish he had earlier caused them by gifts that proved to be snare (*cf.,* 44:1-2).

When the brothers reached home and told their extraordinary tale to their father "his heart fainted" (v. 26), or, as the NAB puts it, "he was dumbfounded." When the truth that Joseph was alive gradually dawned on him, the old man's vitality gradually revived, and he resolved then and there to go and see his favourite son.

JACOB—ISRAEL IN EGYPT
46:1-34 (JEP)

46:1-7

46 So Israel took his journey with all that he had, and came to Beer-sheba, and offered sacrifices to the God of his father Isaac. ²And God spoke to Israel in visions of the night, and said, "Jacob, Jacob." And he said, "Here am I." ³Then he said, "I am God, the God of your father; do not be afraid to go down to Egypt; for I will there make of you a great nation. ⁴I will go down with you to Egypt, and I will also bring you up again; and Joseph's hand shall close your eyes." ⁵Then Jacob set out from Beer-sheba; and the sons of Israel carried Jacob their father, their little ones, and their wives, in the wagons which Pharaoh had sent to carry him. ⁶They also took their cattle and their goods, which they had gained in the land of Canaan, and came into Egypt, Jacob and all his offspring with him, ⁷his sons, and his sons' sons with him, his daughters, and his sons' daughters; all his offspring he brought with him into Egypt.

According to 45:28 and 46:1 Jacob made up his own mind to migrate into Egypt. Before leaving the land of promise, he passed through Beer-sheba where Isaac had erected an altar (*cf.,* 26:25, J). There Jacob offered a sacrifice to the God of his father, doubtless with a view to ensuring divine protection on his long journey. In 46:2-4 (E) we are given a somewhat different picture. According to these verses it was God himself who instructed the patriarch in "visions of the night" (*cf.,* 20:3, 6; 31:11, 24, E) to go to Egypt. The Elohist thus shows that Jacob's decision to leave the promised land was not motivated by a mere desire to see his son. The departure for Egypt which was to give an important new twist to the story of the chosen family of Abraham was the result of a direct divine command. In Egypt, the promise of numerous descendants (*cf.,* 12:2; 18:18; 35:11), so long delayed, would be fulfilled (v. 3). The assurance that God would bring Jacob back from Egypt (v. 4) refers directly to the fact that the patriarch's corpse would be brought back to Canaan (*cf.,* 49:29-30; 50:4-14), but it very probably also foresees that Jacob will return in the person of his descendants to take possession of the promised land.

46:8-27

⁸Now these are the names of the descendants of Israel, who came into Egypt, Jacob and his sons, Reuben, Jacob's first-born, ⁹and the sons of Reuben: Hanoch, Pallu, Hezron, and Carmi. ¹⁰The sons of Simeon: Jemuel, Jamin, Ohad, Jachin, Zohar, and Shaul, the son of a Canaanitish woman. ¹¹The sons of Levi: Gershon, Kohath, and Merari. ¹²The sons of Judah: Er, Onan, Shelah, Perez, and Zerah (but Er and Onan died in the land of Canaan); and the sons of Perez were Hezron and Hamul. ¹³The sons of Issachar: Tola, Puvah, Iob, and Shimron. ¹⁴The sons of Zebulun: Sered, Elon, and Jahleel ¹⁵(these are the sons of Leah, whom she bore to Jacob in Paddan-aram, together with his daughter Dinah; altogether his sons and his daughters numbered thirty-three). ¹⁶The sons of Gad: Ziphion, Haggi, Shuni, Ezbon, Eri, Arodi, and Areli. ¹⁷The sons of Asher: Imnah, Ishvah, Ishvi, Beriah, with Serah their sister. And the sons of Beriah: Heber and Malchiel ¹⁸(these are the sons of Zilpah, whom Laban gave to Leah his daughter; and these she bore to Jacob — sixteen persons). ¹⁹The sons of Rachel, Jacob's wife: Joseph and Benjamin. ²⁰And to Joseph in the land of Egypt were born Manasseh and Ephraim, whom Asenath, the daughter of Potiphera the priest of On, bore to him. ²¹And the sons of Benjamin: Bela, Becher, Ashbel, Gera, Naaman, Ehi, Rosh, Muppim, Huppim, and Ard ²²(these are the sons of Rachel, who were born to Jacob — fourteen persons in all). ²³The sons of Dan: Hushim. ²⁴The sons of Naphtali: Jahzeel, Guni, Jezer, and Shillem ²⁵(these are the sons of Bilhah, whom Laban gave to Rachel his daughter, and these she bore to Jacob — seven persons in all). ²⁶All the persons belonging to Jacob who came into Egypt, who were his own offspring, not including Jacob's sons' wives, were sixty-six persons in all; ²⁷and the sons of Joseph, who were born to him in Egypt, were two; all the persons of the house of Jacob, that came into Egypt were seventy.

This Priestly genealogy which interrupts the account of Jacob's descent into Egypt, lists the members of Jacob's family who settled in the Nile valley. Most of the names in the list occur again in Num 26 (P) which lists "the people of Israel, who came forth out of the land of Egypt." The compilers of the present list arrive at seventy persons (v. 27), the traditional number of those who settled in Egypt (*cf.*, Exod 1:5; Deut 10:22), only by including Jacob himself and Dinah among Jacob's "descendants." It is generally agreed that this genealogy is an artificial Priestly reconstruction that cannot be taken as an actual record of the number of those who accompanied Jacob to Egypt.

46:28-34

²⁸He sent Judah before him to Joseph, to appear before him in Goshen; and they came into the land of Goshen. ²⁹Then Joseph made ready his chariot and went up to meet Israel his father in Goshen; and he presented himself to him, and fell on his neck, and wept on his neck a good while. ³⁰Israel said to Joseph, "Now let me die, since I have seen your face and know that you are still alive." ³¹Joseph said to his brothers and to his father's household, "I will go up and tell Pharaoh, and will say to him, 'My brothers and my father's household, who were in the land of Canaan, have come to me; ³²and the men are shepherds, for they have been keepers of cattle; and they have brought their flocks, and their herds, and all that they have.' ³³When Pharaoh calls you, and says, 'What is your occupation?' ³⁴you shall say, 'Your servants have been keepers of cattle from our youth even until now, both we and our fathers,' in order that you may dwell in the land of Goshen; for every shepherd is an abomination to the Egyptians."

After the lengthy intrusion of the Priestly genealogy the account of Jacob's descent into Egypt is taken up again in v. 28. Judah, who has been given such a prominent place in the Yahwist tradition (*cf.*, 37:26-27; 43:8-10; 44:18-34), was sent

ahead to inform Joseph about his father's imminent arrival.
With a brevity and a sobriety that lend dignity to the scene
the author describes the emotional encounter between
Jacob and the son whom he had considered dead (v. 29; *cf.*,
42:38). The aged father's happiness at seeing his long-lost
son is forcefully expressed in v. 30 which portrays Jacob as
declaring his readiness to die, now that he has seen Joseph
alive.

Joseph, exhibiting some of that diplomacy which must
have served him so well in his elevated political role, prepared his family for their meeting with Pharaoh and briefed
them for the occasion. By instructing his brothers to identify
themselves as shepherds (vv. 33-34), Joseph hoped to influence the king into assigning the land of Goshen — a territory
that was suitable for grazing — to the newly arrived family.
There they could live apart from the main Egyptian population, and continue their shepherd way of life in peace and
prosperity. The statement that "every shepherd is an abomination to the Egyptians" (v. 34c) cannot be supported by
evidence from Egyptian sources. However, settled people in
general distrusted nomads and treated them with hostility,
and the Egyptians would have been no exception to this
rule.

SETTLED IN EGYPT
47:1-28 (JP)

47:1-12

47 So Joseph went in and told Pharaoh, "My father and
my brothers, with their flocks and herds and all that they
possess, have come from the land of Canaan; they are
now in the land of Goshen." ²And from among his brothers he took five men and presented them to Pharaoh.
³Pharaoh said to his brothers, "What is your occupation?" And they said to Pharaoh, "Your servants are
shepherds, as our fathers were." ⁴They said to Pharaoh,
"We have come to sojourn in the land; for there is no

pasture for your servants' flocks, for the famine is severe in the land of Canaan; and now, we pray you, let your servants dwell in the land of Goshen." [5]Then Pharaoh said to Joseph, "Your father and your brothers have come to you. [6]The land of Egypt is before you; settle your father and your brothers in the best of the land; let them dwell in the land of Goshen; and if you know any able men among them, put them in charge of my cattle."

[7]Then Joseph brought in Jacob his father, and set him before Pharaoh, and Jacob blessed Pharaoh. [8]And Pharaoh said to Jacob, "How many are the days of the years of your life?" [9]And Jacob said to Pharaoh, "The days of the years of my sojourning are a hundred and thirty years; few and evil have been the days of the years of my life, and they have not attained to the days of the years of the life of my fathers in the days of their sojourning." [10]And Jacob blessed Pharaoh, and went out from the presence of Pharaoh. [11]The Joseph settled his father and his brothers, and gave them a possession in the land of Egypt, in the best of the land, in the land of Rameses, as Pharaoh had commanded. [12]And Joseph provided his father, his brothers, and all his father's household with food, according to the number of their dependents.

At this point the chapter division actually breaks the flow of the narrative, since 47:1-6 is a direct continuation of chap. 46. Joseph introduced his family to the Pharaoh, adding casually that they are settled in Goshen (v. 1). We may surmise that the five brothers whom Joseph chose to represent the group were those who were most likely to make a good impression at court. In accordance with the instructions which Joseph had given them (*cf.,* 46:33-34) the brothers proclaimed their pastoral avocation, and went on to request permission to settle in Goshen (vv. 3-4). The fact that the Pharaoh placed "the best of the land" (v. 6) at their disposal must have been a proof for the new immigrants of the extraordinary favour which the once hated brother now enjoys at the royal court. Besides granting Jacob's family an ideal dwelling place Pharaoh invited Joseph to appoint his family as superintendents of the royal herds. Since the Pharaoh owned large herds, and since much attention was paid to cattle-breeding in Egypt, this was no mean appointment, and the biblical author wishes us to see it as a royal gesture of respect and trust toward Joseph and his family.

Verses 7-12 (P) describe a new scene. Only now is the aged patriarch presented to the monarch. The statement that "Jacob blessed Pharaoh" (vv. 7, 10) simply means that the guest greeted the king with the appropriate salutations and good wishes. Jacob's one hundred and thirty years can be regarded as few (v. 9) when compared with the one hundred and seventy-five years of Abraham's life (*cf.*, 25:7, P) or with Isaac's one hundred and eighty years (*cf.*, 35:28, P). We who know the story of Jacob's turbulent life can understand what he meant when he said that his days were evil. Jacob describes his life as a "sojourning." This word which occurs frequently in the patriarchal narratives (*cf.*, 17:8; 28:4; 36:7; 37:1) describes the semi-nomadic life style of the ancestors of the Israelite people. It also reminds us that it was God's design that the patriarchs should live a life of homeless wandering until he should assign to them the land that was the object of his promise (*cf.*, Heb 11:13).

47:13-28

¹³Now there was no food in all the land; for the famine was very severe, so that the land of Egypt and the land of Canaan languished by reason of the famine. ¹⁴And Joseph gathered up all the money that was found in the land of Egypt and in the land of Canaan, for the grain which they bought; and Joseph brought the money into Pharaoh's house. ¹⁵And when the money was all spent in the land of Egypt and in the land of Canaan, all the Egyptians came to Joseph, and said, "Give us food; why should we die before your eyes? For our money is gone." ¹⁶And Joseph answered, "Give your cattle, and I will give

you food in exchange for your cattle, if your money is gone." 17So they brought their cattle to Joseph; and Joseph gave them food in exchange for the horses, the flocks, the herds, and the asses: and he supplied them with food in exchange for all their cattle that year. 18And when that year was ended, they came to him the following year, and said to him, "We will not hide from my lord that our money is all spent; and the herds of cattle are my lord's; there is nothing left in the sight of my lord but our bodies and our lands. 19Why should we die before your eyes, both we and our land? Buy us and our land for food, and we with our land will be slaves to Pharaoh; and give us seed, that we may live, and not die, and that the land may not be desolate."

20So Joseph bought all the land of Egypt for Pharaoh; for all the Egyptians sold their fields, because the famine was severe upon them. The land became Pharaoh's; 21and as for the people, he made slaves of them from one end of Egypt to the other. 22Only the land of the priests he did not buy; for the priests had a fixed allowance from Pharaoh, and lived on the allowance which Pharaoh gave them; therefore they did not sell their land. 23Then Joseph said to the people, "Behold, I have this day bought you and your land for Pharaoh. Now here is seed for you, and you shall sow the land. 24And at the harvests you shall give a fifth to Pharaoh, and four fifths shall be your own, as seed for the fields and as food for yourselves and your households, and as food for your little ones." 25And they said, "You have saved our lives; may it please my lord, we will be slaves to Pharaoh." 26So Joseph made it a statute concerning the land of Egypt, and it stands to this day, that Pharaoh should have the fifth; the land of the priests alone did not become Pharaoh's.

27Thus Israel dwelt in the land of Egypt, in the land of Goshen; and they gained possessions in it, and were fruitful and multiplied exceedingly. 28And Jacob lived in the land of Egypt seventeen years; so the days of Jacob, the years of his life, were a hundred and forty-seven years.

Verses 13-26 (J) have no logical connection with the preceding passage but much in common with chap. 41 which describes Joseph's rise to power. We are told how Joseph's economic policies eventually forced the Egyptians to sell themselves into serfdom and to hand over their land to the Pharaoh in order to get bread. The remark that the priestly caste did not lose their land (v. 22) tallies well with what is known of the Egyptian priesthood who were extremely wealthy and therefore well cushioned against the rigours of famine. The biblical author makes the point that the people gratefully acknowledged Joseph as their saviour in time of crisis (v. 25), and he wishes the reader to admire the wisdom of the chief administrator who so shrewdly saved the Egyptians from disaster. It is very likely, too, that the passage describes a system of land-tenure and serfdom that actually existed in Egypt in the writer's day. However distasteful that system might be to freedom-loving Israelites, the author traces its origins back to Joseph.

With vv. 27-28 (P) we return to the story of the settlement in Egypt that was interrupted at v. 12. The remark that the family of Jacob was "fruitful and multiplied exceedingly" (v. 27b) shows the Hebrews firmly established in Egypt, and sets the scene for the Exodus events (*cf.,* Exod 1:7).

JACOB'S LAST WISH
47:29-31 (J)

> [29]And when the time drew near that Israel must die, he called his son Joseph and said to him, "If now I have found favor in your sight, put your hand under my thigh, and promise to deal loyally and truly with me. Do not bury me in Egypt, [30]but let me lie with my fathers; carry me out of Egypt and bury me in their burying place." He answered, "I will do as you have said." [31]And he said, "Swear to me"; and he swore to him. Then Israel bowed himself upon the head of his bed.

The deathbed setting renders the patriarch's last request particularly solemn. The seriousness is also shown by the solemn oath which he exacted from Joseph. The placing of one's hand under another person's thigh solemnized an oath formula (*cf.*, 24:2, J; see comment above p. 136). The burial place which the author had in mind is probably the cave of Machpelah (*cf.*, 49:29-31, P), where Abraham (*cf.*, 25:9, P) and Isaac (*cf.*, 49:29-31, P) had been buried. Burial in the family tomb was, of course, a matter of great importance for the ancients, since it symbolized a bond with one's ancestors and a loyalty to the traditions and goals that had been theirs. For Jacob, burial in Canaan was particularly important, since it represented a claim to that land, and the prospect of finding repose there was an implicit assertion that his people's stay in Egypt would be temporary.

EPHRAIM AND MANASSEH
48:1-22

48:1-7

48 After this Joseph was told, "Behold, your father is ill"; so he took with him his two sons, Manasseh and Ephraim. ²And it was told to Jacob, "Your son Joseph has come to you"; then Israel summoned his strength, and sat up in bed. ³And Jacob said to Joseph, "God Almighty appeared to me at Luz in the land of Canaan and blessed me, ⁴and said to me, 'Behold, I will make you fruitful, and multiply you, and I will make of you a company of peoples, and will give this land to your descendants after you for an everlasting possession.' ⁵And now your two sons, who were born to you in the land of Egypt before I came to you in Egypt, are mine; Ephraim and Manasseh shall be mine, as Reuben and Simeon are. ⁶And the offspring born to you after them shall be yours; they shall be called by the name of their brothers in their inheritance. ⁷For when I came from Paddan, Rachel to my sorrow died in the land of Canaan on the way, when there was still some distance to go to Ephrath; and I buried her there on the way to Ephrath (that is, Bethlehem)."

Having heard of Joseph's solemn encounter with his father who was on the point of death (47:29-31, J), we are surprised to be told that Joseph had to be informed about his parent's illness (48:1-2), until we realize that these latter verses stem from the Elohist. Verses 3-6 (P) describe how the failing patriarch adopted Joseph's sons, Ephraim and Manasseh, as his own sons, and gave them equal status with his own natural offspring. Referring to the promise he had received at Bethel (*cf.,* 35:6, 9-12, P) Jacob incorporated Ephraim and Manasseh among those through whom his progeny would be multiplied. Ephraim and Manasseh must here be seen as personifications of the central Palestinian tribes that bore their names. The "tribe of Joseph," or "the house of Joseph" (*cf.,* Josh 17:14; Judg 1:22-23, etc.) ceased to exist as a unified tribe, and survived in the tribes of Ephraim and Manasseh who lived side by side in Palestine. The present passage thus reflects the historical reality that there was no tribe of Joseph among the group of tribes that formed Israel. It also explains the legal basis for the fact that Ephraim and Manasseh, who were not natural sons of Jacob, became leaders of tribal groups within the Israelite confederacy.

48:8-22

⁸When Israel saw Joseph's sons, he said, "Who are these?" ⁹Joseph said to his father, "They are my sons, whom God has given me here." And he said, "Bring them to me, I pray you, that I may bless them." ¹⁰Now the eyes of Israel were dim with age, so that he could not see. So Joseph brought them near him; and he kissed them and embraced them. ¹¹And Israel said to Joseph, "I had not thought to see your face; and lo, God has let me see your children also." ¹²Then Joseph removed them from his knees, and he bowed himself with his face to the earth.

¹³And Joseph took them both, Ephraim in his right hand toward Israel's left hand, and Manasseh in his left hand toward Israel's right hand, and brought them near him. ¹⁴And Israel stretched out his right hand and laid it upon the head of Ephraim, who was the younger, and his left hand upon the head of Manasseh, crossing his hands, for Manasseh was the first-born. ¹⁵And he blessed Joseph, and said,

"The God before whom my fathers
   Abraham and Isaac walked,
the God who has led me all my life
   long to this day,
¹⁶the angel who has redeemd me from
   all evil, bless the lads;
and in them let my name be per-
   petuated, and the name of my
   fathers Abraham and Isaac;
and let them grow into a multitude in
   the midst of the earth."

¹⁷When Joseph saw that his father laid his right hand upon the head of Ephraim, it displeased him; and he took his father's hand, to remove it from Ephraim's head to Manasseh's head. ¹⁸And Joseph said to his father, "Not so, my father; for this one is the first-born; put your right hand upon his head." ¹⁹ But his father refused, and said, "I know, my son, I know; he also shall become a people, and he also shall be great; nevertheless his younger brother shall be greater than he, and his descendants shall become a multitude of nations." ²⁰So he blessed them that day, saying,

"By you Israel will pronounce blessings,
   saying,
'God make you as Ephraim and as
   Manasseh'".

and thus he put Ephraim before Manasseh. ²¹Then Israel said to Joseph, "Behold, I am about to die, but God will be with you, and will bring you again to the land of your fathers. ²²Moreover I have given to you rather than to your brothers one mountain slope which I took from the hand of the Amorites with my sword and with my bow."

This story, which presumes that Jacob is meeting his two grandsons for the first time (vv. 8-11; *cf.,* vv. 3-6), has about it some of the touching drama that marked the reunion of Jacob and Joseph (*cf.,* 46:28-30). Verse 12 allows us to conclude that Jacob had placed his two grandsons on his knees. This gesture symbolized his formal adoption of the two boys (*cf.,* 30:3; 50:23), and thus had the same effect as the ritual act of adoption described in vv. 3-6. But Jacob's symbolic act had, as it were, to be ratified by his blessing the boys. So Joseph brought his sons to his father, taking care to place Manasseh at Jacob's right hand (v. 13), that is, in the position of honour that belonged to him as first-born. However, the old man upset Joseph's careful arrangement, when, crossing his hands, he lay his right hand on the head of the younger Ephraim (v. 14), thus granting him precedence over his brother.

Although v. 15a says that Jacob blessed Joseph, it is obvious from the wording of the blessing (vv. 15b-16) that it was addressed to the boys. Jacob invoked his God under three titles, each of which tells us something about the patriarch's concept of the deity. By invoking the God before whom his ancestors walked (v. 15b; *cf.,* 17:1), Jacob associated himself with his forebears' worship and prayer as well as with their concept of what was right and just in God's eyes. The phrase rendered as "the God who has led me all my life long" (v. 15c) is more faithfully translated as "the God who has been my shepherd from my birth" (NAB and *cf.* NEB). The image of God as shepherd occurs frequently in the Old Testament (*cf.,* Pss 23:1; 28:9; Isa 40:11), and it suggests God's concern for his people. The "angel" to whom Jacob refers (v. 16a), is, of course, God. By referring to this God as his "redeemer," Jacob is recognizing him as the God who had answered him in the day of his distress, and who had been with him wherever he had gone (*cf.,* 35:3; 28:15; 31:5, 42). Having invoked the deity as God, Shepherd and

Angel, Jacob prayed that Ephraim and Manasseh would be blessed with numerous descendants who would ensure a glorious name for Jacob himself. The ancient Israelite readers of this blessing, who knew of the political prominence of the tribes of Ephraim and Manasseh in Palestine, would have attributed the success of the two tribes to the efficacious deathbed prayer of Jacob. We have another version of the deathbed blessing in v. 20, where the terminology is similar to that of 12:3b (see comment above p. 91).

The comment that Jacob "put Ephraim before Manasseh" (v. 20c) aptly sums up the meaning of the story of the blessing of the two boys. By telling us that Jacob placed his right hand on the head of Ephraim, thus conferring superiority over his older brother on him, the author is continuing a theme which we have encountered several times in the Genesis narrative. Thus Abel (and then Seth) rather than the older Cain was chosen by God (chap. 4); Ishmael was superseded by the younger Isaac (17:19-21); Jacob acquired the blessings that rightly belonged to Esau (chap. 27); Perez seized the rights of Zerah (38:27-30). In the present story, Ephraim and Manasseh represent the two tribes that are said to have stemmed from them. Biblical history tells us that the tribe of Ephraim outranked the tribe of Manasseh. Indeed, so prominent was Ephraim among the tribes of Israel that the prophets sometimes referred to the whole northern kingdom as "Ephraim" (*cf.,* Isa 11:13; Hos 6:4). The present story of how Jacob placed the younger Ephraim in the place of honour as he blessed his two grandsons was meant to be seen as an explanation of Ephraim's political supremacy.

The promise that Joseph would return to the land of Canaan probably envisages both Joseph's burial there and his descendants' return to the land of their ancestors (*cf.,* 46:4; see comment above, p. 251). The promise in v. 22 refers not to Joseph in person, but to his children, the tribes of Ephraim and Manasseh, who were destined to inherit "one mountain slope" in Palestine. The Hebrew word rendered "mountain slope" is *Shechem* (*cf.,* NAB), which can also be taken to refer to the city of that name which was located in the territory of Ephraim and Manasseh. Jacob's claim that he took the "mountain slope," or Shechem, by violence contradicts what we know from chap. 34 (*cf.,* especially 34:25-30). Behind this "contradiction" distinct historical moments of Israel's history converge, some of victory, others of defeat and flight.

JACOB'S BLESSING
49:1-27

This complex poem is a compilation of several poetic fragments and detached sayings. It is generally agreed that vv. 8-12 date from the period when David's brilliant achievements brought glory to the tribe of Judah, so that the poem *as we now have it* cannot pre-date the tenth century B.C. The praise of Joseph in vv. 22-27 probably comes from an earlier period—before the rise of the Judah tribe to prominence ca. 1000 B.C.—and has been harmed textually in its transmission. Although the opening verse gives the impression that Jacob's words are a prediction of what was to befall his sons and their descendants, the various statements in the chapter are obviously based on knowledge of the fortunes of the different tribes of Israel. The text refers to Jacob's sons not as individuals, but as representatives of the tribes of Israel.

49:1-7

49   Then Jacob called his sons, and said, "Gather yourselves together, that I may tell you what shall befall you in days to come.

²Assemble and hear, O sons of Jacob
    and hearken to Israel your father.

³Reuben, you are my first-born, my might,
    and the first fruits of my strength,
    pre-eminent in pride and pre-eminent in power.

⁴Unstable as water, you shall not have pre-eminence
    because you went up to your father's bed;
    then you defiled it—you went up to my couch!

5Simeon and Levi are brothers;
  weapons of violence are their swords.
6O my soul, come not into their council;
    O my spirit, be not joined to their company;
  for in their anger they slay men,
    and in their wantonness they hamstring oxen.
7Cursed be their anger, for it is fierce;
  and their wrath, for it is cruel!
  I will divide them in Jacob
  and scatter them in Israel.

Verse 3 obviously presumes that the tribe of Reuben once enjoyed political prominence. We know, however, that the tribe disintegrated as an independent unity as early as the eleventh century B.C. This loss of glory is implied in v. 4a-b, and in v. 4c it is attributed to Reuben's incestuous crime (*cf.,* 35:22). *Simeon and Levi* are sharply berated for their brute force (vv. 5-7). The violence for which they are condemned seems to be that involved in their fierce act of revenge for the rape of Dinah (*cf.,* chap. 34). The weakness of the two tribes (see comment on 34:30, above p. 196) is here attributed to their cruelty on that occasion.

49:8-12

8Judah, your brothers shall praise you;
    your hand shall be on the neck of your enemies;
    your father's sons shall bow down before you.
9Judah is a lion's whelp;
    from the prey, my son, you have gone up.
  He stooped down, he couched as a lion,
    and as a lioness; who dares rouse him up?
10The scepter shall not depart from Judah,
    nor the ruler's staff from between his feet,
  until he comes to whom it belongs;
    and to him shall be the obedience of the peoples.
11Binding his foal to the vine
    and his ass's colt to the choice vine,
  he washes his garments in wine

and his vesture in the blood of grapes;
¹²his eyes shall be red with wine,
and his teeth white with milk.

Verse 8 portrays Judah as a fearful warrior who has won the allegiance of the fraternal tribes and who has conquered all his enemies. The image of the lion (v. 9) suggests the power of the Judah clans and their unchallenged position among the confederates. The archaic Hebrew text of v. 10 resists all efforts at interpretation, and every translation is hypothetical. If we accept the RSV translation, which has its own merits, then the "scepter" and the "staff" are symbols of authority which the king held between his legs as he sat on the royal throne. The words "until he comes to whom it belongs" leave the verse open to a messianic interpretation. The verse can be taken to mean that the sovereignty shall not pass from the house of Judah until it has been exercised by some great leader of the future whose authority will be recognized by all peoples. This messianic interpretation is supported by the following verses which describe the reign of Judah in paradisiacal terms. A territory where vines are so plentiful that a man can tie his donkey to one (v. 11) without thought for the damage a nibbling animal may cause, and where wine is so plentiful that one can use it for washing purposes, is a veritable paradise. A ruler who is satiated with wine and milk (v. 12) is one who lives in affluence in a prosperous land. Similar language was to become familiar in messianic passages of later times (*cf.,* Amos 9:13-14; Ps 72:16).

49:13-21

¹³Zebulun shall dwell at the shore of the sea;
he shall become a haven for ships,
and his border shall be at Sidon.
¹⁴Issachar is a strong ass,
crouching between the sheepfolds;
¹⁵he saw that a resting place was good,
and that the land was pleasant;

so he bowed his shoulder to bear,
and became a slave at forced labor.
[16]Dan shall judge his people
as one of the tribes of Israel.
[17]Dan shall be a serpent in the way,
a viper by the path, that bites the horse's heels
so that his rider falls backward.
[18]I wait for thy salvation, O Lord.
[19]Raiders shall raid Gad,
but he shall raid at their heels.
[20]Asher's food shall be rich,
and he shall yield royal dainties.
[21]Naphtali is a hind let loose,
that bears comely fawns.

We are told nothing about the tribe of *Zebulun* (v. 13) except that it was located by the sea, and that it engaged in maritime trade. The oracle about *Issachar* (vv. 14-15) is anything but flattering. The image of an ass "crouching between the sheepfolds" suggests the security which that tribe enjoyed at the price of servitude to the Canaanites. The tribe of *Dan*, whose city is often mentioned as the most northern town of Israel (*cf.*, 1 Sam 3:20; 2 Sam 17:11, etc.), is spoken of in laudatory terms (vv. 16-18). In the phrase "Dan shall judge" (the play on words is evident in the Hebrew, *dan ya-din*), the remark is taken to mean that Dan will establish justice in his own territory, and thus prove his autonomy. The terms "serpent" and "viper," as applied here, do not suggest treachery, but rather the small tribe's ability to achieve victory against mighty foes. Verse 18, which has no connection with the rest of the oracle, seems to be a prayer which expresses the tiny tribe's awareness of dependence on God's assistance if it is to survive as an independent group. The territory of *Gad* lay in the Transjordan and was subject to the raids of marauding nomadic tribes. However, the brave men of Gad continually put their attackers to flight (v. 19). The tribe of *Asher* was located north of Mount Carmel, in a fertile area that produced rich foods that were fit for a king's table (v. 20). The tribe of *Naphtali* had its home to the north and west of Lake Gennesaret. The text of v. 21 is obscure, and commentators despair of finding any meaning in it.

49:22-27

> ²²Joseph is a fruitful bough,
>   a fruitful bough by a spring;
>   his branches run over the wall.
> ²³The archers fiercely attacked him,
>   shot at him, and harassed him sorely;
> ²⁴yet his bow remained unmoved,
>   his arms were made agile
>   by the hands of the Mighty One of Jacob
>   (by the name of the Shepherd, the Rock of Israel),
> ²⁵by the God of your father who will help you
>   by God Almighty who will bless you
>   with blessings of heaven above,
>   blessings of the deep that couches beneath,
> blessings of the breasts and of the womb.
> ²⁶The blessings of your father
>   are mighty beyond the blessing of the eternal
>   mountains,
>   the bounties of the everlasting hills;
> may they be on the head of Joseph,
>   and on the brow of him who was
>   separate from his brothers.
> ²⁷Benjamin is a ravenous wolf,
>   in the morning devouring the prey,
>   and at even dividing the spoil."

Although the text of the *Joseph* oracle (vv. 22-26) is badly damaged, its general meaning is fairly clear. The Joseph tribe is settled in a fertile area and enjoys economic and political prominence. The fact that Joseph alone is mentioned, and not Ephraim and Manasseh, suggests that this blessing may have been composed before the tribe was divided (*cf.,* comments to chap. 48; above pp. 260-264). The image of "a fruitful bough by a spring" suggests freshness and vigour (*cf.,* Ps 1:3; Jer 17:8, etc.). Verses 23-24 celebrate the Joseph tribe's ability to resist all adversaries with the help of its divine protector. In the first title given to Joseph's God (v. 24b) the name "Jacob" may be taken as national rather than personal, so that the title "The Mighty one of Jacob" (*cf.,* Ps 132:2, 5; Isa 49:26; 60:16) can be seen to correspond to the name "the Mighty One of Israel" (*cf.,* Isa 1:24). Concerning the application of the title "Shepherd" to God, see comment on 48:15c (above p. 262). The epithet "Rock of Israel" (*cf.,* 2 Sam 23:3; Isa 30:29) points to the absolute reliability of God (*cf.,* Pss 62:2, 6; 95:1). The name "God of your father" (v. 25) is unusual, but can be compared with similar titles that suggest a relationship with the ancestral God (*cf.,* 31:5, 42; 48:15; Exod 15:2). For a comment on the title "God Almighty" see the remarks on 17:1 (above p. 108). The "blessings of heaven above" (v. 25c) refer to the dew and rain that fertilize the soil, while the waters beneath the earth that send forth fructifying rivers and streams are personified as "the deep that couches beneath" (*cf.,* Deut 33:13). By qualifying Joseph as the one "who was separate from his brothers" (v. 26b) the author is referring to Joseph's distinguished position among the tribes and to the primacy that must have been his when the present oracle was composed (*cf.,* Deut 33:16). Verse 27 celebrates the valour of *Benjamin,* the smallest of the tribes (*cf.,* 1 Sam 9:21; Ps 68:27).

JACOB'S DEATH
49:28-33

> [28]All these are the twelve tribes of Israel; and this is what their father said to them as he blessed them, blessing each with the blessing suitable to him. [29]Then he charged them, and said to them, "I am to be gathered to my people; bury me with my fathers in the cave that is in the field of Ephron the Hittite, [30]in the cave that is in the field at Machpelah, to the east of Mamre, in the land of

Canaan, which Abraham bought with the field from
Ephron the Hittite to possess as a burying place. [31]There
they buried Abraham and Sarah his wife; there they
buried Isaac and Rebekah his wife; and there I buried
Leah—[32]the field and the cave that is in it were purchased
from the Hittites." [33]When Jacob finished charging his
sons, he drew up his feet into the bed, and breathed his
last, and was gathered to his people.

Jacob's deathbed address as recorded here (vv. 29-32) by
the Priestly author parallels the Yahwist speech of 47:29-31.
The present text points out that Jacob is to be buried in a site
that had been legally acquired by Abraham in the land of
Canaan. We have already learned that Machpelah, the site
which Abraham acquired as a family grave, was the burial
place of Sarah (*cf.,* 23:19) and Abraham (*cf.,* 25:8-10). Only
here are we told that Isaac, whose death took place at
Hebron (*cf.,* 35:27-28), as well as Rebekah and Leah, whose
deaths are not recorded, were buried there.

JACOB'S BURIAL
50:1-14

50   Then Joseph fell on his father's face, and wept over
him, and kissed him. [2]And Joseph commanded his servants the physicians to embalm his father. So the physicians embalmed Israel; [3]forty days were required for it,
for so many are required for embalming. And the Egyptians wept for him seventy days.

[4]And when the days of weeping for him were past,
Joseph spoke to the household of Pharaoh, saying, "If
now I have found favor in your eyes, speak, I pray you, in
the ears of Pharaoh, saying [5]My father made me swear,
saying, 'I am about to die: in my tomb which I hewed out
for myself in the land of Canaan, there shall you bury me.'
Now therefore let me go up, I pray you, and bury my
father; then I will return." [6]And Pharaoh answered, "Go
up, and bury your father, as he made you swear." [7]So

Joseph went up to bury his father; and with him went up all the servants of Pharaoh, the elders of his household, and all the elders of the land of Egypt, [8]as well as all the household of Joseph, his brothers, and his father's household; only their children, their flocks, and their herds were left in the land of Goshen. [9]And there went up with him both chariots and horsemen; it was a very great company. [10]When they came to the threshing floor of Atad, which is beyond the Jordan, they lamented there with a very great and sorrowful lamentation; and he made a mourning for his father seven days. [11]When the inhabitants of the land, the Canaanites, saw the mourning on the threshing floor of Atad, they said, "This is a grievous mourning to the Egyptians." Therefore the place was named Abel-mizraim; it is beyond the Jordan. [12]Thus his sons did for him as he had commanded them; [13]for his sons carried him to the land of Canaan, and buried him in the cave of the field at Machpelah, to the east of Mamre, which Abraham bought with the field from Ephron the Hittite, to possess as a burying place. [14]After he had buried his father, Joseph returned to Egypt with his brothers and all who had gone up with him to bury his father.

Verses 1-11, 14 give us the Yahwist's account of how Joseph carried out the burial instructions which his father had given him personally (*cf.,* 47:29-31, J). The Egyptian embalming procedure was accompanied by religious rites, prayers, and incantations, and its purpose was to preserve the body so that it would be a suitable residence for the soul which was expected to return to it some day. Jacob's embalming is given no religious significance, and the author probably regarded it simply as a means of preserving the body for the long journey to Canaan. The protracted period of mourning (v. 3b), and the splendid retinue which formed the patriarch's funeral procession (vv. 7-9), indicate the great esteem in which both Jacob and Joseph were held in Egypt. Although v. 13(P) informs us that Jacob was buried at Machpelah, the Yahwist (vv. 10-11, 14) tells us that he was buried in Transjordan in a tomb which he himself had dug (*cf.*, v. 5). Verses 12-13 (P) tell how the prescriptions laid down by Joseph in 49:28-33 (P) were carried out.

PROVIDENTIAL CARE
50:15-21

[15]When Joseph's brothers saw that their father was dead, they said, "It may be that Joseph will hate us and pay us back for all the evil which we did to him." [16]So they sent a message to Joseph, saying, "Your father gave this command before he died, [17]'Say to Joseph, Forgive, I pray you, the transgression of your brothers and their sin, because they did evil to you.' And now, we pray we, forgive the transgression of the servants of the God of your fahter." Joseph wept when they spoke to him. [18]His brothers also came and fell down before him, and said, "Behold, we are your servants." [19]But Joseph said to them, "Fear not, for am I in the place of God? [20]As for you, you meant evil against me; but God meant it for good, to bring it about that many people should be kept alive, as they are today. [21]So do not fear; I will provide for you and your little ones." Thus he reassured them and comforted them.

In this passage, which is rich in its theological comment, we have the climax of the Elohist's Joseph story. Joseph's brothers eventually came to him for reassurance that their father's death would not be an occasion to take revenge on them for their cruelty towards him (vv. 15-17). Joseph's reply was remarkable for its magnanimity and for its profound theology. With the words "Fear not, for am I in the place of God?" (v. 19) Joseph implies that God has forgiven, and that consequently he himself cannot condemn or punish. The words of v. 20, the high point of the Elohist story, assured the brothers, as they now assure the readers, that

God has foreseen and directed the history of the whole family. The brothers had intended evil, but God had directed events to a good end (*cf.,* 45:5, 7, 8). The brothers had been unconscious instruments in God's plan for the salvation of the whole family of Jacob. This remark gives a religious colouring to the whole Joseph story which often seemed so profane, and it assures us that God's sovereignty cannot be thwarted by human malice and passion.

JOSEPH'S DEATH
50:22-26

²²So Joseph dwelt in Egypt, he and his father's house; and Joseph lived a hundred and ten years. ²³And Joseph saw Ephraim's children of the third generation; the children also of Machir the son of Manasseh were born upon Joseph's knees. ²⁴And Joseph said to his brothers, "I am about to die; but God will visit you, and bring you up out of this land to the land which he swore to Abraham, to Isaac, and to Jacob." ²⁵Then Joseph took an oath of the sons of Israel, saying, "God will visit you, and you shall carry up my bones from here." ²⁶So Joseph died, being a hundred and ten years old; and they embalmed him, and he was put in a coffin in Egypt.

In this passage the Elohist records the events of Joseph's last days. The statement that the children of Machir were born on Joseph's knee means that the latter adopted them as his own sons (*cf.,* 30:3; 48:5, 12). The reason for conveying this piece of information is that Machir was to have a place in latter Israel's tribal confederacy (*cf.,* Num 32:39-40; Judg 5:14), a place which, the present text suggests, he owed to his adoption by the aged Joseph.

Before his death Joseph assured his brothers that they, in the persons of their descendants, would eventually settle in the land that had been promised to their ancestors (v. 24).

Thus, the promise of land which had been made at the beginning of the patriarchal story (*cf.,* 12:7) is reiterated as the narrative ends, and the reader's attention is turned from the exiled family in Egypt to the people that will one day dwell in the land of Canaan. Joseph's solemn deathbed request to have his bones transferred to the promised land (v. 25) echoes his father's dying wishes (*cf.,* 47:29-31; 49:29-30). His descendants fulfilled that request, when, on leaving Egypt, they took the ancestor's bones and had them buried in Shechem (*cf.,* Exod 13:19; Josh 24:32).

However, if Joseph's last words are a reassurance that the stay in the land of the Pharaohs will be temporary, the Book of Genesis ends with the family of Jacob still in exile. The land made holy by the sojourn of the patriarchs was still not theirs, and it would become theirs only after the harsh experience of a prolonged enslavement. Thus, at the end of the Joseph story the scene is set for a new drama, and for what was to be the most formative experience in Israelite history.

EPILOGUE

The Book of Genesis begins with a couple in Paradise and ends with a family exiled in Egypt. The primeval history (chaps. 1-11) tells of all the nations that were spread abroad on the earth (*cf.,* 10:32), while the rest of the book traces the story of the family of Abraham. The combined stories, the universal history of chapters 1-11 and the patriarchal narratives of chapters 12-50, have the whole Middle East for a stage. The first eleven chapters have a distinctly Mesopotamian flavour, while the Joseph story (chaps. 37-50) develops in Egypt, and the intervening chapters tell of wanderings in Mesopotamia, Syria, Canaan, and Egypt. The "primeval history," is not history in the ordinary sense of that word, but "pre-history," about a period which antedates written documents and can be reconstructed only by vague relics of human presence. It sets Israel within the context of the nations and describes a world where sin threatened to destroy humankind, if God's justice had not been tempered by a saving mercy. Abraham, whose name appears at the end of the last genealogical list that occurs in the primeval history (*cf.,* 11:26), belongs to the sinful world where humanity appears under divine judgment.

The divine call which Abraham received (*cf.,* 12:1-3) ushered in a new era, an era in which one family became the bearers of God's promise and the agents of his blessing. The patriarchal history (12-50) tells the story of that family, and outlines the gradual unfolding of a divine plan for the ultimate triumph of humanity over sin. Abraham's family was gradually separated from the tribes that were related to it, as the God who created the world and all peoples showed himself to be the friend and protector of the Patriarchs.

As we read the patriarchal stories we do not expect to find raw material for the modern historian, nor precise data from which we might construct a biography of Abraham and Sarah, Isaac and Rebekah, etc. Indeed, if we were asked whether these worthies who have made such an impression on the minds of countless generations of believers, ever existed, we would have to admit that we cannot prove that they did. But neither can we prove that they did not. In spite of the claims of those (*e.g.*, T.L. Thompson; see bibliography) who would argue that we cannot establish any kind of historicity for the patriarchal narratives, one can still hold that these narratives represent a valid historical memory of the experiences of Israel's ancestors. It is futile to attempt to reconstruct actual events, or to establish precise dates, but we can assert that the patriarchal stories fit into the world of the second millennium B.C.

However, the biblical narrative was not written from a historical perspective, but from the point of view of faith. The patriarchal saga begins with a vaguely defined divine promise of land (*cf.*, 12:7), and it ends with a confident assurance that that promise will be fullfilled (*cf.*, 48:21; 50:24). The God who guided the complex train of events that brought Abraham's tribe from Mesopotamia to Egypt was with Abraham (*cf.*, 21:22), Isaac (*cf.*, 26:28), Jacob (*cf.*, 28:15), and Joseph (*cf.*, 39:3), ensuring that in spite of human failings his plans for his chosen family and for the world would not be frustrated. If the patriarchal stories end with the seemingly hopeless picture of Jacob's family exiled in Egypt, that is because Genesis is only the first chapter in the long history of God's relationships with the world. Where Genesis leaves off Exodus takes up, and goes on to describe the next steps in the realization of God's mysterious plan for Israel and indeed for all humanity.

Select Bibliography

Coats, W., *From Canaan To Egypt. Structural and Theological Context for the Joseph Story. (The Catholic Biblical Quarterly Monograph* Series, 4) Washington, D.C., 1967.
Denies the existence of a separate E source in the Joseph story. This is the work of one author, possibly J. Some ethical applications of the Joseph story.

Davidson, R., *Genesis 1-11.* (The Cambridge Bible Commentarty, N.E.B.). Cambridge University Press, 1973.

idem, Genesis 12-50. (The Cambridge Bible Commentary, N.E.B.). Cambridge University Press, 1979.

These two works by Davidson provide the New English Bible text of Genesis with a concise commentary that is always lucid and reliable.

de Vaux, R., *The Early History of Israel.* Westminster, Philadelphia, and Darton, Longman & Todd, London, 1978.
In the chapters devoted to Genesis the author examines the historical, archaeological, and literary data that cast light on the biblical text. Detailed. Masterly.

Herbert, A. S., *Genesis 12-50. Abraham and His Heirs.* (Torch Bible Paperbacks.), SCM Press, London, 1962.
More interested in exegetical and theological matters than in literary and historical questions, although the latter are not ignored. Commentary is brief but clear.

Maher, M., *When God Made a Promise. A Christian Appreciation of Genesis.* Koinonia, Manchester, 1976.
Aims at making the theological and spiritual riches of Genesis available to the non-specialist reader of the Bible.

Von Rad, G., *Genesis, A Commentary*. Revised Edition, (Old Testament Library), translated by J. H. Marks, Westminster, Philadelphia, 1972.
A slightly modified edition of a book that first appeared in English in 1961. Became a classic. Still a must for the serious student of Genesis.

Richardson, A., *Genesis 1-11. The Creation Stories and the Modern World View*. (Torch Bible Paperbacks), SCM Press, London, 1953.
A theological commentary. Aims at making the Genesis text relevant to the needs of an ordinary congregation.

Speiser, E. A., *Genesis* (Anchor Bible, 1), Doubleday, Garden City, New York, 1964.
Offers a new translation of Genesis. Provides a long introduction to the sources of Genesis. Particularly interested in literary, historical and archaeological information that helps to elucidate Genesis.

Thompson, T. L., *The Historicity of the Patriarchal Narratives. The Quest for the Historical Abraham* (BZAW, 133), Walter de Gruyter, Berlin/New York, 1974.
This very scholarly work is severely critical of the arguments that have been used to support the historicity of the patriarchal stories.

Vawter, B., *On Genesis. A New Reading*. Doubleday, Garden City, New York, and Chapman, London, 1977.
A full and detailed commentary. Superbly written. Provides a wealth of literary, archaeological and historical data that clarifies the Genesis text.

Westermann, C., *Creation*. translated by J. J. Scullion, S.J., Fortress Press, Philadelphia, 1974.
This volume presents the conclusions of Westermann's massive German commentary on Gen. 1-3.